STIPENDS
and SPOUSES

STIPENDS and SPOUSES

*The Finances
of American Arts and Science
Graduate Students*

JAMES A. DAVIS
*with David Gottlieb, Jan Hajda,
Carolyn Huson, and Joe L. Spaeth*

National Opinion Research Center.

THE UNIVERSITY OF CHICAGO PRESS

Library of Congress Catalog Card Number: 62–12630
THE UNIVERSITY OF CHICAGO PRESS, CHICAGO & LONDON
The University of Toronto Press, Toronto 5, Canada
© *1962 by The University of Chicago. All rights reserved*
Published 1962
Printed in the United States of America

Introduction

AMONG THE MAJOR changes in our economy that have occurred over the past two decades has been a tremendous increase in the personnel and funds allocated to research and development. Private enterprises and government have multiplied their commitments to these activities, giving rise to a demand for technical, scientific, and professional personnel that must be considered enormous relative to pre-World War II levels.

The increased level of manpower demand inevitably led, first of all, to an examination of the institutional mechanisms charged with the responsibility for training beyond the undergraduate levels. Graduate and professional schools have therefore become the subject of much discussion and some empirical research. The next step in the search for understanding of the issues involved in this particular type of manpower shortage was to consider the scientists, professionals, and scholars in the process of development. This study of graduate students in the liberal arts and sciences represents an endeavor in this direction. It is concerned with how graduate students support themselves while pursuing their studies.[1]

This is a study of one important aspect of graduate training in the traditional arts and sciences. We have taken a close and careful measure of the financial circumstances of American graduate students. There are many other aspects of graduate study today which are more important than this topic and still others which might be considered as important. Yet the crucial characteristic of finances is their malleability. It is easier for an affluent society to alter

[1] Many other issues were also studied at the same time — for example, orientations toward teaching versus research; the influence of peer groups upon graduate students; and the assimilation of professional and career values. These topics will be treated in another report to be published next year.

the financial circumstances of American graduate students than to transform many other of the circumstances which play important roles in graduate training. But, in order to construct rational social policy, we need to know what are the financial problems of American graduate students and how these problems affect their careers. This is the concern of the study reported here.

The Office of Scientific Personnel of the National Academy of Sciences — National Research Council has long been concerned with fellowship and scholarship policies and has sponsored a number of studies in this area. The present study is one of this series.

In the spring of 1958 the Office of Scientific Personnel requested the National Opinion Research Center to design and execute a study particularly aimed at yielding a detailed and insightful report on the way graduate students are financed. The Office of Scientific Personnel had arranged the financing for this study through a grant from the Fund for the Advancement of Education of the Ford Foundation. An advisory committee was set up which represented the Social Science Research Council, the American Council of Learned Societies, as well as the National Research Council.

The members of the original committee were: Dr. Ralph E. Cleland (chairman) and Dr. M. H. Trytten, representing the National Research Council, Dr. Robert Hoopes and Dr. J. Fletcher Wellemeyer for the American Council of Learned Societies, Dr. Elbridge D. Sibley and Dr. Donald Marquis for the Social Science Research Council.

The present membership is as follows: Dr. Ralph E. Cleland (chaiman) and Dr. M. H. Trytten, National Research Council, Dr. Elbridge Sibley, Social Science Research Council, Dr. Gordon B. Turner, American Council of Learned Societies.

The committee has met from time to time with the staff of the National Opinion Research Center assigned to carry out the study, and NORC has enjoyed the benefit of their advice and suggestions. However, full responsibility for the content of this report lies with the staff of the Center.

Dr. James A. Davis, Senior Study Director, designed and directed the study. His insightful understanding and technical skills are manifested throughout this report.

Under Dr. Davis at NORC, David Gottlieb, assistant study director, was the coding supervisor and the original analyst for the materials on stipends. Jan Hajda, assistant study director, participated in the design of the questionnaire and built most of the codes. He left the project to join the staff of the Johns Hopkins University and did not participate in the analyses reported here. However, they could not have been done without his dedicated and insightful contributions. Carolyn Huson was responsible for the tabulations and calculations for all the tables in the revised report. Joe L. Spaeth, assistant study director, participated in the design of the questionnaire and sample, supervised most of the original field work, and was the original analyst for the chapter on financial worries and expectations.

Numerous graduate assistants and NORC staff members in Chicago and in our national field staff participated in this study. Among those whose contributions were outstanding are William Erbe, field supervisor for the follow-up study; Dorothy Pownall, coding supervisor for the follow-up study; Martin Levin and Joe Zelan, clerical assistants; Sanford Abrams, assistant supervisor of machine tabulations; and Selma Monsky and Marlene Simon of NORC's field department.

Mrs. Helen R. Miller, who typed and typed and then retyped the various drafts of this report deserves particular thanks for her skill and patience, as do Patrick Bova and Grace Osgood for work on Index and proofs.

We should like to acknowledge the fine co-operation and assistance of the graduate deans, the registrars, and the field representatives at the 25 sampled universities. The splendid "take rates" in the two waves of the study are due to their hard work and efficiency. The co-operating institutions and field representatives are as follows:

Boston College (Mrs. Mildred Raeder)
Boston University (Mrs. Mildred Raeder)
Brown University (Dr. Nissem Levy, Mr. James Kearns)
University of California, Berkeley (Mr. Herbert Maccoby, Miss Jane O'Grady)
Catholic University (Mrs. Barbara McLoney, Miss V. Rebecca Finkelstein)
University of Chicago (Mr. R. Branson Frevert)
Columbia University (Mrs. Pearl Zinner)
Cornell University (Dr. William Delaney, Mrs. Pearl Zinner)
Georgetown University (Mrs. Barbara McLoney, Miss V. Rebecca Finkelstein)
Harvard University (Mrs. Mildred Raeder, Mr. Anthony Wiener)
Indiana University (Mr. Stuart Hills, Dr. William Chambliss)
University of Kansas (Dr. E. Jackson Baur, Mr. Shepard Wolman)
University of Michigan (Dr. David Bordua)
University of Minnesota (Mrs. Mildred Roe)
New York University (Mrs. Pearl Zinner)
Ohio State University (Jacqueline J. Clarke, Mr. John H. Behling)
University of Oklahoma (Dr. Charles D. Whatley, Jr., Mrs. M. K. Read Lima)
University of Oregon (Dr. Lionel Wishneff, Dr. John C. Pock, Mr. R. Branson Frevert)
University of Pennsylvania (Mrs. Kailly B. Sass)
Pennsylvania State University (Mrs. Virginia Luchek, Mrs. T. A. Hardes)
Rensselaer Polytechnic Institute (Mrs. Selma Axelrod)
University of South Carolina (Dr. David L. Hatch)
University of Tennessee (Dr. William E. Cole, Mrs. Lawrence Coe)
University of Wisconsin (Dr. Robert Davis, Mrs. Lois L. Davis, Mr. Lionel C. Barrow, Jr.)
Western Reserve University (Dr. Eugene S. Uyeki, Mr. Donald C. Hildum)

Successfully carrying through a survey and an analysis of the sort reported here requires the application of considerable ingenuity, technical skill, sensitivity, and perserverance. James A. Davis and his assistants have full measures of these characteristics and have employed them with considerable effectiveness in this report. It is a great pleasure to commend their efforts to the reader.

PETER H. ROSSI
Director, NORC

Contents

		INTRODUCTION *by Peter H. Rossi*
3	1	SEVEN GRADUATE STUDENTS
13	2	THE ACADEMIC WORLD OF THE GRADUATE STUDENTS: A COMPOSITE PORTRAIT
24	3	THE LIFE HISTORIES OF THE GRADUATE STUDENTS: A COMPOSITE PORTRAIT
35	4	GRADUATE STUDENTS' INCOMES: SOURCES, TOTALS, AND PERCEIVED ADEQUACY
50	5	GRADUATE STUDENTS AS CONSUMERS OF EDUCATION: EXPENDITURES, PRICES, AND DEMAND
58	6	STIPENDS
74	7	THE PATTERN OF NON-STIPEND INCOME
92	8	CONCERNS ABOUT MONEY: WORRY AND EXPECTATIONS
106	9	THE OUTCOME ONE YEAR LATER
121	10	SUMMARY
131		APPENDIX I: THE SAMPLE
139		APPENDIX II: SAMPLING ERROR
145		APPENDIX III: TABLES
287		INDEX

STIPENDS
and SPOUSES

■ Chapter 1

Seven Graduate Students

IN ORDER TO illustrate some specific instance of the generalizations we will develop and to give the reader some feel for the sort of people who make up America's arts and science graduate students, let us begin by describing seven graduate students selected from among the 2,842 respondents in the sample. Here then are the vignettes we can construct from reading questionnaires 2545, 1260, 2624, 2377, 2562, 1962, and 2603.

BILL NORTON [1]

Bill Norton is a second-year graduate student in botany at a state university. Unlike many of our biological science students, he doesn't come from a small town but grew up in New York City. He says that he first seriously considered botany while in high school, and he majored in it at New York University where he got his bachelor's degree in 1957. The only other fields he has seriously considered are zoölogy and biochemistry.

His father and mother were both college graduates, and his father owned a small wholesale business. Both parents died when Bill was an undergraduate. Bill was reared as an Episcopalian but now checks his religion as "None." His political preference is "conservative Republican," but he says he is not much interested in politics. He says he is an intellectual only "in some ways."

When it came time to apply for graduate school, Bill applied to three Big Ten universities and another state university in the Midwest. The former did not admit him, but his present school not only accepted him but offered him a $1,300 a year teaching assistantship.

[1] For obvious reasons, names of specific people, universities, academic subspecialties, cities, etc., have been changed. Financial materials have not.

Although he is progressing in his work—since the questionnaire was administered he completed his master's degree and is now working for his Ph.D.—his academic abilities are not outstanding. Both of his faculty raters put him in the third fifth of his class, and one checks that "he may have difficulty in meeting Ph.D. standards, but will probably make it eventually."

Bill is aiming for an academic career. Five years after completing his graduate work he expects to be "teaching in a university," and if not that, "teaching in a small liberal arts college." If his highest aspirations were realized at the peak of his career he would have "a full professorship."

Although he dares to hope for a full professorship, his financial expectations are modest. He predicts a starting salary of $5,000 a year (in terms of annual income from all sources before taxes) and a salary of $8,500 at age 45. He guesses that if he were to go into non-academic work at age 45 he could make a minimum of $5,000 a year and a maximum of $7,000, which puts him in the very small minority of graduate students who see greater salary opportunities in academia.

Bill is a teaching assistant, handling three laboratory sections in a biology course, for an annual pay of $1,400. He expects to withdraw $200 of his $300 in savings, all of which came from a summer research assistantship which paid him $600. He has no debts, and expects to pay $155 for educational expenses: $105 in tuition and fees, $50 for books.

Thus his financial status is as follows:

Income	$1,600
Stipend	1,400
Savings	200
Professional Expenses	155
Debts	None

In rating his financial situation he checks, "I worry about it a lot, but it isn't my most serious problem," and on another question "I'll have enough money for my necessary expenses, but nothing left over for emergencies."

He is 24 years old and single.

HARVEY PEARLMAN

Harvey Pearlman is a single, 25-year-old first-year graduate student in philosophy in an Ivy League school. Like many philosophy students he did not take kindly to the fixed categories of the questionnaire. He filled it out carefully and at the end rated it as "Interesting throughout," but he added a large number of comments and qualifications (after his rating of the questionnaire he added, "though ambiguously and uncarefully phrased") which gives us more insight into his intellectual style than we get from most of our schedules.

Like Bill Norton, Harvey grew up in New York City. He was raised as a Jew but now checks "None." His father, an executive in a large women's wear firm, and his mother, a professional artist, both completed two years of college.

Harvey has just returned to his alma mater after two years in the army. He definitely plans to get a doctorate, and he is aiming for an academic career. As he notes when he leaves blank a series of questions comparing academic and non-academic jobs: "In philosophy, non-academic jobs are non-existent. This question doesn't apply." Although in the past he has considered psychiatry and social work as possible careers, he predicts that five years after completing his graduate work he will be doing "philosophy in a college." In terms of his highest aspirations he writes, "My highest aspirations include no reference to position."

He is a very good student. His two faculty raters placed him in the first or second fifth of his class, and both checked the category "Superior — stands out among the general group of graduate students, but there are a number here who are equally able." One year later he was still in school working on his master's degree.

He rates himself as a "liberal Democrat" and "definitely an intellectual."

With philosophical disdain for material matters, he estimates a starting salary of $3,000 a year and a peak of $7,500 at age 45. Unlike Norton, Pearlman sees a considerable differential between the money he could make in academic and non-academic jobs. At age 45 he sees an academic minimum of $6,000 and a maximum of $8,000. If he were to go into a non-academic job, however, he thinks he could make a minimum of $10,000 and a maximum of $25,000 to $50,000.

This year he expects an income of $3,000, all of which will come from his existing savings of $3,000. He didn't work last summer, although there is an eight-month gap in his chronology between the army and graduate school, during which he might have saved some of this money. He adds that his parents will contribute "as much as needed." He didn't apply for any stipend which was refused him or receive a stipend offer which he turned down, but he does say that all other things being equal he would like a teaching assistantship.

Tuition bills at his Ivy institution will be $1,000 and he expects to spend $85 on books, making his total professional expenditures $1,085. He has no debts.

His financial status is as follows:

```
Income  . . . . . . . . . . . . . . . . . . . . . . . . . . . . $3,000 (savings)
Professional Expenses  . . . . . . . . . . . . . . . .  1,085
Debts  . . . . . . . . . . . . . . . . . . . . . . . . . . . . . None
```

Harvey checks his immediate financial situation as, "I'm not very worried about it," and his long-run financial situation as, "I'm not very worried about it." Beside each of these questions he penciled in, "I DO NOT THINK ABOUT IT."

6   *Seven Graduate Students*

FRANKLIN R. CARRUTHERS

Franklin R. Carruthers, a Ph.D. student in physics at a Great Plains state university, is older (28) than our first two students and further along in his studies.

He comes from a middle-class, small-town midwestern family. His father, a college graduate, was an insurance salesman, who died when Franklin was in high school. His mother, who had two years of college, worked as a secretary.

Franklin started undergraduate work at a southern state university but apparently was drafted after a year. On discharge from the military, he completed his bachelor's work at Duke where he got a bachelor's degree in physics, in June, 1954. He applied to three smaller state universities and Syracuse, in addition to his present school. He was admitted to all but Syracuse and was offered $1,200 assistantships at two state universities.

He is aiming for a Ph.D. and a career in industrial research. His most probable job five years after completing his graduate work is "research (pure) in industry" and his next most probable job is "research (development) in industry." If his highest aspiration should be realized, he would "design, conduct, and analyze experiments in pure research with several people under me."

Carruthers expects a starting salary of $9,000 a year (after he gets his Ph.D.) and at age 45 when he has those several people working under him he predicts an annual salary of $20,000 a year. If he were to go into academic work he sees a minimum of $7,500 and a maximum of $18,500 at age 45.

Both of his faculty raters place him in the second fifth of his class, and both rate him as "competent." Although in 1958 he predicted he would get his degree in August, 1959, at the time of the follow-up in Fall, 1959, he was still in school.

He was reared and still is a Methodist, he leans toward the "more conservative Democrats," and rates himself as an intellectual "in some ways."

In the summer of 1958 two things changed his financial situation considerably. He got married to a girl he met four years before and shortly thereafter had a serious operation which resulted in medical bills of $2,000. His wife's father is a jeweler.

He has two stipends, a university fellowship worth $1,250 and a research assistantship working on apparatus for a government project which pays $700. His wife is a dietician and works full time, making $4,300 during the academic year. In addition, he will receive $70 from "investments."

The Carruthers' have $2,450 in debts: $2,000 to a bank for medical bills, $300 to a bank for a car loan, and $150 to their university for "traveling expenses for vacation."

His professional expenses are $250 for tuition and fees, and $25 for books.

In sum, then —

Income	$6,320
Stipend	1,950
Spouse	4,300
Investments	70
Professional Expenses	275
Debts	2,450

In rating his financial situation, Franklin checks, "I'll have enough money for my necessary expenses, and enough left over for emergencies," and in terms of worry about his immediate financial situation, "I'm not very worried about it." He pencils in a note saying, "My medical bills are the only money I have had to borrow in order to continue in school. My graduate expenses prior to marriage were paid by stipends and the GI Bill."

CARL ERICKSON

Carl Erickson, a second-year graduate student in English at a world famous private university, is a late starter. He did his undergraduate work in business at a small denominational college in the Midwest and went into the Navy after his bachelor's degree in 1952. He says that he has seriously considered careers in business and career military service and only seriously considered English after being out of college three years. (This pattern is much more common in humanities and social science than among physical science students.)

After a year's work at a liberal arts college (possibly to pick up prerequisites for graduate work in English) he applied to the University of Southern California, University of Minnesota, and his present school. Each accepted him, but none offered him aid.

Carl's father was an immigrant from Scandinavia, who didn't go beyond eighth grade. His mother, a native-born American, stopped at eight grades too. The father is an electrician with his own small business.

We got only one faculty rating on Carl, the rater terming him "competent" in terms of ability for Ph.D. work, but placing him in the third fifth of his class.

Like almost all students in the humanities Carl wants to be a liberal arts teacher, but his decision is not definite. His second most probable job five years after completing his graduate work is "administrative work in a large industry," and his reply to the question on highest aspiration is, "I don't know."

He predicts a starting salary of $4,500, and a salary of $6,500 at age 45. He sees academic jobs offering a range of $6,000 to $6,500 at age 45, and non-academic jobs offering a range from $6,500 to $7,000.

Carl was reared and still is a Presbyterian, checks himself as a "liberal

Republican," "very interested in politics," and says he is an intellectual "in many ways."

He is now 28 and has been married three years to a girl he met when he was 20. She is also a Presbyterian and her father owns a furniture store.

Carl has no university stipend but receives $1,100 in veterans' benefits. His wife is a school teacher, and she makes $2,400 a year. The Ericksons have two other sources of income. They expect to spend all of their $700 in savings, $400 of which came from Carl's work on a construction gang the previous summer. He also expects to work as a substitute high school teacher and make $400 during the year.

They have no debts, but there are professional costs of $1,355, of which $1,280 goes for tuition and fees, $50 for books, and $25 for master's thesis costs.

The Ericksons' books read as follows:

```
Income .................................... $4,600
    Spouse ................................. 2,400
    Veterans' Benefits ..................... 1,100
    Part-time Work ......................... 400
    Withdrawals from Savings ............... 700
Professional Expenses ..................... 1,355
Debts ..................................... None
```

He checks, "I'll have enough money for my necessary expenses, but nothing left over for emergencies," and in terms of financial worry, "I worry about it a lot, but it isn't my most serious problem."

One year later Carl had dropped out of school and was teaching high school. The faculty informant tells us that this is because of a family problem which we cannot explain in detail because it might identify Carl.

BILLY JOHN WILLIAMS

As you might guess from his name, Billy John in a southerner. He is working for his Ph.D. in physiology in a state university, was 36 years old when he filled out the questionnaire, married, and had three children.

He grew up in the South, where his father, who didn't get past the eighth grade, was a railroad fireman. He started college in 1941 at a teachers college in the South Central states, but was drafted before he could finish. Upon discharge in 1946 he entered the state university in his home state and received a B.S. in physiology in 1950. His chronology is a little confusing, but since 1950 he has been in service again and got a master's at Tulane. In 1957, upon his second military discharge, he applied at Tulane and two state universities, one of which was his bachelor's degree alma mater. He was offered a $1,800-a-year research assistantship at his alma mater and began his doctoral studies there, although he says that he would have continued at Tulane if he had been offered a stipend.

Like Franklin Carruthers, Billy John is aiming for a non-academic research career. Five years after finishing his degree he expects to be doing medical research at the National Institutes of Health, and, if not that, medical research for the Army. His highest aspiration would be "director of a research laboratory."

Despite his long time in getting his degree, he is well thought of by his department. Both raters say he is "competent" and in the second fifth of his class. Both pencil in comments stressing that he is a good student.

Billy writes, "I have no [political] party leanings" and thinks of himself as an intellectual "in many ways."

Billy John has been married five years, has three children, and expects another child in the next two years.

His financial situation is as follows. He has four sources of income, a teaching assistantship "preparing laboratory demonstrations" which pays $1,800 a year; $400 from other part-time work during the year; $400 aid from his wife's parents; and $400 in veterans benefits. In addition, the couple were living with Billy John's family, and, although the questionnaire does not ask this, their rent was probably free.

They owe $500 to a credit union for a washer and dryer, and $200 to Mrs. Williams' father, who lent them money at no interest with no repayment deadline for "current expenses."

Academic expenses total $260 a year: $200 for tuition, $30 for books, and $30 for professional journals.

In summary:

Income	$3,000 (plus)
Stipend	1,800
Veterans Benefits	400
Spouse's Parents	400
Part-time Work	400
Free Rent	(?)
Professional Expenses	275
Debts	700

His subjective financial self-ratings are contradictory. On the one hand, he checks, "It's doubtful that I'll have enough money to cover my necessary expenses," but in terms of current financial worry he checks, "I'm not very worried about it." One reason for this may be that he has $1,300 in savings which he doesn't expect to tap during the year.

The following year Billy John had dropped out of school and was working full time for his department as a research aid, but his professors both predicted he would be back in school the following year.

RALPH AMATO

Ralph Amato has an esoteric specialty, being a 33 year old Ph.D. candidate in Sanskrit, at a world-renowned private university in a large metropolis.

Ralph's father, a janitor, and his mother were born in Italy, and Ralph was reared and still is a Roman Catholic. He grew up in Philadelphia and got a bachelor's degree in English at Temple in 1948. He was married immediately after graduation and worked for five years as a salesman. Apparently his original inclinations were literary, for he says that at one time he seriously considered "literary criticism" as a career and only seriously considered foreign languages after being out of college two years. In 1954-55 he got a Master's degree at Princeton in languages, and then went to work for the United Nations as a language specialist. In 1957 he returned to school for his Ph.D., switching to an equally renowned private university, after being admitted to Princeton and Cornell. None of the three schools offered him any aid.

Five years after completing his studies he expects to be doing "teaching and research at a university," and, if not that, academic administration. His highest aspiration is as follows, "professor of Indic studies, specializing in comparative, historical, and descriptive studies."

As befits a specialist in comparative, historical, and descriptive studies, Ralph predicts a salary of $10,000 a year at age 45. He sees a minimum of $10,000 and a maximum of $15,000 in the academic world, and a range from $13,000 to $18,000 in non-academic jobs.

He is one of the few students who gets a split decision in his faculty ratings, one rater placing him in the top fifth of the class, the other in the third.

He defines himself as a "liberal Democrat," "very interested in politics," and an intellectual "in some ways."

The Amatos' have three children.

Ralph will be working full time while going to school, working as a translator for a large bank with many customers in Asia. He expects $3,060 from this and will also withdraw $200 from his savings of $500.

He owes $300 to a bank, borrowed at 12 per cent interest, to pay for a child's operation. His academic expenses total $1,052: $1,000 for tuition, $25.00 for university fees, $15.00 for books, and $12.00 for professional journals.

Ralph's bookkeeping goes as follows:

Income	$3,260
Full-time job	3,060
Withdrawals from savings	200
Professional Expenses	1,052
Debts	300

In the fall of 1958 Ralph checked, "It's doubtful that I'll have enough money to cover my necessary expenses" and said that his immediate financial situation is "my most serious problem right now."

One year later he had dropped out of school and was working full time for the bank.

Whitney Dunn

Whitney Dunn differs in many ways from most of the students in our sample, but he is representative of a small subgroup of students with a very particular pattern of finances and career plans.

He is twenty-three years old and a first-year graduate student in economics at a moderate prestige private university in a large metropolis.

Whitney grew up in New England. His father, a college graduate, was in "middle management" in a very large industrial firm. Whitney was reared as and still is a Congregationalist.

He was graduated from Dartmouth in 1957 with a B.A. in economics. Although he considered economics as a career during his senior year in college, he went to work immediately as a management trainee in an electronics firm, where he is still employed full time.

Five years after completing his graduate work he expects to be "in management or staff work" for "industry," and his highest aspiration is "president of my own company." He might, however, get a C.P.A. and go into accounting.

At age 45 he expects a salary of $25,000 a year. If he were to go into academic work he sees a minimum of $7,000 and a maximum of $10,000 at age 45. In non-academic work he sees a range from $10,000 to $30,000.

Both of his faculty raters said they didn't know him very well (not untypical for part-time students). One rated him in the second fifth, and one in the third fifth of his class. Both, however, rate him as "Problematical — may have promise, but hasn't found himself yet."

Whitney defines himself as "a liberal Republican" and "definitely" an intellectual.

He was married upon graduation to a girl he met in college. Mrs. Dunn, who is a schoolteacher, is the daughter of an architect.

The Dunns will have a total income of $9,850 during the academic year. Whitney's work will bring $5,250 (three-quarters of an annual salary of $7,000), his wife's job, $4,500, and investments, $100.

They owe $500 for money borrowed for undergraduate tuition, and Whitney will incur $620 in professional expenses, $500 for tuition, $100 for books, and $20 for journals.

To summarize the Dunn's finances:

Income	$9,850
Full-time Job	5,250
Spouse's Job	4,500
Investments	100
Professional Expenses	620
Debts	500

He checks, "I'll have enough money for my necessary expenses, and enough left over for emergencies." And in terms of immediate financial worry, he first wrote, "I worry about it a lot, but it isn't my most serious problem," but crossed that out and checked, "I'm not very worried about it."

One year later he was still in school, working for his Master's degree.

Here then, are seven contemporary American graduate students: Protestant, Catholic, Jew; scientist and humanist; bachelor, husband, and father; carefully chosen to be as representative as an infantry squad in a Hollywood movie.

They are not a random sample in the statistical sense, for we chose them to illustrate some important factors in graduate education, and we deliberately chose males for our examples. However, with a couple of minor exceptions noted in our discussions, they seem to us to be a fair sample of the men in our study. In that sense, they are ideal typical, if not typical.

By the end of this report we will have some explanation of most of the characteristics of their financial situations. For now, however, let us merely note their heterogeneity. They range in age from early twenty to middle thirty; in social origins from the very bottom to just below the top (there are upper-uppers in graduate school but not enough to pay particular attention to); in nine-month income from $1,600 to $9,850; in stipend income from zero to $1,950; in anticipated income at age 45 from $6,000 to $25,000; in non-stipend work from none to full-time outside jobs; and from worry to satisfaction with their financial situations.

Why we see this variety, and what factors explain the differences cannot be answered from the cases. When, however, we consider all 2,842 respondents and replace our detailed knowledge of individuals with statistical comparisons made among hundreds of students in similar and differing situations, a new picture begins to emerge, one in which individuals disappear but in which variables and clusters of variables which affect finances and feelings about finances present a more abstract and general picture of the financial situations of American arts and science graduate students.

The remainder of this report is devoted to that analysis.

Chapter 2

The Academic World of
The Graduate Students:
A Composite Portrait

IN THE FALL OF 1958 American graduate schools had about 63,000 students enrolled for the master's or Ph.D. in an arts and science field. This is slightly less than the number of cabinetmakers and a little more than the number of locomotive firemen in the country. Although many of the students will fall by the wayside, the nation depends on the survivors for its future professors, research scientists, psychologists, and college administrators in an era of increasing demand for trained professionals in and out of the academy.

Just as they are rare, they have been highly selected. They survived 12 years of primary and secondary education, four years of undergraduate education, and, according to the best estimates available, their median corresponds to the top 8 per cent of the general population in terms of intellectual ability.[1]

One would think that such an important group would have been extensively surveyed, counted, and analyzed, but as far as we know this is the first national sampling of arts and science graduate students. Although our major attention will be devoted to their financial situations, we will begin with a detailed description of the students, their personal characteristics, and their academic environments. This chapter describes them in terms of their schools, field of study, stage of training, career plans, and evaluations of school. Chapter iii considers their personal characteristics: social origins, age, transition from undergraduate to graduate training, and their family situations.

GRADUATE SCHOOLS

There are approximately 140 institutions in the United States which offered the doctorate in one or more arts and science fields in 1958, the exact

[1] The estimate is derived from data presented in Dael Wolfe, *America's Resources of Specialized Talent* (New York: Harper & Bros., 1954), p. 200.

number varying somewhat with one's definition of arts and science fields. Just as the students are a tiny fraction of all the students in higher education, so these schools make up only a minuscule part of the roughly 1,000 accredited colleges and universities in the country.

At first glance, even this tiny, if not cozy, little world seems to include a wild array of schools ranging from giant public institutions (the University of California at Berkeley had some 2,500 graduate students in arts and science in 1958) the ancient Ivy League dowagers, new schools (Brandies), well-known institutions with relatively small graduate schools (in 1958 Notre Dame, Vanderbilt, and Tulane each had fewer than 400 graduate students), independent medical schools with a dozen or two graduate students in biological sciences, to highly specialized schools with no undergraduates such as the Rockefeller Institute or the Institute of Paper Chemistry.

Although the schools vary in prestige, size, offerings, control, and location, statistical analyses of these characteristics suggest that we can cover most of them by locating the schools on two independent dimensions.

The first dimension, which we will call "stratum," involves prestige, number of students, and departmental offerings, which seem to hang together in such a fashion as to produce a scale of institutions from large, high-prestige schools with wide offerings, through lesser-known institutions with few students and narrower offerings, to small schools with offerings in only the most common areas of study and little academic glamor.

In considering institutional prestige it is important to remember that there are probably no "bad" graduate schools in the sense that there are bad undergraduate institutions, for any school which offers the Ph.D. stands out in comparison with the mass of colleges. Although all graduate schools are good, academics have long known, and a series of research studies have indicated, that many are better, and a few have extremely high prestige. In 1959 Hayward Keniston published the most recent data confirming this generalization.[2] On the basis of rankings by departmental chairmen, Keniston derived departmental and institutional rankings for twenty-five leading graduate schools excluding technological schools and state colleges. He finds a striking consistency between schools' standings in different fields. Thus, even within this elite group of schools the association between a school's rank in chemistry and its rank in philosophy is .96 (using Q as a measure of association).

In many prestige systems, the top group consists of a small elite, as contrasted with a larger middle and bottom. In terms of graduate students and graduate schools, this is not true, and there is a considerable concentration of students in the highest ranking schools.

Enrolments vary considerably (see Table 2.1). Our estimates for the total

[2] Hayward Keniston, *Graduate Study and Research in the Arts and Sciences at the University of Pennsylvania* (Philadelphia: University of Pennsylvania Press, 1959).

Academic World of Graduate Students 15

140 schools in 1958 show that one-quarter of the students are in the five largest graduate schools, and 85 per cent of the graduate students are enrolled in the 64 largest schools. Seventy-five per cent of America's graduate schools have smaller enrolments than the largest *department* in the largest school.

The relationship between size and prestige is considerable (see Table 2.2). All but one of the 25 schools in Keniston's list have enrolments of 500 or more, and, even within his rarified group, the larger schools are more likely to be in the top ten.

One of the reasons why quantity and quality go together lies in the patterning of offerings in graduate schools. Although there is a wide range in the number of schools offering the Ph.D. in a given field (111 offered the Ph.D. in chemistry in 1958, 65 in economics, 29 in classics, 2 in geochemistry), the patterning is such that schools which offer degrees in rare fields also tend to offer them in the more common ones (see Table 2.3).

Offerings form a pattern of cumulation rather than one of specialization. We can illustrate this by means of a Guttman scale [3] (see Table 2.4). To the extent that the pattern is one of cumulation, the schools should fall into five patterns of offerings in Table 2.4 which form a step-like progression, and a statistic known as the Coefficient of Reproducibility should be .90 or higher. In our example, 90 per cent of the schools fall into the "scale types," and the reproducibility is .974. Thus, in terms of offerings, philosophy and chemistry tend to go together. Of the schools which offer the Ph.D. in philosophy, 98 per cent also offer it in chemistry.

In order to tap this dimension for the purposes of sampling, the 140 schools were divided into three strata:

Stratum I: Schools with ranks 1 to 10 in the Keniston survey plus MIT and California Institute of Technology which were not included in the survey.
Stratum II: Other members of the Association of Graduate Schools, an organization of leading graduate institutions, and/or universities which granted 400 or more arts and science Ph.D.'s between 1936 and 1956.
Stratum III: All other graduate schools.

Our intent was to sort the institutions into the small group of large, extremely high prestige schools; the other major institutions producing high numbers of Ph.D.'s; and the smaller institutions. The operational definition is

[3] For the technical reader, we should note that the criterion for scalability we used was that of high intercorrelations among the items (offerings). The 496 intercorrelations for fields offered by 10 or more schools have a median Q of .69, and, almost without exception, the selection of five or six items of varying marginals gives scales with reproducibilities of .90 or higher. Cf. James A. Davis, "On Criteria for Scale Relationships," *The American Journal of Sociology*, LXIII, No. 4 (January, 1958), pp. 371–80.

strongly related to prestige, size, and extensity of offerings (see Table 2.5). Lacking a good term which refers simultaneously to prestige, size, and variety of offerings, we shall refer to this dimension hereafter as "stratum."

The second dimension for classifying schools involves their control and location. Although throughout the report we shall see that financial matters vary with both dimensions, for now the important point is that control, dichotomized as private versus public, is independent of stratum. At each stratum level about half of the schools are private, half public (see Table 2.6).

The six cells formed by the three strata provide the sampling frame for selection of students in the study. The details of the sample are explained in Appendix I to this report, but, in brief, each of the six cells was given a quota which corresponded to its proportion of all students, schools within a cell were sampled with a probability proportional to their number of students, sample quotas were set within cells so that each student in the nation had the same probability of being drawn for the study, although larger graduate schools had a much larger chance of being drawn. The sample is thus representative of students, but not of schools.

As Table 2.6 shows, the students split about 50–50 between public and private schools, and roughly one-quarter are in Stratum I schools, one-half in Stratum II schools, and a quarter in Stratum III. Three-quarters of the graduate students are in the forty-nine Stratum I and II schools which we will call major producers.[4]

Returning briefly to the control dimension we note an ecological patterning of schools which turns out to be of some significance for understanding the students' financial situations. Public and private institutions comprise an independent dimension not only in the sense that control does not correlate with stratum but also in the sense that the two types of schools tend to comprise geographically distinct systems (see Table 2.7). Private institutions tend to be concentrated in large cities, state schools in smaller towns (see Table 2.7a). Private schools, regardless of stratum, tend to be concentrated in New England and the Middle Atlantic states. Larger, higher-prestige state schools tend to be concentrated in the Middle West and Far West, and smaller public schools tend to be concentrated in the South and Mountain states (see Table 2.7b). Considering region and type of city simultaneously, (see Table 2.7c), half of the private graduate schools are located inside the central city of a standard metropolitan area in the "East," and none of these cities have a public school. Conversely, half of the public institutions are located outside a central city in a region other than the East, as compared with less than a fifth of the private schools.

[4] The fact that in Table 2.6 the sample and universe distributions of students are very similar is not in itself evidence that the sample is representative. The sample quotas were set to give back the same cell distribution as in the universe. Appendix I considers the evidence on representativeness.

The findings have a number of direct and indirect implications for understanding the financial situations of graduate students. We shall develop them as we proceed, but a few conclusions are worth noting now.

The fact that the vast majority of graduate students are trained in a relative handful of high-prestige institutions means that for the students going into academic work theirs is a career line in which one starts at the top and typically moves down when one finishes school.[5]

The fact that schools are geographically differentiated means that the student who lives in a large city and wants part-time graduate training almost always will attend a private institution.

The fact that private schools are concentrated while public schools are dispersed suggests that private schools are more likely to be in direct geographical competition[6] and differentiated in the type of student they attract.

DIVISION OF STUDY

The natural unit of graduate study is not really the school but the department. Unlike undergraduate training, in graduate school course work is centered in one department which has great control over the student's degree work, save for general legislation regarding residence requirements, language examinations, and so forth. We shall not treat departmental differences in this report because of the complications involved in dealing with large numbers of small groups of cases. This does not mean, though, that field of study is unimportant financially. It is extremely important, as we shall see. However, the important differences seem rather to be between more general groupings, which we will call divisions, than departments.

The students in the sample are in forty-seven fields of study (see Table 2.8), which is larger than the fields in Table 2.3 because this classification is finer. The largest field is chemistry with 11 per cent of the sample, the smallest biopsychology with one student. The departments were originally grouped into four divisions, but after preliminary analysis we combined the biological and physical sciences because their situations were so similar, ending with 47 per cent of the sample in natural science, 23 per cent in social science, and 30 per cent in humanities. Eight interdivisional students are excluded from analyses involving divisions.

While considerable attention has been given to the fact that departmental offerings vary with the type of institutions, all three divisions include common fields (chemistry, economics, history) and rare ones (astronomy, anthropology, comparative literature). Consequently there are few divisional

[5] Cf. Theodore Caplow and Reece McGee, *The Academic Marketplace*, (New York: Basic Books, 1958), pp. 225–26.

[6] Using a rough criterion of commutability, New York City has seven graduate schools; Philadelphia, six; Washington, D.C., five; Chicago, four; Boston, four; and Pittsburgh, three, although not all offer work in the same fields.

18   *Academic World of Graduate Students*

differences by stratum and control (see Table 2.9). It is true that the lower the stratum in public schools (but not in private schools) the greater the proportion of students in natural science, but it is also true that, in each of the six cells of the design, natural scientists are the largest group, social scientists the smallest.[7]

Although the division classification plays an important role in the anlysis, we will not discuss it further here, except to note that it adds a third, essentially independent, dimension for classifying students' academic situations and for financial variables which relate to stratum, division, and control; the simultaneous consideration of all three usually produces considerable variation.

STAGE OF STUDY

Graduate study, unlike earlier training, is not laid out in a steady progression of grades. In the first place, there is no yearly promotion in the sense of freshman–sophomore–junior–senior. The graduate student progresses by surmounting various hurdles (course requirements, comprehensives, language examinations, theses), typically at a time of his own choosing. In the second place, the hurdles are not laid out in standard form. Some students go straight for the Ph.D., without getting a master's, some departments do not require a master's thesis, and so on. Thus, academic age can be plotted on two separate axes, years of study and progression toward meeting degree requirements. In terms of its financial implications, this "looseness" is probably the most significant organizational aspect of graduate study, but right now it is important because it raises the problem of measuring degree progress.

A combination of degree sought and current academic work gives a measure of progression toward meeting requirements (see Table 2.10). The students were asked whether they were taking courses or seminars, preparing for comprehensives, or working on a thesis. Respondents were allowed to check more than one alternative, but, if it is assumed that comprehensives come later than course work and theses come last, the index provides a rough ordering. The sample splits evenly between master's and doctor's candidates,[8] and within each degree about 60 per cent are beginning and 40 per cent nearing the last hurdles.

[7] In our original enrolment estimates, history was classified in the social sciences. Preliminary tabulations indicated that the financial situation (perhaps "lot" is the better word) of the history student is more akin to those in humanities than those in social sciences, and they are grouped in humanities. Thus, it is impossible to compare the classification used in the report with the figures for the universe. Table 2.9 shows the sample results for both classifications. Because history is a large field, the relative proportion in humanities and social sciences varies considerably when one moves history back and forth.

[8] In this report, we shall not limit candidacy to the formal status but shall consider anyone working for a given degree as a candidate for it.

Progression toward a degree is, naturally, related to years of graduate study completed (see Table 2.11). Of the first-year students 85 per cent are master's candidates, while 85 per cent of those who have completed three or more years are Ph.D. candidates. The relationship is not perfect, however, for 34 per cent of those who have completed two years and 15 per cent of those who have completed three or more years are still master's candidates.

Although they vary in where they stand now, the sample as a whole is very much Ph.D. oriented. Sixty-three per cent say they "definitely plan to get a doctorate," 9 per cent say "I do not plan to get a doctorate," the remainder checking a qualified alternative. In the nature of the sample and in the nature of arts and science graduate training, the students are heavily professionally oriented toward future work for which the Ph.D. has great value.

Just as the Stratum Index was derived to tap the complex variables of school prestige, size, and offerings, the index of academic stage combines years and degree progress as a measure of where the students stand in their training (see Table 2.12). The index divides the sample into four stages:

Stage I: First-year students, regardless of degree sought or type of academic work.
Stage II: Master's candidates who have completed one or more years of graduate work.
Stage III: Ph.D. candidates who have completed a year or more of graduate study, but who are not working on their thesis.
Stage IV: Ph.D. candidates who have completed a year or more of graduate study and are working on their thesis.

For convenience, Stages I and II will be called "master's candidates," although first year students working on their Ph.D. are included; while stages III and IV will be termed "Ph.D. candidates."

The Stage Index is not independent of the three previous dimensions of academic life (see Table 2.13). In each division and in both public and private schools, the higher the stratum, the greater the proportion of Ph.D. candidates. Similarly, within stratum and control type, natural science students are more likely to be Ph.D. candidates, humanities students less likely, with social science students tending to be in between. The disparity is of some importance, for such differences could arise either if some students take longer to reach a given stage or if some students are more likely to drop out of school early in their studies, and both of these possibilities raise important questions about financial factors in delay and drop-out. There is a third possibility, that students in lower-stratum schools and in humanities are less Ph.D. oriented. Examination of the proportion who state "I do not plan to get a doctorate" among master's candidates (Table 2.14) shows more self-defined terminal master's students in the lower-stratum schools, but no divisional difference.

Removing these students does not eliminate the original differences (see Table 2.15). Among Ph.D. oriented students, as in the total sample, students in lower-stratum schools and in humanities tend to be at earlier stages.

Career Expectations

The career plans and expectations of the students have no direct importance for their immediate financial situations, although, because career expectations are associated with other variables, students with different career plans tend to be characterized by different financial situations. Career plans do affect the students' perception of their future financial situations, and they are of some intrinsic interest. Therefore, we will review them briefly.

For present purposes, the students are simply divided according to what they expect to be doing five years after they complete their graduate work (see Table 2.16). Fifty-seven per cent expect to be in academic jobs (defined as teaching or research while employed by a college of university), 33 per cent expect a non-academic job in their field of study (e.g., a biochemist who expects to do research for a drug firm), 3 per cent expect to be in non-academic jobs in a different field (e.g., a career military officer working for a degree in Spanish who expects to be a military attaché), 5 per cent expect to be in primary or secondary teaching or administration, and 2 per cent do not expect to be working.

Actually, the degree of orientation toward academic jobs is somewhat higher than the figure of 57 per cent might indicate. On a separate question, students were asked about their preferences, as opposed to their expectations. Of the 2,744 students with an opinion, 70 per cent preferred academic jobs, 9 per cent preferred academic and non-academic jobs equally, and 22 per cent preferred non-academic jobs. Because of the difference in the two figures, there are necessarily a number of students who prefer academic jobs, but do not expect them (see Table 2.17). Sixteen per cent of the total sample and 23 per cent of the students who prefer academic jobs are "frustrated academics." Detailed analyses of these data by Joe L. Spaeth indicate that the frustrated academics are more likely to have poor grades, and regardless of their grades, they are more likely to be women. If the academy is not receiving enough recruits, these data suggest that the problem lies in something other than motivations. More students prefer academic jobs than expect them, and our follow-up materials suggest that more students expect them than get them.

The academic-minded students are not distributed randomly in the academic worlds described by our indexes (see Table 2.18). Ph. D. candidates in every comparison are more likely to expect academic jobs than are master's candidates. In most comparisons, there is a regular increase in academic expectations as one moves up the stratum classification. Humanities students, whose skills have less extra-academic market value, are consistently more academic in their expectations, but interestingly there is no consistent difference between natural and social scientists. The fact that there is no pattern by control is in accordance with the interpretation of public and private schools as parallel rather than differentiated systems of education.

Table 2.18 shows that when stratum, division, and stage are considered simultaneously they produce considerable variation in career expectations. At the extremes, only a minority of Stratum III natural and social science master's candidates expect academic jobs, while about 90 per cent of the Stratum I humanities Ph.D. candidates envision academic futures.

Thus, in contrast with professional schools such as law, medicine, education, or engineering, the arts and science graduate schools mingle together students with considerable differences in their future career lines.

EVALUATIONS OF SCHOOL

Our concern with the financial situation of the students is not essentially economic. Rather, financial matters are considered important to the degree that they affect the career plans, academic progress, and continuity of study of the graduate students. Therefore, it is important to view financial variables in the light of other factors which affect career progress and decisions. Important among these is the degree to which the students are satisfied or dissatisfied with their academic world. For the student who is unhappy with his school or sees no advantages to getting his degree even the rosiest monetary circumstances may not keep him in school.

It is commonly believed that graduate school is a period of tension and anxiety and that graduate students tend to be worn to a frazzle by the ordeal of getting their degrees. Thus, Caplow and McGee write:[9]

> As graduate students they have been tested in many ways and over a period of years for intelligence, persistence, and conformity. The ordeal is sufficient to eliminate the vast majority of graduate students before they reach the doctorate. For those who survive, the habit of insecurity and a certain mild paranoid resignation are standard psychological equipment.

The data from the sample suggest that such conclusions overstress the negative (see Table 2.19). The students tend to be pleased with their choice of schools, 74 per cent being fairly sure they made the best choice, 7 per cent being regretful. Although they see few job opportunities in their field for those who do not go beyond the bachelor's degree, 72 per cent think non-academic opportunities are excellent or good for a person with a master's, and almost all think academic and non-academic job opportunities for Ph.D.'s

[9] Caplow and McGee, *op. cit.*, p. 223.

are excellent or good (see Table 2.20). They seem to believe that a master's degree is a guarantee of a good non-academic job and a Ph.D. will get them a good position in or out of academia. Such optimism may enable them to put up with a considerable amount of frustration in their immediate situations because they see considerable gain in completing their studies.

A more direct measure of their satisfaction comes from a question simply asking them whether they have a good time in graduate school (see Table 2.21). Sixty-nine per cent say they have a good time, 5 per cent say they have a bad or rotten time.

All of this does not mean that they are uncritical of graduate training. When presented with a list of twelve common criticisms of graduate education (ten are summarized in Table 2.22) 92 per cent checked one or more and 51 per cent checked four or more as "valid" or "somewhat valid." The most common complaints were, "It has too many formal 'hurdles' which are really initiation rituals, not genuine training" and "It doesn't provide enough training for teaching," each being checked by about half of the sample.

Whether such figures indicate high or low morale cannot be determined without some standard of comparison. Such a yardstick is given by one of the most famous questionnaire items of all time, "in general, how would you say you feel most of the time?" The question was used in extensive researches on the personal *esprit* of American soldiers in World War II (see Table 2.23). Fifty-eight per cent of the students checked "I am usually in good spirits," 2 per cent "I am usually in low spirits." Comparing various categories of soldiers with the students (Table 2.24), it turns out that graduate student spirits are higher than any group of enlisted men, although lower than commissioned officers who came up from the ranks. Considering that the students probably have the simulated rank of non-commissioned officers in the army of higher education, it seems fair to conclude that, for people in marginal statuses, they are in good shape psychologically.

One of the most important findings about morale is that it does not correlate with any of the variables described in chapters ii and iii. When a morale index, combining the questions on spirits and good time, is cross-tabulated against stratum, control, division, stage, and career expectations, there is almost no variation. In chapter viii of the report there is a detailed discussion of the variables which do correlate with morale and the role of financial problems in affecting morale. The important point here is that, while the variables describing the students' academic world indicate considerable differences among them, their morale seems more related to how they adjust to their situations than to the nature of the situations. One might think that advanced students would be tired out or, conversely, that their morale might be boosted by being near their goal; one might think that students in the elite universities would be in better spirits; or one might expect divisional differences, but none of these inferences is supported by the data.

Summary

This chapter has described the academic world of American arts and science students in terms of five measures:
1. Stratum Classification of Universities
2. Control of University
3. Division of study
4. Academic Stage
5. Career Expectations

In considering their interrelationships and data on evaluations of school, the following substantive conclusions were suggested:

1. High-prestige graduate schools tend to have more students and to offer work in the same fields of study as smaller schools plus offerings in additional rare fields. Consequently, graduate students are heavily concentrated in large, diverse, high-prestige institutions.

2. Public-private control is unrelated to the stratum dimension of size-offerings-prestige, but private universities are concentrated in the urban East, large public universities in the less urbanized areas of the Midwest and Far West, and small public universities in the less urbanized areas of the South and Mountain states. The result is that America has two geographically differentiated systems of graduate training of about the same size and stratum level.

3. A little less than half of the graduate students are in the natural sciences, a little less than one-quarter are in the social sciences, and a little more than one-quarter are in the humanities. Divisional differences by control and stratum are small.

4. About half of the students are in the beginning or master's degree stage, about half are in the advanced or Ph.D. stages of training. Students in humanities and in lower-stratum schools tend to be at earlier stages, which is suggestive of problems of speed and retention in these groups.

5. Very few of the students eschew the Ph.D., although a number are not certain that they will get one.

6. A clear majority of the students prefer academic jobs, and a slight majority expect them, the discrepancy being accounted for by 16 per cent of the sample who prefer academic jobs but do not expect them, often because of their sex or academic record.

7. Although often critical of specific aspects of graduate study, the students tend to be pleased with their choice of school and optimistic about their vocational futures. Their personal *esprit* compares favorably with the highest morale groups of enlisted men in the World War II American army.

8. There is no relationship between a student's location in the academic world described here and his morale.

Chapter 3

The Life Histories of
The Graduate Students:
A Composite Portrait

AMERICAN EDUCATION has grown by adding layers of advanced study to the existing structures underneath, without subtracting from the previous programs or building strong institutional bridges between the layers. Graduate study has been added to sixteen previous years of formal education, which means that it is rather difficult to begin graduate work before the age of 22. In addition, colleges and universities typically have no planned curriculum for feeding students into advanced training, in the sense that premedical and prelaw programs tend to funnel students into professional schools and require commitment fairly early in the game. When, in addition, it is noted that in America the age at marriage has been declining steadily and graduate education is no longer (if it ever was) defined as the province of celibate gentlemen scholars, the suggestion is that graduate students will be characterized by rather high age levels, delays in beginning graduate study, and a considerable number of wives, children, and chattels.[1]

Because all of these trends have important implications for understanding the students' financial situations, we must describe the sample in terms of age, family origins, marital status, and explore the career histories of the students before our strictly financial data can be interpreted with understanding.

Chronological age is the key variable here, and its most important consequence is the general tendency for the student's progress in the "family cycle"

---

[1] Eighteen per cent of the graduate students live in single-family houses, as contrasted with 10 per cent in university dormitories. Among those in single-family houses, two thirds own rather than rent.

to correlate strongly with age, while his progress through academic stages is only loosely related to it. Although the students range from 20 to over 60 (see Table 3.1) they are concentrated in the middle and late twenties, the median age being near 26.5, and half of the sample being between 24 and 29. The distribution has a definite skew. For obvious reasons, none of the students are under 20 (although a handful of students report that they had started graduate work while under 20), but one-quarter are 30 or older. While the typical graduate student is in his middle and late twenties, many are still continuing their education in their fourth decade.

Given every possible break, a student could complete his bachelor's degree by 22 and a Ph.D. in three or four years beyond that. Because 26.5 is the median age, rather than the upper limit, it would appear that not every possible break has been given, and in order to understand the gap between practice and the ideal it is necessary to reconstruct the student's past career histories, beginning with the families from which they come.

CLASS ORIGINS OF THE STUDENTS

In terms of education graduate students are conspicuously upwardly mobile (see Table 3.2). Forty per cent of their fathers did not finish high school, only 30 per cent are college graduates. Their occupational mobility is less obvious (see Table 3.3), 70 per cent of the students reporting that their fathers had a white-collar job when the respondents were in high school. Because of the age differences among the students, precise comparisons are impossible, but in 1950 18 per cent of the employed men in the country were managers or professionals, as contrasted to 58 per cent of the students' fathers.

There are two ways of looking at such results. Absolutely, most graduate students come from modest social origins, which implies that not many of their parents would find financial aid for a student son or daughter easy. Relatively, however, they are highly selected in terms of social class.

Because the United States Census classification of occupations presents some difficulty when used as a measure of prestige, the prestige level of the father's occupation was coded as one of five groups:[2] Low Status (garbage collectors, janitors, truck drivers, etc.), 7 per cent of the sample; Respectable Working Class (postmen, barbers, mechanics, clerks in retail stores, etc.), 16 per cent; Working Class Elite and Bottom-Middle (plumbers, carpenters, owners of small retail businesses, white-collar supervisors with minimum staff and discretion, etc.), 32 per cent; Middle-Middle (engineers without a professional degree, schoolteachers, middle managers, etc.), 27 per cent; and Elite (major professions, presidents of medium to large firms, top management in large firms, etc.), 19 per cent (Table 3.4).

[2] Sociological readers will recognize this as a modification of the Warner occupational prestige scale.

It is difficult to validate such scales, but in effect we asked the students to validate it for us. Each was asked, "In your opinion, how would the *general social standing* of your father's type of job compare with that of a professor in a small liberal arts college?" Professor in a small liberal arts college was picked as a reference point because it is a median position in the social world into which these students will move. Sixty-one per cent said their father's job was lower, 20 per cent said it was the same, and 19 per cent said it was higher. When this item is cross-tabulated against father's occupation (see Table 3.4), there is a strong relationship. Among those coded Low Status, 99 per cent said their father's job was lower. At the opposite end, among those coded "elite," 7 per cent checked lower. All of which suggests that we classified the fathers much as the respondents would have (or that graduate students have a similar bias whether they are filling out a schedule or are hired as coders for NORC).

In subsequent analyses father's occupation will be used as a measure of the class or prestige levels of the students' parental families.

Class origins are unrelated to most of the variables involved in the students' academic world (see Table 3.5). There is no relationship between father's occupation and academic stage, career expectations, or division. Despite the belief of many that social scientists are particularly upwardly mobile or that humanists are from high-status origins, the range by division is 4 per cent. There is a slight difference by type of school. Private I students come from higher class origins than those in the other five cells of the school classification. Inspection of the data for specific schools does indicate considerable class variation, institutions ranging from 27 per cent to 72 per cent of their students from middle-middle and elite class levels. Although the differences are perfectly sensible to anyone familiar with specific institutions, the important point is that class origins do not vary systematically with the dimensions of school classification which are significant for us.

A much more important finding, however, is that although there is no relationship between class and stage, there is one between class and age. Thus, at each stage of academic progress, students from lower-status origins are older, i.e., have taken longer to get there. We shall soon see some of the reasons.

Religion is the other aspect of the students' family origins which plays some part in the financial story (see Table 3.6). About half of the sample were reared as Protestants, about one-quarter as Roman Catholics, and 13 per cent as Jews. Today 39 per cent have maintained their identification and attend church "regularly, almost without exception," or "fairly regularly"; 30 per cent have maintained their identification, but attend church "occasionally," "seldom," or "never"; 26 per cent report no religion, and 5 per cent were converted to another faith (switches within Protestantism are not counted as conversions). Twenty-five per cent of the sample have shifted from an original denomination to "none," such changes being most frequent among Jews

(33 per cent shifting to "none") and least frequent among Catholics (12 per cent of the Catholics shifting to "none"). In terms of finances, the important statistic is that in terms of current religion, 22 per cent of the sample are Roman Catholics whose religious doctrines affect their family situations.

AGE AT BACHELOR'S DEGREE

One critical event in the student's academic histories is graduation from college. A bachelor's degree being necessary for graduate study, any delay in receiving it will be reflected in the age distribution of the sample.

Twenty-two, the "ideal" age, is the most common single age, but only half received their A.B.'s by then (see Table 3.7). Almost a quarter (23 per cent) were 25 or older when they finished undergraduate college. Presumably academic difficulties are not the explanation for differences in age at A.B. The survey did not ask questions about this problem, but a suggestive pattern develops from the cross-tabulation of father's occupation, sex, and age at A.B. (see Table 3.8). Among both men and women, students from lower-status origins were more likely to have been delayed in getting their bachelor's degree, and in both status levels men are slower than women.[3] Although military service plays some role, we get the same differences among students who have never been in service. More directly relevant is the contribution of self-help. The respondents were asked to estimate the "percentage of your undergraduate expenses which was met by: scholarships and fellowships, own earnings, parents, and other" (see Table 3.9).

Men are more likely to have been self-supporting than women, and in both sexes students from lower-status origins are more likely to report self-financing for the A.B. (There is no difference by status in the percentage reporting high scholarship help, the higher-status student's advantage coming almost entirely from parental support.) If the class and sex differences in delay come from work, when self-support is controlled, the sex and status differences should disappear (see Table 3.10). Self-support is indeed a factor. In each comparison, and particularly among the women, the self-supporting student is more likely to have been 23 or older when he or she finished undergraduate studies. Self-support is not the entire story, though. Among those who worked their way through, sex and status have no effect on delay, but, among those supported by stipends or parents, men are slower, and lower-status students slower than higher status students. The coding did not cover military service before the bachelor's degree, which may explain the sex difference. Regardless of the reason, for a man, being from a low-status back-

[3] This does not mean necessarily that this is true of all undergraduates. It could be that men are more interested in graduate school and that the delayed man is more likely to go on to graduate school than the delayed woman. Such selection problems should be borne in mind in interpreting all of the analyses in this section.

ground has about the same slowing effect as working one's way through school.

Remembering that men outnumber women considerably; that one-third of the graduate students earned half or more of their undergraduate expenses; and that a majority of the sample come from status levels in which graduation after 22 is more common than not; it follows that graduate schools typically recruit students who are a little behind the ideal at the time they get their bachelor's degrees. While it is perhaps a tribute to the channels of mobility in American education that so many working students and lower-class students can go on for graduate work, the system charges measurable years of their lives for this privilege (see Table 3.11). Although in the total sample, half are 27 or older, among those who got their A.B.'s after age 22, 71 per cent are that old. All other things equal, if all students going to graduate school got their A.B.'s by 22, the proportion of older students would be cut by a third or more.

A good share of the remaining age discrepancy comes from the fact that more than 40 per cent did not go to graduate school immediately after they earned their A.B.'s (see Table 3.12). At each age of receiving the bachelor's, between 40 and 48 per cent of the students report a gap of one year or more between their degree and first enrolment in graduate study in their current field. Between 20 and 30 per cent report a gap of five years or more.

What were they doing? Were they reluctant draftees? Or impoverished students who had to work to save up money for graduate school? Each student was asked to indicate what he was doing during his hiatus and also to indicate whether "if at that time you would have preferred to stay in school." By combining the type of activity and reported attitude toward graduate study, six major types can be defined (see Table 3.13). Although a large number of cases turned out to be uncodable, the general picture is not one of a frustrated group prevented from pursuing their studies. Rather it is one that includes a considerable number who were in no hurry to begin. The two most common categories are "willing work," and "study in another field." "Military service" and "employment" combined with "preference for school" are each reported by about one-fifth of the sample. When we consider patterns and combinations (see Table 3.14) it turns out that "unwilling work only" and "draft only" are each reported by 11 per cent of those with a break. Considering the "preferred school" item only, for students with one or two breaks, 28 per cent checked "preferred school" for their entire hiatus, 72 per cent reported one or more periods when this was not true. It would appear that the student with a gap is not typically one who was prevented from getting into graduate school, but one who had not as yet been attracted by it.

Two pieces of indirect evidence buttress the idea that a number of graduate students become motivated for graduate work only after they have been out of school some time. First, there is *no* relationship between father's occupation and a gap (see Table 3.15). Because low-status origins are generally associated with financial frictions which delay motivated students, and they are not associated with the hiatus phenomenon, the suggestion is that lack of money is *not* the important thing. A more direct line of evidence comes from answers to the question, "When did you first seriously consider going into this field?" Of the 2,831 students who answered the question, 26 per cent checked a period before college, 29 per cent the freshman or sophomore year, 28 per cent the junior or senior year, and 17 per cent a period after graduation. There is considerable variation by field (see Table 3.16). The natural sciences have large majorities of early choosers, but the social sciences and philosophy tend to be distinctly acquired tastes. In sociology, philosophy, political science, clinical psychology, and history, a fifth or more of the students first considered graduate work after they had been out of college; and, of sixteen fields with sufficient cases for tabulations, in only six is the proportion of students who first considered graduate study after college below 15 per cent.

There certainly are a number of students who have to postpone their graduate study, but probably an even large number of the students with a hiatus are late recruits. Perhaps they are people who found the non-academic world unsatisfying or perhaps they discovered the advantages of graduate study for success in their work, but either way the suggestion is that exposure to undergraduate work is not sufficient to provide motivation for graduate studies and that post-collegiate experience, positive or negative, plays an important part in the decision for graduate work.

Delay in getting the bachelor's degree and breaks between bachelor's degree and graduate work being independent, they produce an additive effect on age levels (see Table 3.17). Among the 30 per cent who graduated at 22 or younger and went straight to graduate school, only 17 per cent are 27 or older; among the 23 per cent who were delayed in their undergraduate work and also had a hiatus, 88 per cent are 27 or older. The high age level of graduate students can be pretty well explained by delay in getting to graduate school, although the fact that 17 per cent of those who started at 22 or before are now 27 or older is important too.[4]

So far, delay factors have been considered in the total sample. Late bachelor's degrees and late recruiting are unequally distributed among the cells of

[4] We should note that the dependent variable here is the age distribution of the population in school. The factors associated with dropping out of school, completing degrees in absentia, and slow progress toward degrees, which have not been considered here, play a part in the dolorous figures on age at receipt of the Ph.D. In 1957, the percentage of new Ph.D.'s who were 30 or older for selected fields is: foreign languages, 84; English, 84; social sciences and geography, 79; history, 78; philosophy, 71; psychology, 67; biological sciences, 59; earth sciences, 52; mathematics, 52; physics and astronomy, 46; and chemistry, 31; according to tabulations provided by the National Academy of Sciences–National Research Council.

the academic world indexes, which means that in some divisions and schools there is very little postponement, and in others delay is endemic (see Table 3.18). Although there are no divisional or control differences in age at bachelor's degree, in every comparison the lower the stratum of the school the greater the proportion of students who were 23 or older when they finished undergraduate training. Gaps between graduate and undergraduate work are similarly more common among students in lower-stratum schools. As Table 3.16 would suggest, natural science students are much less likely to report a gap (see Table 3.18b). Combining the two forms of delay (see Table 3.18c) produces a considerable divisional and stratum difference. Over 80 per cent of the Stratum III humanities and social science students got a late start in terms of the "ideal," as contrasted with 51 per cent in Private I natural science.

As a result, the age distribution of graduate students varies considerably with their division and type of institution (see Table 3.19). At each stage of academic progress, natural science students are younger (one exception turns up in Public II); and students in higher-stratum schools are younger. These effects are stronger in the private than in the public schools (which is congruent with our idea that private institutions are more differentiated than are public ones) so that Private II and III social science and humanities *master's* candidates are older than Private I natural science *Ph.D.* students. Although Ph.D. candidates under 27 are typically a small minority, in private schools there are twice as many proportionally in Stratum I as in Stratum III, and twice as many proportionally in natural science as in the other divisions.

We can now trace out the following factors involved in the fact that the age level of the graduate students is shifted several years above a priori norms. Many graduate students come from modest economic backgrounds and work their way through undergraduate college. Because of this and other reasons associated with class and sex, about half of the graduate students got their bachelor's degrees after the typical age of 22. Independent of this friction, a considerable number did not go on to graduate school immediately, some because they were drafted or forced to work, but many, particularly in the social sciences and humanities, because they were not motivated for graduate study at that time. Because students with either type of delay factor are more likely in lower-stratum schools and because natural scientists are less likely to report a hiatus, older students are more common in lower-stratum schools and in social sciences and humanities. This chain of factors comes close to explaining the general age level of the graduate students and the particularly high age levels in lower-stratum schools and among social science and humanities students.

AGE AND FAMILY CIRCLE

The fact that graduate students are typically a few years behind the optimum progress at a given age has a number of implications in terms of lifetime earnings, professional working lives, etc. More directly of concern, however, is the relationship between advanced age and family situation. Among the men there is a steady increase in marriage rates along the age scale (see Table 3.20). Some believe that marriage rates are particularly high in graduate school, but among men 26 or younger, less than one-half are married, and it is only in the group 30 or older that two-thirds are married. When these figures are compared with data for the U.S. population of college graduates in 1950,[5] it appears that up to age 24 marriage rates are similar for male graduate students and the general population of college graduate men. In the older ages, male graduate students are a little less likely to be married. There are some technical problems involved in making this contrast,[6] indicating that one should not make too much of it, but it suggests that the fact that half of the men are married is more a function of their advanced ages than of any precipitous rush to the altar on the graduate campuses. Because the survey data are from a cross-section in time rather than a cohort study, the finding is not conclusive, but the suggestion is that progress in family life (and responsibilities) proceeds steadily with increased age, while, because of differences in delay, academic progress does not.

The situation is a little different for women. After age 23, marriage percentages do not increase so steadily, and from 22 on the women have lower proportions married than do the men. Possibly graduate school disproportionately attracts women who are not tempted by matrimony, but, equally possible, women students who marry are likely to quit school. Single women were asked, "During the first five years after you finish graduate work, which of these would you prefer: marriage only, marriage with occasional work in my field, combining marriage with a career, or career only?" Of the single women, 20 per cent of 361 chose the last or anti-marriage alternative. Similarly, when the marital expectations of single men and women are compared (see Table 3.21), up to age 34 single women are more likely to expect marriage in the immediate future than are single men. These indirect pieces of evidence suggest that the low marriage rates of the women come from attrition among the recently married rather than high spinsterhood.

Considering men only, we can trace out the following sequence. By the time they have been married three years [7] (see Table 3.22) a slight majority of the men have a child, by the time they have been married five years, about

[5] Christopher Tietze and Patience Lauriate, "Age at Marriage and Educational Attainment in the United States," *Population Studies*, IX (November, 1955), 159–66.

[6] The U.S. data are from 1950, the survey from 1958. The U.S. data are for whites only, while Negroes make up 2 per cent of the survey sample, etc. More important is the possibility that married men are more likely to drop out of school. This is discussed in chapter ix.

[7] Duration of marriage was measured by subtracting reported age at marriage from reported age to nearest birthday.

two-thirds have a child, and after six or more years all but a small minority are fathers. A similar table for second children shows that after six or more years of marriage a clear majority have two or more children. Interestingly, in the general population people who marry earlier are more likely to have children within a given duration of marriage, but among graduate students it is the late marriers who have higher fertility. Perhaps some of the men postpone marriage and then have children quickly to catch up.

Each married student was asked, "Do you expect to have any (more) children in the next two years?" When fertility expectations are cross-tabulated against duration of marriage and number of children, the general pattern is as follows (see Table 3.23). Those with one child are rather likely to expect another within two years (perhaps because they believe that being an only child is undesirable), but those with two or more tend to have low expectations. Among the childless, the proportion expecting a child increases with duration of marriage up to five and six years.

It may well be that these fertility expectations are lower than among other groups in the population, but the conclusion is that, until they either have two children or have been married seven or more years without any, the majority of married male graduate students expect a child in the next two years.

These patterns do not vary much with other social characteristics. One might expect that those students who anticipate academic jobs would have lower fertility since they anticipate smaller future incomes, but the difference between academics and non-academics in fertility and fertility expectations is only a few percentage points. There is, however, a clear religious difference (see Table 3.24). At each duration of marriage, Catholic men are more likely to be fathers, and, regardless of their number of children (see Table 3.25), they are more likely to expect another. Differences among other religious positions are inconsistent and students reared as Catholics who have shifted to "none" have lower fertility, which suggests that the underlying factor is acceptance of Roman Catholic doctrine on birth control, rather than ethnic or value differences between religions.

If one thinks of the progression from adolescence to marriage to parenthood as a progression along stages of the life cycle, it would appear that for male graduate students life-cycle progression is ahead of progression through the stages of academic progress. The Family Role Index (Table 3.26) was constructed as a measure of progress in the family cycle. It combines sex, marital status, and the presence or absence of children to yield six types. The very small number of ex-married students (1.5 per cent of the sample) are treated as "single" if childless and are excluded from the typology if they have a child. The components of this index give the following findings:

82 per cent are male, 18 per cent female
51 per cent are single, 21 per cent married but childless, 28 per cent are parents

Among the men, 47 per cent are single, 28 per cent are childless husbands, 30 per cent are fathers

Among the women, 71 per cent are single, 13 per cent are childless wives, 16 per cent are mothers

The Family Role Index can be used to document the claim that the students' family progress is ahead of their academic progress (see Table 3.27). Among the men, as one moves from the early 20's to the 40's, the proportion single declines from 72 per cent to 19 per cent, the proportion of fathers increases from 8 per cent to 65 per cent, and there is a similar but less strong trend among the women. If the age distribution of the students were brought down to that characteristic of those who received their A.B.'s by 22 and went straight to graduate school, the proportion of fathers among the men would decline from 30 per cent to 19 per cent. However, because of the variability in starting graduate work and looseness in the relationship between academic stage and years of graduate study, the relationship between age and academic progress is not very strong (see Table 3.28). What there is comes from the obvious fact that very few of the 20–23 year-olds are Ph.D. candidates. After 23, however, there is no linear relationship between age and stage, each age group having one-third or more master's students. The third side of this triangle is that, necessarily, the relationship between family role and academic stage is loose. From Stage II on there is very little relationship between family role and academic stage in either sex (see Table 3.29).

Although progress in the family cycle is strongly related to age, especially among men, academic progress is not so closely tied to age, making for a considerable variety of family situations in every stage of academic progress.

SUMMARY

In this chapter we described three additional background characteristics — father's occupation, age, and family role — and looked at the interrelationships of these variables with some of the academic characteristics introduced in chapter ii. Our major conclusions were as follows: Absolutely speaking, graduate students are considerably older than is necessary. Relatively speaking, their progress in the life cycle tends to keep up with their age, while their progress in the academic cycle does not.

Specifically:

1. From the viewpoint of the society as a whole, graduate students are disproportionately recruited from higher-class levels, but in absolute terms they come from families of modest economic circumstances, and about one-third work their way through undergraduate college.

2. About half of the students were over 22 when they got their bachelor's degree, delay of this type being associated with undergraduate self-support, being a male, and lower-class origins.

3. A little over 40 per cent of the students were out of college a year or more before they began graduate work.

4. Delay in starting graduate school after receiving the A.B. is only partly due to military service and economic difficulties. More commonly it seems to be due to late development of motivation for graduate studies, particularly in the humanities and social sciences.

5. Because delay in receipt of the A.B. and gaps between bachelor's degree and graduate study in current field are statistically independent, their additive effect comes close to explaining the high ages of the students. All other things equal, if all graduate students received their A.B. at 22 and went to graduate school in their field immediately, only 17 per cent of the students in residence would be over 26 as contrasted with half of the sample.

6. Overage students are disproportionately concentrated in lower-stratum schools and in the social sciences and humanities.

7. Regardless of his academic progress, the *typical* male graduate student marries around age 26, is fairly likely to have a child by the time he has been married three years, and expects a child within the next two years unless he has two already or has been married seven or more years without any.

8. The only social characteristic which affects fertility and fertility plans among the men is that Roman Catholics have and expect more children.

9. Women students have lower marriage rates and higher marriage expectations than men, which suggests that women tend to drop out of graduate school when they get married.

10. Because progress in the family cycle is strongly related to age, and progress in academic stage is loosely related to age, at every stage of academic progress there is considerable variation in family situations.

■ Chapter 4

**Graduate Students' Incomes:
Sources, Totals,
And Perceived Adequacy**

During the academic year 1958–59 the students in the sample expected to receive approximately ten million dollars in income from sources ranging from National Science Foundation fellowships to royalties on a popular song. This grand total provides little information for understanding the students' financial resources and problems. Even translating it into an average of $3,900 raises more questions than it answers. Detailed analysis of sources of income, variation in total income, and perceived adequacy of income is necessary to bring the picture into clearer focus.

To begin with, one wonders where all this money is coming from. What are the major and minor income sources for the students? How much comes from stipends — scholarships, fellowships, assistantships? Probably more than any other group of American students, the arts and science graduate students receive sums of money from their schools and outside agencies to advance their training. What proportions receive a stipend? What proportions of their total incomes come from stipends? Are stipends a minor source of income or are the students heavily dependent on them? Where does the rest come from? Do their parents help them much? Are their wives putting them through school? How many are borrowing money to get through school? How many of the students are working their way through full- or part-time employment? Taken together the answers to these questions tell us how much of the costs are borne by the representatives of the larger society, by the students' families, and how much must be raised by the students' own employment or borrowing.

Graduate Students' Incomes

When income from all these sources is added up and divided by the number of students, we get our average-income figure. It is a very deceptive one, however, for among some groups of students only the most affluent are "average," and among others the average is typical only of the least affluent. At the center of things here lie family situations and a process whereby progression in the family cycle is associated with changes in income levels and sources of income along with increasing financial responsibilities. The extent to which the incomes analyzed here are family incomes is one of the most important aspects of graduate student finances. The differences between students who live alone, students whose spouse is the breadwinner, and students who must be breadwinners for their families are strong differences indeed.

None of these analyses, however, treat the most important question of all, whether incomes are high enough so that graduate students get along pretty well, or whether a considerable proportion are expecting to be in the red before the end of the year. Whether a given income level is adequate for the fullest development of personal and spiritual values is a question which we shall not tackle, but the less ambitious question of whether students expect to show a surplus or deficit — and who expects which — is amenable to research.

In this chapter we shall treat in turn sources of income, total incomes, and perceived income adequacy.

Sources of Income

The survey classified the income sources of the students into eleven categories:

1. *Stipend*: any source of income which is: (*a*) not to be repaid, (*b*) not provided by kin or personal friends, (*c*) supposed to enable the recipient to continue or complete his training, and (*d*) if work is required: (1) the work must be research, teaching, or professional internship in the student's field, and (2) the employer must be the university or an agency affiliated with the university or if a non-university agency (e.g., a VA hospital) the work is officially named as an internship or the like and there is presumable supervision and training involved.

2. *Veteran's Benefits*: any stipend provided by a governmental agency which is limited to veterans of military service (includes "G.I. Bill" and vocational rehabilitation).

3. *Withdrawals from Savings*.

4. *Part-time Job*: employment which is not a stipend and which is less than 37½ hours per week throughout the academic year.

5. *Full-time Job*: employment which is not a stipend which requires 37½ hours per week or more throughout the academic year.

6. *Spouse's Job*: income from husband's or wife's employment regardless of hours per week, but excluding spouse's stipend employment.

7. *Aid from Parents*.

8. *Investments*.

9. *Loans*: money expected to be borrowed during the year.
10. *Aid from Spouse's Parents.*
11. *Other.*

It should be noted that the classification is necessarily somewhat arbitrary. The frequency or infrequency of a given source could be increased or decreased by combination or subdivision of categories. Thus, if investments were divided into real estate and other, frequencies would be smaller, while, if savings and investments were combined as "capital," the frequency would be higher. For most analyses, stipends and veteran's benefits are combined. In addition, it should be noted that the unit involved is the academic year, not the calendar year, the fruits from the previous summer's employment (two-thirds of the sample worked the previous summer) appearing as available savings and money from the subsequent summer not being available to pay 1958–59 bills. It should also be noted that by these definitions, high income does not necessarily represent a favorable economic position because borrowings are treated the same as earnings or gifts. Thus, the question is how much money the student has available, not how much is available free of an obligation to repay it or work for it. Finally, married students reported on incomes for a family unit, single students for an individual.

The eleven sources vary considerably in their frequency (see Table 4.1), suggesting a number of conclusions about income sources.

1. Stipends, even when segregated from veteran's benefits, are clearly the most common source of income for graduate students. Seventy-four per cent report some stipend income and half (50 per cent) receive $150 a month or more.

2. Every other source is reported by only a minority of the students. Although only 3 per cent receive income from "other," no specific source except stipends is reported by much more than a third of the sample. Thus, there is considerable heterogeneity in the income patterns of the students.

3. Withdrawals from extant savings, reported by 35 per cent, is the second most common source, although it seldom represents a high amount, only 8 per cent reporting $100 a month or more.

4. A little more than a quarter (29 per cent) report income from a part-time job. Less than a half of the part-time workers expect $100 a month or more from their job.

5. Income from a spouse's job is a rather common source. Remembering that about half are married, the fact that a quarter of the students receive income from a spouse's job and 15 per cent receive $100 a month or more indicates that this is an important source of income.

6. Parents are, as informal observers of graduate student life have noted, a relatively infrequent source of income. Twenty-two per cent receive some help, and 7 per cent receive $100 a month or more.

7. Sixteen per cent of the sample receive income from veteran's benefits, 9 per cent receive $100 a month or more. GI income is absolutely rare, but aid from Uncle Sam is almost as common as aid from Dad and Mother. Clearly, the GI era in higher education is now history, but, among older students and those in fields of study which receive few stipends, veteran's benefits are of some importance.

8. Full-time work for graduate students is rare, being reported by 18 per cent of the sample. Because, however, it brings in higher wages, it ranks high among the sources which bring in large amounts and is the most common source yielding $300 a month or more.

9. Investments, hardly unexpectedly, are not the modal means of support of American graduate students. Despite the relatively high status origins of the sample, only 3 per cent receive as much as $100 a month from this source.

10. Although investments are rare, they are more common than borrowing. Nine per cent of the sample expect to borrow money during the year, 2 per cent expect to borrow $900 or more. Because loans are a major issue in higher education policy, the picture should be filled out in more detail. First, *this research was conducted before the advent of National Defense Act Loans*, and the current situation may well be quite different. Second, the figure refers to anticipated borrowing only. Students who had borrowed money before the beginning of the term should not (according to the questionnaire wording) have reported it as a source. In a separate question, students were asked to list their extant debts and the purposes for which they were incurred. When debts are separately classified as for "non-durables" (living costs, medical bills, tuition, etc.) or "durable goods" (anything with a resale or investment value, such as a mortgage, life insurance, or instalment credit) it turns out that 21 per cent of the sample have non-durable debts of $100 or more, 7 per cent have non-durable debts of $1,000 or more. Because these debts have been incurred over a number of years, it is fair to conclude that in any given calendar year prior to the National Defense Act, few graduate students borrowed money.

11. Only 3 per cent of the students have income from any other sources. Four students had money from inheritances, 16 reported aid from relatives other than parents or spouse's parents, 27 reported income from a spouse's stipend, and 39 fell into a residual pile — including one student who expected royalties on a song he had written.

Table 4.1 summarizes quite a bit of information and provides a reasonable picture of income sources, but there is another way of looking at these same figures, which can supplement it. The data in Table 4.1 are in terms of dollars, but $100-a-month means something different to a student with a total income of $1,800 a year than to a student with a total of $5,400. Therefore, for each student the same data were calculated as a percentage of his total income (see Table 4.2).

The table may be read across the rows or down the columns. Reading across, for spouse's job, as an example, we note that 25 per cent expect some income from this source, 21 per cent receive a fifth or more of their total from it, 12 per cent get half or more of their income from spouse's job, and only 1 per cent are totally supported by a wife or husband's work. Reading down the column headed 50 per cent, for example, we see that stipends are the most common source providing half or more of total income, with full-time work and spouse's employment next, but well behind.

There are a number of inferences to be drawn from Table 4.2. Very few students seem to have a single source of support, only 23 per cent falling into any of the 100 per cent categories. While savings are the second most common source, only 13 per cent get as much as a fifth of their income from savings withdrawals. Nobody is totally supported by his in-laws. Only 2 per cent can be thought of as gentlemen scholars, receiving half or more of their income from investments.

The data can be viewed a little more systematically, by summarizing the same numbers in a slightly different fashion (see Chart 4.1). The vertical dimension of the chart is the percentage of students who receive any income from a given source and the horizontal dimension is the percentage who get half or more of their income from a given source among those who receive any. The dimensions are analogous to frequency and intensity, the vertical scale measuring over-all frequency, the horizontal dimension measuring intensity of contribution among recipients.

When we think of a given source as being "important," we probably mean either that it is quite common or, regardless of its frequency, it is a major source of income for those who receive it. The chart tells us that these two criteria of importance are not strongly related, some sources being high on one dimension and not on the other. We can then think of four basic kinds of sources: 1. *Very important*: sources which are both frequent and yield a high proportion of the total income among recipients; 2. *Supplementary*: sources which are rather common but bring in only a low proportion of the total income of the recipients; 3. *Concentrated*: sources which are relatively infrequent but which contribute a high proportion of the incomes of those who have access to them; 4. *Unimportant*: sources which do not occur very often and which, when they do, account for only a low proportion of the income of recipients.

Allocation of specific sources to these categories depends upon an arbitrary cutting point. On the intensity dimension, any source contributing 50 per cent or more was termed high, and on the frequency dimension, given the high scatter, any source reported by 20 per cent or more of the students was termed high. The vertical dashes in the chart correspond to the division point on intensity, the horizontal dashes mark the division point on frequency, with the result that the chart is divided into four pigeonholes corresponding to the four types of importance.

The specific sources group as follows:

Very Important: By the criteria, there is only one source which is very important and one which is on the border line. *Stipends are the most important source of income for American arts and science graduate students*, in terms of dollar income, frequency, or in terms of the classification in Chart 4.1. Spouse's employment although to the left of the cutting point is a borderline candidate here.

Supplementary: The four supplementary sources, which are relatively frequent but typically a minor part of total income, are withdrawals from savings, part-time jobs, aid from parents, and spouse's job.

Concentrated: There is only one source which can be considered relatively rare but extremely vital to its recipients and that, of course, is full-time work. Only 18 per cent are working full time, but, among those who do, 94 per cent get half or more of their total income from their jobs.

Unimportant: The relatively unimportant sources are veteran's benefits, investments, loans, aid from spouse's parents, and other.

Because so many of the sources account for low proportions of the students' total incomes, it follows that graduate students tend to rely on multiple income sources (see Table 4.3). Three-quarters of the sample have more than one income source, and a little less than half have two or more sources each of which accounts for a fifth or more of their total income. Examination of the various combinations and patterns of income sources discloses a wide variety. Considering sources which amount to 20 per cent or more of total income, although 44 per cent of the sample have two or more such sources, the most frequent combination — spouse's employment plus stipend (including veteran's benefits) — is reported by only 13 per cent of the sample.

In general, graduate students tend to have multiple and diverse income sources, of which income from stipends is clearly the most important. For about one-fourth of the students, income from spouse's employment is an important source; for a small minority, full-time work is the predominant source. Withdrawals from savings, part-time work, and aid from parents tend to be relatively (but not absolutely) common supplementary sources; and all other sources of income are relatively unimportant.

Total Income

The total income of each student was determined by summing his expected returns from each of the eleven specific sources. When stipends included board and room, an estimate of their cash value was made from consulting university catalogues.

About half of the sample (see Table 4.4) anticipated incomes amounting to $400 a month or more. The distribution shows considerable variation, however, with one-third reporting total incomes of less than $300 a month (assuming a nine-month academic year) and one-third reporting $500 a month or more.

At first glance, it is possible by a careful (and biased) selection from the data to make the case that graduate students are remarkably prosperous. Thus (1) half (48 per cent) of the students had $500 or more in savings at the beginning of the year; (2) two-thirds own an automobile; (3) more students receive income from investments than expect to borrow. In order to gain a more realistic perspective, it is necessary to consider a number of additional factors.

In the first place, graduate students have expenses connected with their education. A large number receive stipends which help pay for these expenses, but, because stipends are counted in the total-income figures, it is only fair to take into consideration that a portion of these funds go for tuition, books, thesis costs, etc. Chapter v discusses academic expenditures in detail, but for present purposes it is enough to note that, on the average, the students spend 15 per cent of their total income on education. There is considerable variation in this proportion, and it works out in such a way that lower-income students spend much higher proportions of their income for schooling, but on the average a factor of between 10 and 20 per cent may be subtracted to give a fair picture of the money available for "living expenses."

Second, it is easy to forget that we are living in a wealthy nation in a period of high incomes and inflation. Statistical analyses controlling for age, sex, family situation, education, region, race, etc., would be necessary before one could compare their situation with similar people in the general population. Furthermore, the survey includes some sources of income which are excluded in data for the general population (loans and withdrawals from savings). However, a brief review of some 1958 income data for the American population as a whole may give useful perspective if one does not demand too much precision (see Table 4.5).

Although in 1958 the national per capita income was only $2,474, the family (defined by the Census as "a group of two or more persons related by blood, marriage or adoption and residing together") is the typical economic unit for adults, and median family incomes range from about $3,000 for working women with no family to about $7,000 for families with a working husband and wife.

Income also varies considerably with the occupation and education of the worker. Table 4.5 shows that family incomes for college graduates are higher than for Americans as a whole, the medians being above $7,000 a year for all groups under 65 years of age. For comparison, the same Census data give the following median family incomes for other educational levels in the 25-34 group: elementary school, $3,544; part high school, $4,765; high school, $5,399.

Remembering that all of the sample are college graduates, one-half are married, and the majority are in the 25-34 age range, our very rough guess would be that a similar population with comparable educations and family situations but not in graduate school would have a median income well above that reported by graduate students. Thus it is probably fair to say that the typical graduate student is receiving less income than he could make if he were to drop out of school, although his studies may well have a long-range benefit on his income level in later life.

Seen in perspective, the incomes of graduate students appear less opulent, but, because their major source of income is stipends which seldom run to $400 a month, one wonders how they amass this much.

When the incomes of students with and without specific sources of income are compared, two sources — full-time work and spouse's employment — stand out as being associated with high incomes (see Table 4.6). In fact, income levels of $400 a month or more are pretty much limited to students who receive money from one or both of these sources (see Table 4.7). Among students with income from one or both, three-quarters or more have yearly totals of $3,600 or more, while for students with no income from either, three-quarters have incomes below $3,600.

Because the students typically have multiple income sources, these figures do not mean that all the spouses are employed at salaries of $5,000 a year or more. Rather it means that unless a graduate student can supplement his other income sources with money from full-time work or spouse's employment he has a rather low chance of receiving $400 a month or more in total income. One way of thinking about this is to think of two separate economic worlds: the university world characterized by stipends, low paying part-time jobs, half-time assistantships, etc., where wages are not especially high, hours of work tend to be low, and the situation is defined as one of training. In contrast there is the "real labor force" of full-time jobs and competitive wages. Unless students are receiving income from real labor force participation, their total incomes seldom go over $400 a month. The high income levels of the students stem essentially from the fact that 42 per cent of them are receiving money from their own or their spouse's employment in the real labor force.

High incomes stem from access to real labor force wages, and real labor force wages, in turn are a function of family role. Possibly the most important table in this study comes from the cross-tabulation of family role, full-time work, and spouse's employment (see Table 4.8). Among single men the high income sources are almost non-existent, as only 10 per cent have full-time jobs and single men have no spouses to help out. When a man gets married, however, the situation changes. Although his chances of working full-time do not increase, in 76 per cent of the cases he will receive income from his wife's employment. In total, 83 per cent of the husbands have income from one or both of the high-income sources. What happens when the stork arrives? Among fathers, the proportion working full-time almost triples, (38 per cent as contrasted with 13 per cent of the husbands) and the proportion with income from wife's employment declines sharply (from 76 per cent to 25 per cent).

As a result, 58 per cent of the fathers have access to one or both of the high-income sources.

We shall have cause many times to note the consequences of the curvilinear process in which at first marriage adds an important income source for the male graduate student, but then soon children tend to subtract that source, add to the budget, and apparently increase the work levels of the students.

Among women the process is slightly different. Only a few women, regardless of their life-cycle position, have full-time jobs, but both wives and mothers have high rates of support from husband's jobs. To put it simply, it appears that married women can afford to go to graduate school only if their husbands can support the entire family, whether or not there is a child.

Having a near monopoly on the high-income sources, married students tend to have a near monopoly on the high incomes (see Table 4.9). For single students of either sex, incomes are concentrated between $1,000 and $2,999 for the academic year. Two-thirds of the single students report incomes in this range and about 90 per cent have incomes between $1,000 and $4,999. The married students have much higher incomes and more variation. Beginning with the men, very few have incomes below $3,000. Only 12 per cent of the married men, as contrasted with 67 per cent of the single students, have incomes below $3,000. Married men's incomes are concentrated in the range from $3,000 to $6,999, which includes 74 per cent of the husbands and 70 per cent of the fathers. Fourteen per cent of the husbands and 18 per cent of the fathers fall in the high-income levels of $7,000 or more. The highest incomes among the students are reported by married women, 33 per cent of the wives and 42 per cent of the mothers reporting family incomes of $7,000 or more for the academic year, 60 per cent of each group reporting incomes of $5,000 or more for the nine-month period. Our inference is that while a man's graduate training can be considered an important investment, graduate training for married women is an economic luxury, and the high-income levels of the married women probably stem from the fact that married women typically go to graduate school only when their husbands are making enough money to pay for such a luxury.

The median income figure of around $400 a month for the entire sample conceals the fact that the vast majority of single students have incomes well below it and a majority of married students have incomes above it.

Although access to the high-income sources is a major factor in the high incomes of the married students, it is not a complete explanation (see Table 4.10). Married students have higher incomes than single students, whether or not they are tapping the high-income sources. Examination of the detailed data on the married students who are not working full time and whose spouses are not working discloses no particular additional source, leading to the conclusion that they just get more from the same sources. Thus, life-cycle position is related to income levels independent of the special sources of income associated with later stages in the family cycle.

With minor exceptions, the further along a student is in school and the older he is, the higher his income, regardless of marital status and income from the two high paying sources (see Table 4.11). It is important to note that older students and students with families are characterized by higher incomes for reasons above and beyond their access to the two high-income sources.

These data have a number of implications for policy in the area of graduate education.

To begin with, the support of American graduate students is rather expensive. Whether or not their incomes are lower than those of comparable non-graduate students, their family situations and ages are such that incomes equivalent to $5,000 a year are as common as not. This in turn suggests that even with a substantial increase in stipend money the traditional academic sources of income cannot be sufficient to support these students. Given the kinds of people in graduate school, half of the American graduate students almost of necessity must have a representative in the real labor force or, failing that, will have to go to work to support their families. It is our impression that policy makers in the area of graduate education do not systematically allow for the fact that the graduate student is no longer (if he ever was) typically young, unattached, and inexpensive.

Second, the evidence suggests that fathers, who comprise 25 per cent of the students and 30 per cent of the men, present particular financial problems, although their income levels are high. Single students of either sex typically have a low income, but presumably their income requirements are also modest; the married woman typically has an employed husband or she would not be in graduate school (the loss of talented women through marriage is of course a problem, but it is not purely economic); the husband has an expensive menage to support, but he usually has a working wife to help him; but the father has the heaviest financial burdens and lesser help from his mate (although the fact that a quarter of the wives of married men with children are working is a striking one). Among married men there is a strong negative association between full-time work and spouse's employment ($Q = -.68$) which suggests that, if spouse's employment is absent, fathers solve their dilemma by taking full-time jobs (or not giving up full-time jobs when they start graduate work). In terms of income this is a satisfactory solution, but, as we shall see, the fathers tend to pay a price in terms of low academic loads and high drop-out rates. Our later analysis will show that fathers do not worry much more than other students about their finances, but the academic world may legitimately worry that 31 per cent of the Ph.D. candidates, who represent the cream of the crop in terms of training and selection, are caught in these financial cross-pressures.

Third, as our non-financial analyses would imply, age seems to be a key background variable here. Because age is related to family role and contributes independently to high incomes, among students under 27, one-third (34 per cent) have incomes of $3,600 or more during the academic year, as contrasted with 59 per cent among students 27 or older. Thus, the American pattern of late beginning and endings for graduate study is also one of high income levels for graduate students.

ADEQUACY OF INCOME

Probably the most important question about money is not how much, but whether there is enough. Because family responsibilities and styles of living vary among the students, total income data need to be supplemented by information on whether that total is sufficient to pay the bills. By and large the students are fairly optimistic about their chances of striking a favorable balance during the academic year (see Table 4.12). Half of the sample predicted sufficient margin to provide a hedge against emergencies, and 84 per cent thought they had enough money to cover their necessary expenses. Sixteen per cent, however, were doubtful about the chances of having an adequate income to get through the academic year.

The basic variables which explain variation in perceived adequacy of income are the amount of income and the student's family situation. The higher the income and the smaller the family, the more likely the student is to say that he will have enough money to get through the year (see Chart 4.2). While the relationship is hardly surprising, some of the trends in the chart require discussion. Single men and women seem to have about the same expense situation, for their curves are almost identical. In the lowest income categories (under $200 a month) roughly three-quarters expect to balance their books, and the proportion rises steadily until after $400 a month 90 per cent are optimistic, and at $600 a month almost all single students can avoid a deficit. For married men the pattern is a little different. In the low-income group again roughly three-quarters predict solvency, but among married students the proportion drops in the group expecting between $200 and $299. Presumably married students living on less than $200 a month constitute a particular group which can adapt to a minimum budget. After $300 a month, there is a recovery for both husbands and fathers, but a difference in the rate of recovery. For husbands, an income level of $300 or more a month brings the curve up to near the figures for single students, but it takes an income level of $500 a month or more before the fathers are reporting the same net position as husbands report at $300–$399. Because of the small number of cases, married women were excluded from this analysis.

Putting it another way, it takes an income level of $300 a month or more to put husbands in the same net position the single students are in at $200–$299, and it takes over $500 a month for the fathers to achieve the same proportion of solvencies. The big differences, of course, are in the $200–$399 a month range, which is clearly comfortable for single students and marginal for the fathers. In this range roughly 15 per cent of the single students anticipate deficits, in contrast to about 40 per cent of the fathers.

As we have seen, those who need larger incomes tend to have them, and there is some tendency for the situation to come out even (see Table 4.13). In each type of family role the vast majority expect to balance their books. However, we do note that married women, as one would have expected from their (husbands') high incomes have somewhat fewer hardship cases, and fathers have somewhat more, their financial needs being greater and their incomes not much higher than husbands.

None of the other major variables seems to contribute to perceived adequacy. One might expect that students from lower-class origins would be more used to tightening their belts and could get along better at the same income level, or one might predict that those who expect academic jobs might have more modest levels of living because they clearly anticipate lower future salary levels. Nevertheless, we find no relationship with father's occupation, stage, division, age, academic expectations, or type of school. The negative finding on type of school is perhaps the most surprising, for a case could be made that the lower-stratum public schools, which tend to be in smaller towns, would have a lower cost of living. However there is no consistent difference by stratum or control in the proportion of students anticipating solvency in a given family situation and income level (see Table 4.14). This does not mean that there are no differences in the objective cost of living, but it does imply that such differences are not translated into consistent effects on subjective adequacy.

What this section has shown then is that: (1) the vast majority of students expect enough income to get through the year; (2) the amount of income necessary to produce a favorable situation varies widely with the students' family situations; (3) with the possible exception of the fathers, income and needs tend to balance out so that there are no differences in the percentage who see themselves as comfortably fixed by the standard variables of our analysis—father's occupation, career expectations, age, stage, division, stratum, and control.

Summary

1. Graduate students tend to have multiple and diverse income sources. The only source which is important for a majority of students is stipends. Seventy-four per cent receive stipend income, half receive $150 a month or more in stipend income, and 41 per cent receive half or more of their income from stipends.

2. For about a quarter of the students, income from spouse's employment is an important source; for a small minority, full-time work is the major income

Graduate Students' Incomes

source; and for a considerable minority withdrawals from savings, part-time work, and aid from parents are important supplementary sources. Investments, borrowing, veteran's benefits, and other sources are relatively unimportant.

3. The sample reports a median income of approximately $400 a month during the academic year, which appears to be fairly high, but needs to be qualified by the fact that on the average 15 per cent of this must be spent on graduate school and incomes for comparable people in the general population are probably higher.

4. High incomes are concentrated among married students, low incomes among single students. Part of the high income levels of the married comes from their access to income from full-time jobs and income from spouse's employment, but, even among those without income from these sources, total incomes run high.

5. Eighty-four per cent of the students believe that they have enough income to cover their expenses, 53 per cent believe they have enough for their expenses plus a surplus for emergencies.

6. Whether incomes are seen as adequate or not depends on the size of the income and the size of the family it must support. On the average, it takes an income of $300 a month to put husbands in the same financial position as single students who get $200–$299 a month, and it takes over $500 a month for the fathers to achieve the same proportion who believe their incomes are adequate.

7. Because students with larger families tend to have larger incomes, perceived adequacy of income does not vary much with family role (or with other major variables), although married women are a little more comfortable and fathers somewhat less comfortable than the others.

8. Family role position is the major determinant of financial situations.

Single students have low incomes, low income needs, and seldom work full time.

Married women tend to have high incomes and to be supported by a working husband.

Husbands tend to have high incomes, high income needs, and working wives to supplement their totals.

Fathers have higher income needs than husbands, about the same income levels as husbands, and appear to compensate for the loss of spouse's employment by taking up full-time work. Of all the groups, only the fathers seem to have financial troubles, and these are not due to low incomes but to income sources which divert them from their studies.

Implications

This chapter has been concerned primarily with documenting specific details — the proportion receiving aid from parents, comparison of student incomes and incomes in the general population, the importance of withdrawals from savings as a source of income, etc. Along with some materials which will be presented in later chapters, these findings suggest three generalizations about graduate student finances.

The ubiquity of solvency.—To a surprising degree, graduate students appear to be able to balance their books each year. This is a rare enough feat in the general population and indeed remarkable in a group who are still going to school. Ninety-one per cent expected to get through the year without borrowing, and only a handful did not expect enough income to cover expenses. A number of academic statesmen have urged the students to borrow, arguing from the idea that graduate training should be considered an investment which adds to earning power. Prior to the National Defense Act loan program, and perhaps still, few students were tempted to study now and pay later. This is in sharp contrast to the field of medicine, for example, where in 1959, a representative sample of graduating medical students reported an average non-durable indebtedness of $1,800.[1] We are not taking a position on this issue, and not even the most optimistic would claim that graduate students have the repayment potential of future physicians, but the point remains that arts and science graduate study is essentially on a pay-as-you-go basis.

The paucity of subsidy.—Having documented at length the importance of stipends as the major source of income for graduate students, it may appear illogical to conclude that they receive very little subsidy. Partly it is a "is the glass half full or half empty" semantic trick, since the fact that 61 per cent receive stipends can also be stated as "roughly four out of ten receive no stipend at all."[2] More important, however, chapter vi will show that most stipend holders are assistants who are only partly subsidized, since they must work for their money. Thus, although a little less than two-thirds receive a stipend, only one-third receive *any* money, above and beyond tuition, for which they did not have to work. Because, in addition, parental help is rare and when provided is typically a small amount, it is fair to conclude that the vast majority of students, while surely aided by stipends or parents, are hardly subsidized in the sense of having to be unconcerned in the raising of the bulk of their incomes. Again, we wish to take no position for or against such subsidies but merely stress that the high proportions receiving stipends and the high income levels of students do not in any sense mean that graduate students are living on the dole.

[1] These figures are not exactly comparable, but the different definitions of debt cause, if anything, the underestimation of the average debt of the medical student. Dr. J. Frank Whiting of the Association of American Medical Colleges kindly supplied this information.

[2] In neither private nor public schools does tuition pay the full costs of college education at any level. Thus even students without stipends are receiving help from donors or tax payers.

The costs of maintaining solvency without subsidy. — A person who does not intend to borrow money, who does not receive a total subsidy, and who expects a reasonable income is in a rather delicate situation. The finding that few graduate students borrow money or run up debts appears to indicate that the students' financial situations are optimal. However, there are some less happy ways of stating the same conclusion. For instance, "Graduate students will stay in school only so long as they can meet their expenses without borrowing," or "Graduate students will avoid debt even at the price of prolonging their studies through employment." The extent to which these statements are true is the subject of subsequent chapters, but even without detailed data, a priori reasoning tells us that long periods of uninterrupted full-time study are incompatible with non-borrowing and low rates of total subsidy, except perhaps for the small number of husbands who are supported by their wives (and our data on fertility and fertility expectations suggest that this halcyon state seldom lasts more than one or two years). Our data suggest that graduate students pay for their money with time, either through interruptions in their studies or light course loads.

The typical graduate student (whether he knows it or not) is faced with a dilemma. On the one hand there is the siren call of the research and teaching assistantship for many, and for others the imperative claim of bills to be paid and families to be fed. It is entirely possible that, through assistantships or other employment in combination with other income sources, he can end his academic year in the black. On the other hand, heavy work loads are hardly congruent with heavy course loads. Light course loads, in turn, probably provide enough delay to make it unlikely that a Ph.D. student (who begins his graduate work typically around age 25) will elude the stork, whose arrival exacerbates the entire situation.

It is perhaps not surprising that America's system of graduate education, which delays entry into graduate studies until the ages of family formation, which tacitly encourages part-time and full-time work in combination with studies, and which extracts no tangible penalties for prolonging the period of study, is characterized by high student incomes and low student debts. What would indeed be surprising would be a finding that such a system is compatible with getting any schoolwork done. It is to this obverse side of the coins that the next chapter turns.

■ Chapter 5

Graduate Students as
Consumers of Education:
Expenditures, Prices, and Demand

IN A WAY, the system of graduate education can be thought of as a market place in which academic credits and degrees are sold by institutions and purchased by graduate students. This "market" has a number of bizarre features: the sellers lose money on every transaction; a number of the buyers get their funds by working as salesmen in the basement departments of undergraduate education; the sellers have the right to demand intellectual accomplishment before delivering the merchandise; and the buyers have little opportunity to shift to alternative suppliers if the delivered merchandise is shoddy or overpriced.

Pursuing this analogy a little further, it will be useful to think of the purchase of graduate education as similar to the purchase of a home furnace. There is an initial decision, say, to get a gas, coal, or oil furnace, but after this decision is made it is very expensive to alter it, although the customer can control his expenditures by turning the thermostat up or down. As in furnace economics, the costs to the students of graduate education are a function of the kind of instalation and the *rate* of consumption. In this chapter we shall consider first the prices and second the great variation in rates of consumption.

ACADEMIC COSTS

Table 5.1 gives the distributions of expenditures for specific categories of academic expenses (tuition and fees, books, journals, theses, and other). For tuition the amount covered by a stipend is included in the costs, just as it was

Graduate Students as Consumers 51

included in the students' incomes. For theses, however, only out-of-pocket costs were considered, since such subsidies as the availability of a manuscript collection or a cyclotron are hard to compute in dollars.

Total professional expenditures (expected in 1958–59) are rather variable. The median expectation is close to $450 a year, but one-fifth expect to pay $900 a year and somewhat less than one-fifth will pay $225 or less. Expressing these same figures as a percentage of total income, one-third will spend less than 10 per cent of their total and about two-thirds will spend less than a fifth of their total income on schooling. At the opposite extreme, a fifth (22 per cent) will spend 30 per cent or more of their total income on graduate training. In short, for a considerable majority of students the absolute and proportional costs of graduate education are fairly low, but for a minority these costs will take a big bite.

When we turn to the specific categories involved, we see quickly that when we consider "total professional expenditures" we are concerned essentially with tuition. Thus, the median for tuition and fees is about $350 a year, while the median for total costs is about $450. The difference is accounted for by books, journals, theses, and other. Tuition varies considerably, one-quarter of the students expecting to pay less than $200 a year and one-quarter $700 or more. Half of the sample will pay between $200 and $700, and the median is about $350. Other categories of costs are perhaps interesting in themselves but cannot be viewed as creating severe financial problems for the students. We note that 8 per cent of the students in the apex of the American educational system avoid the financial burden of book costs by not buying any at all, and only 35 per cent expect to spend $55 a year or more on professional books. If books are estimated at the very unrealistic low value of $5 a copy, this means that close to two-thirds of America's graduate students buy less than ten books a year. About half plan to subscribe to a professional journal, and a little less than one-fifth plan to pay $20 or more for journals. Less than one-quarter of the sample reported expected expenditures for their theses. This last figure is deceptive, since it applies only to those expecting to be working on their theses. Among those reporting such costs, about a third reported expected costs of $100 or more.

About 80 per cent of the sample expected no other costs in addition to those considered above, and only 4 per cent reported other costs of $100 or more. These "other" costs scatter over a number of categories, the only frequent ones being dues to professional societies (12 per cent mentioned this, although this is not a valid estimate of such memberships, since many societies provide a journal along with membership and such costs were probably reported as journal costs), travel to professional meetings (5 per cent of the sample), and laboratory equipment (5 per cent). Three students (or .13 per cent) reported expected costs of publishing a paper or book.

Because tuition and fees make up such a great part of total expected professional costs, the total variation in professional expenditures is primarily a function of variation in tuition payments. As our furnace analogy suggests, tuition costs vary with two things, the type of institution and the rate at which education is consumed.

We can begin by examining the list price. Estimates of "normal" tuition costs are hard to make because of the complexity of the tuition rate schedules involved and the looseness of graduate training requirements. For example, in public schools, in-state and out-of-state tuitions vary; one university in the sample charges a special discounted tuition to religious workers of its faith who make up a goodly portion of the students; one of the schools charges a higher tuition in one and only one of its arts and science departments. However, using the university catalogues, we made the best rule-of-thumb estimate we could of the total in tuition and fees which would be paid by a *full-time* graduate student (see Table 5.2).

Table 5.2 should be read with some caution. First, in each cell there are a small number of schools. Second, our sample is not a sample of *schools* but of *students*. In order to make our *students* representative of American graduate *students*, schools with many graduate students had a greater chance of being drawn. Hence our tuition costs are biased toward the costs of big graduate schools. However, there are more students in big graduate schools, and these figures give a good picture of the tuition situation faced by the typical graduate student.

The striking difference in Table 5.2 is that between the private and public institutions. Not only are state university tuitions lower for their own residents, but, comparing the 13 private institutions with the 12 state schools, there are only two public schools whose *out-of-state* fee is higher than the *lowest* private school in the sample. The two distributions are almost mutually exclusive.

Comparing schools in terms of stratum, however, does not present as clear a picture. In the state schools there is no linear relationship between fees and prestige, the cheapest school in the sample being in Stratum III, the second least expensive school being among the ten most highly rated institutions in the country, the two most expensive public schools being in the middle stratum.

Among private schools, there is a progression in the averages, as prestige increases ($774 to $860 to $1,100) and the high-prestige private schools are fairly expensive. However within each prestige group there is a lot of variation, such that the cheapest school in each stratum is less than the highest in any other. Thus there are private institutions of quite modest academic reputation whose tuition costs run up to ten times as much as schools solidly in the academic upper class.

Now let us see what the students actually expected to pay during the academic year 1958–59.

Considering only students who actually were registered for the entire academic year 1959–60, expected payments show the same trends as "normal costs." In each stratum, students in private schools anticipated at least twice the costs of students in public institutions, and the same slight stratum differences shown in Table 5.2 reappear in Table 5.3.

The figures in Table 5.3, however, are much smaller. In the private schools, expected payments run considerably smaller than the normal costs for full-time students, and, presumably, if we had the data to segregate residents and non-residents in public schools the same difference would appear. The suggestion is that course loads often run under those suggested by the catalogue norms.

One year after the original survey, NORC representatives collected the grades and course credits for students in all but one of the sample schools. Credits actually received were then expressed as a fraction of the catalogue norm for a full year's full-time work. There are some difficulties in the data — students who received incompletes and failing grades in many cases still paid tuition for the courses although they did not receive credit for completion, students writing questionnaires in the fall may not be accurate in predicting their course loads for the entire year — but on the whole there is a considerable association between tuition and fee expectations and academic work completed (see Table 5.4). Private school students with the lightest completions still expected to pay more than public students with heavy loads; but within a control category the variation by course load is greater than the variation by stratum. Considering that our biases are such as to underestimate rather than to overestimate the relationship, we conclude that course loads play a major part in determining tuition and fee expenditures.

Viewing the same figures as a proportion of total income, we see that the burden of academic costs is quite variable. Among part-time students in state schools, only a handful spend 30 per cent or more of their total income for graduate training, but, among private school students who completed more than two-thirds of a full year's load, a majority spend this much (see Table 5.5).

Because single students have lower incomes and carry somewhat heavier course loads, academic expenses consume a considerable share of their incomes even in public institutions and to a more striking degree in private institutions (see Table 5.6). At first glance, it would appear that the general prosperity of graduate students conceals groups for whom educational costs are a considerable burden. The matter is not that simple, however, for a burden has to be perceived as such before it becomes a serious problem. When perceived income adequacy is cross-tabulated by income and proportional professional costs (Table 5.7) no effect appears. The lower the income, the less likely the student is to anticipate solvency, but within an income group there is no systematic difference in perceived adequacy whether academic expenses are less than 10 per cent or more than 30. Possibly the students adjust their other expenditures to make up for tuition costs, but, equally possible, students keep their academic expenses under control by completing only as much work as they can afford without going into the red. Under either interpretation, the high costs absolutely and relatively in private schools do not appear a subjective burden to the customers.

We may summarize as follows:

1. Median total expenditures for graduate education amount to about $450 a year, the bulk of this going for tuition which has a median of $350. Viewed as a proportion of total income, the average student spends about 15 per cent of his total income on academic expenses.

2. Academic expenses are highly variable: One-fifth of the students spend $900 or more, 22 per cent spend 30 per cent or more of their total income on schooling; while 16 per cent spend less than $225 a year and 36 per cent spend less than a tenth of their total income.

3. Variations in academic expenditures are essentially due to two factors, lower tuitions in public institutions and highly variable course loads in all types of institutions.

4. It may be (and we have no figures to back up the idea) that at the undergraduate level state institutions provide mass education for students from lower status origins, while private institutions provide "elite" educations for students from higher status origins, but this difference does not hold among graduate students. Public and private graduate students are essentially similar in their "quality," students' class origins, and student incomes. Thus, essentially similar students are receiving essentially similar types of education at very different costs in the two types of schools.

5. Although for some students (e.g., single students with high course loads in private schools) academic costs consume a large fraction of their total incomes, the proportion of total income which must be spent for education shows no relationship to perceived financial adequacy. That is, students with higher educational bills are no more likely to anticipate ending up in the red.

Course Loads

So far, the financial analyses have painted a far rosier picture of student finances than was anticipated when this study was commissioned. Graduate students as a whole have adequate levels of income, low levels of debt, and educational expenses which generally run in the neighborhood of $50 a month for the nine-month academic year, or about the level of payments on a used car.

Remembering our furnace analogy, however, it may be worthwhile to find out how much heat is coming through the registers.

Table 5.8 describes the academic work completed by the sample in 1958–59. Of the students who were registered for the entire year, 12 per cent received credit for what their schools' catalogues define as a full-time load, and about 40 per cent received credit for more than two-thirds of a full year's load.

There are a number of perfectly good reasons why these figures should not be taken at face value. Catalogues may set forth unrealistic norms, graduate education places less stress on courses and more stress on independent work, courses may vary considerably in the amount of time they require, and so on. Thus, it is quite possible that graduate students could be putting in large amounts of their time in academic activities and still not amass a large number of credits.

When, however, course loads are tabulated against the students' employment situations, some doubt arises as to whether the excess time is spent in cerebration (see Table 5.9). The fact that the amount of credits amassed in 1958–59 is a strong negative function of the amount of employment expected during the year raises the distinct suspicion that employment and rapid completion of graduate training are somewhat incompatible. Among the students who expected to be employed full- or part-time during the year only a third completed more than two-thirds of a full-time load, while among those without jobs 63 per cent passed the two-thirds mark. While the fact that among those who were not employed full-time loads are not unanimous may reflect the unreality of our measure, the fact that those who were employed (73 per cent of those who were registered all year) completed so much less cannot be explained away so easily.

The indirect evidence in the table is that what is important is the time and not the nature of the work. Among the workers, teaching and research assistants had lower completion rates than those students with only a part-time job, while among the non-workers, fellows completed more work than the rest. Thus the question is not one of "stipends," because stipends which require work have the same interference value as other part-time jobs and stipends which do not require work have no more beneficial effect than other situations which involve exemption from work.

Such data as these do not tell us which is cause and which is effect. It could be that graduate programs vary considerably in the amount of time they require and that students put the excess time in work, or it could be that students vary in the amount of work they require to get along and they put the excess time into school, or it could be that America has evolved a type of graduate program which is particularly adapted to part-time students, but it is now fairly clear that the benign financial situations of America's graduate students go hand in hand with fairly low consumption of academic credits, given the a priori standard of full-time study.

We can add to our understanding of these findings by considering the relationships between academic loads and other variables.

1. Academic loads are unrelated to career plans and to faculty members' ratings of students' ability. In the follow-up study we managed to collect faculty ratings of a high proportion of our students. There is no association between these evaluations and course loads, over-all, or when employment is introduced as a statistical control. Similarly there is no relationship between career expectations and load. Thus, the "part-time student" is by no means of lesser ability or with a more applied vocational aim.

2. Academic loads are unrelated to control, stratum (except that Stratum I private and public institutions show a little higher completion rates) and division. Although the following chapters will show wide variation in the kind of employment by these characteristics, employment per se is endemic in graduate schools and so are low academic loads.

3. Academic loads are unrelated to father's occupation. It is not merely the student from modest economic backgrounds who is working part-time.

4. Family role is associated with course loads (see Table 5.10). The further one is in the life cycle, the lower the completion rates, particularly if there are children. But, when one controls for employment status, the picture changes somewhat. Regardless of employment status, mothers have lower completion rates, but the difference between fathers and other males is slight among those with similar work situations. In short, the low completion rates of fathers are pretty much explained by their high rates of employment. In the context of the analyses of the previous chapter, the inference is that fathers manage to keep up economically with other students but do so at the price of lower academic loads.

5. Stage, age, and income are related to academic loads independent of employment situation. The big difference by stage is between first year and advanced students (see Table 5.11), although, among "thesis" writing stages for both master's and Ph.D. candidates, course loads are naturally lower. Except for the full-time workers, most first-year students complete more than a two-thirds load, but after that the part-time student is in the majority. Employment status, nevertheless, produces a greater range in completed loads within a given stage than occurs in different stages for the same employment status. Since income, age, and stage are correlated, it is necessary to examine them simultaneously (see Table 5.12). In most comparisons older students completed less work than younger students regardless of employment, stage, or income; and students with higher incomes completed less work regardless of their stage, age, or employment. Taken together, these findings suggest a sort of negative relationship between "social status" and academic accomplishment. Among poor, young, beginning unemployed students, 87 per cent completed more than a two-thirds load, but even among the unemployed, less than half of the older, richer, advanced students got that much done.

The fact that employment status and stage contribute independently makes intuitive sense, for advanced graduate work is less based on courses, and employment status is probably a good index of time pressures. Why age and income contribute independently is not really clear. A plausible interpretation of the age effect is that students who carry lighter academic loads take longer to finish and are thus older. Among the workers the income effect could come from differences in hours spent on the job, students with higher incomes putting in more hours on work and fewer on school. Nevertheless, the finding that income has an effect even among non-workers hints that something other than pure economics is going on. It is possible that there is a "psychological" effect such that the older student and the richer student have more distractions, older students perhaps being more involved in their families and communities, richer students being more tempted to spend time in travel, hobbies, puttering around the house or apartment, etc. Our data are not really subtle enough to catch whatever is going on, but there is a suggestion that dire economic necessity is not enough to explain the data and that perhaps there is also a non-economic dimension to "restriction of output" in graduate school.

There are a number of drawbacks to our data and we can only untangle cause and effect by fiat, but the line of interpretation which we favor is something like this.

American graduate schools attract students who are older, have expensive families, and have skills which are quite marketable either to their institution or to employers in the immediate vicinity. The schools (and the society which supports the schools) provide only a few of the students with subsidies which enable them to avoid employment: in fact, the schools tempt the better students into assistantships and are then somewhat hard put to forbid part-time employment for those who do not get stipend jobs. In addition, the structure of graduate education, under the rationalization that independent study is desirable for advanced students, places little pressure on the student to complete his courses, examinations, or theses. As a consequence of all these things, students are free to consume as little or as much education as they please in a given year. With expensive families, low subsidies, and tempting job opportunities, and an apparent aversion to debt, it would appear that the students take as many courses as they literally can afford, and no more.

The financial solvency of American graduate students comes at the price of much less formal education in a given year than the catalogues would have one believe. Or, to paraphrase the poet, the motto of graduate education may well be:

> Ah, take the Cash and let the Credits go,
> Nor heed the rumble of a distant dean!

Chapter 6

Stipends

THE DICTIONARY defines a stipend alternatively as "a gift, donation, given in small coin" or "settled pay or compensation for services." Although our definition of stipends did not come from the dictionary,[1] the distinctions implied by the dictionary definition are important for classifying stipends in a realistic fashion. Thus, although in total dollar amount stipends have been shown to be the major source of income for graduate students, a clearer understanding of stipend allocation requires that one consider the "gift" and "service" aspects separately. In addition, because of the great variation in tuition costs, it is more realistic to consider the gift value of a stipend vis-à-vis tuition, rather than in absolute dollars.

These considerations led to the following rules for classifying stipends:

A. *Duties.* — "A non-duty stipend is any stipend for which no services are required by the giver with the possible exception that the student be registered for classes or be working on his dissertation. This would include scholarships, fellowships, G.I. benefits, vocational rehabilitation grants and out-of-state reductions in tuition and fees."

B. *Types of service required if duty stipend.* — (1) Teaching assistantship, (2) Research assistantship, (3) Traineeship, internship, etc.

C. *Value of Non-Duty Stipend vis-à-vis tuition which the student expected to pay during the year.* — (1) None, (2) Amount less than tuition plus $1,000 (scholarship), (3) Amount equal or greater than tuition plus $1,000 (fellowship).

Because only 28 students had simultaneous research and teaching assistantships and only 28 reported traineeships or internships, the possible combinations can be reduced to nine, which will be called the "Stipend Typology" (see Table 6.1).

The table presents a number of findings in compact form.

[1] For our definition, see above chap. iv, p. 36.

1. A little more than two-thirds (71 per cent) of the students received some sort of stipend.

2. About half (47 per cent) had some non-duty stipend, about one-fourth (23 per cent) receiving $1,000 or more over and above tuition costs from a non-duty stipend.

3. Four out of ten (41 per cent) students had a duty stipend. Teaching assistantships were twice as common as research assistantships, a little more than one out of four students holding a teaching assistantship.

4. Non-duty and duty stipends are by no means mutually exclusive, roughly half of the assistants and half of the non-assistants having some non-duty stipend. Among assistants with a non-duty stipend, however, research assistants (RA's) are more likely to have a high one, teaching assistants (TA's) are more likely to have a low one. The implication is that RA's tend to have fellowships in addition to their research income, while TA's tend to have automatic tuition reductions along with the cash income from teaching.

5. The major groupings in the stipend typology are as follows: TA's with or without non-duty stipends (27 per cent); "Fellows," students with a high non-duty stipend and no assistantships (16 per cent); "Scholars," students with a low non-duty stipend and no assistantship (12 per cent); research assistants with or without a non-duty stipend (13 per cent); students with no stipend (32 per cent). Because many of the "Scholars" are receiving veterans benefits and are thus a special group, we shall consider in most analyses RA's, TA's, and Fellows.

The over-all picture is one of high stipend holding, but not terribly high *subsidy*. Thus, although two-thirds of the sample have some sort of stipend, only half receive any money for which they do not work and only one out of four receive $1,000 or more toward their general support after tuition has been subtracted. This is not to say that assistantships do not provide important training (the students almost uniformly approve of the training they get from their assistantships) or that grants for tuition are not a help; but it does reinforce the previous claim that the frequency and nature of stipends are not such that the average student can enjoy full-time study.

Let us now see how these boons are distributed among various types of students.

STIPEND ALLOCATION

Whether or not a given graduate student has a stipend or a particular kind of stipend is strongly related to: (1) his stage of training, (2) his type of school, and (3) his division of study. These three factors contribute independently, and taken together produce a range from situations where stipend holding is practically a birthright to situations where a stipend holder is an anomaly. What is particularly interesting is that these characteristics tend to be what sociologists call "ascriptive" rather than "achieved." We shall see that the chances of receiving a stipend depend more on "where you are" than on what you need or how good you are academically.

The farther along the student is, the more likely he is to hold a stipend (see Table 6.2). Among first-year students, 61 per cent hold a stipend, 22 per cent a high non-duty stipend, and 31 per cent have an assistantship. At the end of the trail, among those in Stage IV, 92 per cent have a stipend, 37 per cent have a high non-duty stipend, and 49 per cent have an assistantship. The only exception to this progression is the teaching assistantship. TA chances appear to increase up to Stage III and then drop off, for reasons to be discussed later.

The differences are not terribly strong, and later analysis will show that it is difficult to disentangle cause and effect (Are advanced students favored in the distribution of stipends or are stipend holders more likely to continue with their studies?) but the differences are important enough that they will be used as a control variable in analyzing the effects of other variables.

Division of study is a more important and slightly more complicated correlate of stipend holding, involving both quantitative and qualitative differences (see Table 6.3).

Over-all, natural science students have a marked advantage over their colleagues in the social sciences and humanities. Seventy-nine per cent have some sort of stipend, as contrasted with about 60 per cent in social science and humanities, and in every subcategory their stipend holding is higher. The extreme is in research assistantships. One out of five natural science students is an RA compared with one out of nine students in social science and one out of a hundred in humanities.

Despite their anguished cries of relative discrimination, social science and humanities students tend to come out even with each other. They have almost identical proportions with a stipend, with a non-duty stipend, a high non-duty stipend, and with an assistantship. The important difference lies in the type of assistantship. The social science students have an advantage in RA's, the humanists in TA's, but taken together the advantages cancel out, while natural science students have higher proportions of both types of assistantships. We have indirect evidence that holding an assistanship affects career choice, and thus it may be that the assistantship difference affects the research interests of students in humanities and the teaching interests of students in the social sciences, but, generally speaking, the big divisional difference in stipends is between students in natural sciences and those in other fields.

The third correlate of stipend holding, type of school, is equally important and still more complicated. Control and stratum make little difference in the chances for holding a non-duty stipend (see Table 6.4a and 6.4b). Close to half of the students in each of the six types of school have a non-duty stipend, and not far from one-quarter have a fellowship worth $1,000 or more after tuition. There is some tendency for non-duty stipends to be more common in higher-stratum schools among the private institutions, but stratum makes no difference among public schools. Now it has long been believed that

Stipends 61

private institutions have a lot of fellowships and public institutions have a lot of assistantships. Undoubtedly, if one coded the gross cash value of non-duty stipends one would get such a result, but, by treating non-duty stipends vis-à-vis tuition, the difference disappears because the high dollar value of private school stipends is offset by their tuition rates. The essential difference here is whether one gives money or receives money. More money is given per capita for non-duty stipends in private institutions, but apparently no more accrues to the students after they pay their tuition bills.

The common belief about assistantships, however, is quite true (see Tables 6.4c, 6.4d, 6.4e). Half of the students in public institutions have some sort of assistantship as contrasted with between a third and a fifth of the students in private institutions. Again, in private institutions, assistantships are more common in the larger schools. (That is, assistantship probabilities increase with stratum in private schools, but not in public.) Because state universities tend to have large numbers of undergraduates and to make liberal use of TA's, this difference is not surprising. However, it is perhaps interesting that the research assistantship differential is as strong or stronger than the difference in TA's. Students in public institutions have roughly twice the chance for either type of assistantship.

When we put all of these things together (see Table 6.4f), the net result is that in public institutions regardless of stratum, about three-quarters of the students have some sort of stipend; in Stratum I private schools, 70 per cent have some sort of stipend; but in smaller private institutions the proportion drops down to about one-half. We shall see in the next chapter some of the particular characteristics of students in the smaller private schools which help to explain the situations of these high tuition, low stipend students.

Considering stage of study, division, and type of school together, one sees quite a range in stipend holding (see Table 6.5).

Stage of study and division are apparently the most important correlates of fellowships (see Table 6.5a). In each comparison natural science students and Ph.D. candidates are more likely to have a high non-duty stipend. The difference by type of school is consistent only among natural scientists, however. Among social scientists and humanities students, type of school makes little difference, but among natural scientists students in Stratum I private schools appear to have an edge. Putting these findings in another way, the reputed advantage in fellowships for private institutions is limited to students in natural science fields.

Stage, division, and control each make small but independent differences in research assistantships (see Table 6.5b). In each comparison, public school students have greater probabilities than private students; advanced students have more assistantships than beginning students; and natural science students are more likely to be RA's than are students in other fields. At the extremes, a third of the advanced natural science students in public institutions are R.A.'s in contrast with 2 or 3 per cent among beginning social science and humanities students in private institutions.

The TA situation (see Table 6.5c) becomes somewhat complicated when one examines the variables simultaneously. The stage difference disappears among natural scientists but is quite strong in social science and humanities; the divisional difference is quite strong among beginning students but disappears among advanced students, while the order by type of school (public, Private I, Private II–III) remains. A number of complicated explanations could be advanced, but a very simple one is as follows. If one were to add about 20 per cent more TA's to each group of advanced natural scientists, all these asymmetries would disappear, and there would be fairly consistent effects by stage, division, and type of school. Consulting Tables 6.5a and 6.5b one sees that advanced natural scientists are in a particularly felicitous position regarding both fellowships and research assistantships. Since both are relatively rare and have some advantages over a TA, perhaps there is a TA shortage among advanced natural scientists, a shortage of supply, not of demand. Because — indeed Table 6.7d shows that in public schools and Private I schools about 85 per cent of the natural science students have a fellowship or assistantship — the possibility arises that for advanced natural science students stipend offerings have gone beyond the saturation point.

Table 6.7d considers both assistantships and fellowships, the most important and lucrative types of aid. Although there are complications and compensating processes for specific types of aid, the general picture is clear.

1. In every comparison, advanced students are more likely to have high aid than are beginners.

2. In every comparison, natural science students are more likely to have high aid than social science and humanities students.

3. Contrasting private schools as a whole and public schools as a whole, students in public institutions have a distinct advantage in high aid, in each stage and division.

4. Among public schools, stratum has no effect on stipends, but within the private institutions in our sample, Stratum I natural science students receive a considerable amount of support, so that among scientists (but not among social science and humanities students) Private I has levels of support equivalent to public institutions. Because of sampling variability, this pattern should be considered as merely suggestive, however.[2]

5. At the extremes, about 85 per cent of the advanced natural science students

[2] Our sample includes almost 3,000 students, but only 25 schools. Thus, the contrast between Private I and other private schools is based on evidence from only four institutions in Private I and nine in other private, hence in comparing schools (as contrasted with comparing students) we have only 13 independent observations and the sampling error is rather large. While it does not seem unreasonable that the largest and strongest private institutions have higher support levels, we would not claim high statistical reliability for the finding, particularly since it applies only to natural science students.

Stipends

in public or Private I schools have a fellowship or assistantship, while about 25 per cent of the master's candidates in social science and humanities in private schools have such aid.

If we are told a student's choice of school, choice of field, and how far along he is, we can go a long way toward predicting his stipend aid. This is interesting in itself but perhaps even more interesting when we consider that the tables have ignored ability and need. Since students vary in their aptitude and their financial status within each of the cells of our tables, it may be asked whether these two characteristics play a role in stipend allocation, or whether, once a student has made his original choice of field and school, his support probabilities are fixed. Putting it another way, one wonders about the extent to which personal characteristics relate to stipends, or whether stipend distributions are solely a function of location in the academic world.

It would be rather surprising to find no correlation between academic ability and stipend holding, both because many stipend selection procedures are based on some measure of ability (e.g., National Science Foundation fellowships) and because faculty members may tend to include stipend holding in judging ability. The measure of ability comes from faculty ratings of the students. Although one might think that tests would provide a better index, students are ultimately judged by their faculties and, in "the real world," discrepancies between faculty judgments and test scores are almost always resolved in favor of the faculty when specifice decisions are made. Thus, while faculty judgments are undoubtedly in error many times, a student's ability is, pragmatically speaking, what his faculty thinks it is.

An attempt was made to secure two faculty ratings for each student in the sample during the follow-up one year after the original questionnaires were collected. Although the attempt was not entirely successful, at least one rating was collected for 85 per cent of the sample, and two ratings for 67 per cent. The missing ratings were divided fairly evenly between students who were unknown to their department and departmental refusals, most of which stem from one Private I institution which refused to permit collection of the data.

The rating used here is "native ability" and consists of responses to the following question:

IF THE STUDENT IS A PH.D. CANDIDATE — In terms of native ability (ignoring for the moment, motivation, previous background or personality characteristics) required to complete a Ph.D. in this department, this student would rate as:

Exceptional — one of the best we have seen in recent years.
Superior — stands out among the general group of graduate students, but there are a number here who are equally able.
Competent — clearly has the ability to do Ph.D. work, but there are a number who are better, and a number who are worse.
Problematical — may have promise, but hasn't found himself yet.

Problematical — may have some difficulties in meeting the Ph.D. standards, but will probably make it eventually.

Doubtful — this student probably cannot meet the standards required for a Ph.D. in this department.

For master's candidates the same question was repeated but modified to "native ability required for admission to candidacy for the Ph.D. in this department."

The standard implied is the ability to achieve a Ph.D. in the department, regardless of actual degree sought or motivation to do so. Presumably standards vary from department to department and the measure undoubtedly means different things in different schools. However the rating is not merely a ranking within class, for departments were allowed to vary freely in the proportions of their students whom they saw as Ph.D. material.

Because of the high agreement between raters, ratings were pooled [3] and divided into three groups: high, medium, and low. For all practical purposes, "*high*" corresponds to "exceptional" and "superior," "*medium*" to "competent," and "*low*" to "problematical" or "doubtful."

Stipend holders, regardless of stipend type, are more likely to receive high ability ratings (see Table 6.6).

It may be that RA's are given slightly higher ratings than TA's (which is quite true in natural sciences, but diluted by the high ratings of TA's in fields in which RA's are scarce), but over-all the difference is between those with assistantships or fellowships and those without them. The lack of elevated ratings for students with scholarships only probably stems from the fact that many of them have veteran's benefits which are not supposed to be based on ability.

The relative importance of ability and other factors is given by a crosstabulation of the institutional predictors, ability, and stipend holding (see Table 6.7).

The ability difference is consistent within subgroupings by stage, division, and control. In each category students with fellowships or assistantships are rated as more able (although part of this could come from a tendency to use stipend holding as a criterion for ability in making the ratings). Thus, ability seems to count. However, the ability ratings can be used to draw some conclusions about the effect of other variables.

1. Within each stage and control group, natural science students who are seen as poor Ph.D. material have almost the same chance for a stipend as social science and humanities students who are rated as superior or exceptional, and a

[3] William Erbe constructed the combined index. For discrepancies of two or more categories, the student was assigned the median of the ratings; for students with one category discrepancies, the student was assigned the rating of the faculty member who on a separate question reported greater familiarity with the student. Discrepancies which could not be resolved by these rules were solved by assigning the rating closer to the median of the total distribution.

better chance than social science and humanities students who are rated as competent for Ph.D. work.

2. Within stage and division groupings, public school students who are rated as poor Ph.D. material have almost the same chance for a stipend as private school students rated superior or excellent, and a better chance than private school students who are rated as competent for the Ph.D.

3. Although in most comparisons advanced students have better stipend chances than master's candidates, the relationship is not so strong that poor Ph.D. students have a better chance than better master's students.

In short, although ability undoubtedly plays a role in the process of stipend allocations, the institutional factors are strong enough to justify the conclusion that in the favorable school and field situations quite poor students are more likely to have stipends than outstanding students in less favored schools and fields.

The extent to which financial need plays a role in stipend allocation is difficult to assess. What is really necessary are measures of the students' needs prior to the distribution of stipends and some control for the possibility that needy students who did not receive stipends may have dropped out of school. Two indirect measures of need, however, suggest that it plays little role in the distribution of stipends. As a group, students from lower-status origins are more needy. We have seen that more of them worked their way through school and that they took longer to do so. The next chapter will show that their debt levels are slightly higher. When the cases are divided according to the measure of father's occupational status described in chapter iii, there is no association between status and aid, either for fellowships or for assistantships (see Table 6.8).

Controlling for the grouping of the institutional predictors which gives the greatest range, we see that students from lower-class origins have no advantage over students from higher status levels, and no disadvantage. The suggestion is that financial need is not important in the distribution of stipends.

A second indirect measure of need or financial situation is family role. We have seen that, in the nature of things, fathers have more difficult financial situations because, in comparison with single students, they have increased expenses and, in comparison with married women and husbands, they lack an additional breadwinner. Their pattern of stipend holding is an interesting one (see Table 6.9). For fellowships (non-duty stipends worth $1,000 or more after tuition) family role seems to make no difference at all. Neither sex nor progression in the family cycle lead to any consistent difference in fellowship holding. For assistantships, however, fathers tend to be low, particularly where assistantships are common. Does this mean that they are discriminated against? We think not. The fact that fathers are not discriminated against in fellowships implies that there is no systematic tendency to withhold aid from them. Remembering that fathers are very likely to be working and to be supporting an expensive family, perhaps they cannot afford to be assistants. One may speculate that the fathers' need for work income is such that they need more money than can be gleaned from an assistantship. Certainly the pay and hours of assistantships are not designed for the support of families, and possibly those students who must support families must pass up these opportunities for higher paying jobs or those which give them more hours of work.

The factors associated with stipend holding may be thought of as grouped into three types. Division of study, type of school, and stage of study can be considered institutional or situational factors because they are characteristic of institutional contexts for graduate study rather than personal characteristics of the student. Father's occupation and family role may be thought of as need factors in the sense of describing basic financial circumstances which affect the students' monetary situations. Ability, as measured by faculty ratings, is a measure of degrees of relative merit by departmental standards.

The following general conclusions can be drawn:

1. Need appears to play little or no role in the pattern of stipend distribution. Students from lower economic strata have no greater advantage or disadvantage in receiving stipends. Fathers, whose family situations put them under the greatest economic pressures have, if anything, fewer stipends. Thus, the structure of stipends is such that slim economic resources do not provide any competitive edge, and the stipends which are most commonly available are possibly an economic luxury for the students in the most pressing financial circumstances.

2. Ability is related to stipend holding, in the sense that fellowship and assistantship holders as a group are rated higher in native ability than those with no aid and those with scholarships. There is no strong over-all tendency, however, for the very best to receive the more advantageous non-duty stipends.

3. Situational factors are quite important. Depending on stage, division, and type of school, students of clearly lesser ability and need have better chances than outstanding and needy students in less favored academic situations.

In general:

a) Natural science students have a distinct advantage over social science and humanities students, regardless of the type of stipend.

b) Ph.D. candidates have an advantage over master's candidates for most types of stipends.

c) Public school students have an advantage over private school students, for both teaching and research assistantships, although there is little difference by control in net value of fellowships.

In addition, particular combinations of these variables stand out:

a) Advanced natural science students, except possibly in lower-stratum private schools, have such high levels of stipend holding that they appear to have reached something like a saturation point.

b) Advanced humanities and social science students in public institutions have very high rates for teaching assistantships.

c) Beginning social science and humanities students in private schools have very low rates of support. Outstanding students in these groups have a lesser chance of receiving a stipend than non-Ph.D. material in private natural science and public institutions.

The preceding materials considered only the presence or absence of a stipend or a given type of stipend, thus ignoring a rather important aspect — the money. Even though there are sharp differences in the holding of stipends, it is not necessarily true that there are similar differences in money received. The high rates of stipend holding among advanced natural students may not mean that more money is spent on them per capita but merely that the soft-hearted donors divide it up into smaller packages and give more people a little money rather than giving lots of money to a few people. It turns out that this line of reasoning is totally incorrect, but the figures are worth examining.

The simplest measure is the percentage of students receiving $2,000 or more a year from their stipend among students who receive any stipend (see Table 6.10). There is considerable range in gross receipts, and the pattern is not unfamiliar. Advanced students have bigger stipends (14 out of 17 comparisons); natural science students have bigger stipends (15 out of 16 comparisons); and students in private schools have bigger stipends (15 out of 15 comparisons).

When, however, tuition and fees are subtracted from the stipend totals to give an index of net return to the student, the control difference vanishes. If anything, net stipend values are higher in public institutions (10 out of 15 comparisons), but the fairest conclusion is that, after tuition costs have been paid, control does not make much difference in the return to the stipend holders. Division and stage of study, however, maintain rather sprightly effects. Considering those students who have only a non-duty stipend, the average advanced student in natural science receive $1,819 a year over and above tuition and fees, in comparison with $524 among beginners in social sciences and humanities. Not only is the advanced student in natural science more likely to receive a non-duty stipend, but when he gets one it is about three times as large as that of the beginner in social sciences and humanities.

In each of the 16 possible comparisons, natural science students have higher net returns, and in 16 out of 17 comparisons advanced students do better. Although the pattern is consistent for each type of stipend, the evaluation of stipend income among assistants should allow for possible differences in hours worked before a firm conclusion is drawn (see Table 6.12). Regardless of school, division, stage, or type of assistantship, the average assistant reports between 15 and 20 hours per week for his actual duties (the questionnaire asked the students to distinguish between hours "in theory" and "in practice" but there was very little difference). Among those with no non-duty stipend in addition, RA's appear to work a little more than TA's, but among the natural sciences RA's with an additional non-duty stipend labor drops to a gentlemanly ten hours per week, thus, over-all, there is little difference in hours for the two types of assistantship.

Using the arbitrary estimate of a 39-week working year and the students' estimates of their hours and wages, one can calculate the hourly pay for various types of assistants (see Table 6.13). Advanced students tend to have higher hourly rates (10 out of 13 comparisons) and natural science students tend to have higher hourly rates (9 out of 11 differences, plus one tie). There is no consistent control effect, assistants in private schools having higher rates in five comparisons, assistants in public schools being higher in six.

Considering assistants who have no non-duty stipend in addition, the over-all average hourly rate was $2.32 after subtraction of tuition and fees, the actual pay, of course, being somewhat higher.

The major generalizations about the distribution of stipends may now be revised as follows:

1. Natural science students have a distinct advantage over social science and humanities students in terms of:
    a) Probability of holding a stipend of any type.
    b) Amount of money received from non-duty stipends among holders of such stipends.
2. Divisional differences in the pay rates for those with assistantships only are slight, but if there is any tendency it is for higher hourly rates among natural science students.
3. Ph.D. candidates have an advantage over master's candidates in terms of:
    a) Probability of holding a stipend of almost any type.
    b) Amount of money received from non-duty stipends among holders of such stipends.
4. Stage differences in the pay rates for those with assistantships only are slight, but if there is any tendency it is for higher hourly rates among Ph.D. candidates.
5. Public school students have a distinct advantage over private school students for both teaching and research assistantships, but there is little control difference in:
    a) Probability of holding a non-duty stipend for tuition plus $1,000 or more.
    b) Net value (after subtraction of tuition and fees) of non-duty stipends among holders of such stipends.
    c) Hourly pay rates for assistants, after subtraction of tuition and fees.

Or somewhat more succinctly: Students in natural science and Ph.D. candidates have advantages in stipends, regardless of how you look at it. Stu-

Stipends 69

dents in public schools have an advantage in getting teaching and research assistantships.

SOURCES OF STIPENDS

Academia being a mixture of governmental and private enterprise and academic accounting systems having some notorious quirks, it is exceedingly difficult to tell "where the money really comes from" for graduate students' stipends. Thus, for example, stipend money given to students by their universities may become available because a federally financed research project covers the salaries of a given number of faculty members so that more of the instructional budget can be allocated to teaching assistantships. Without seeking a subtle understanding of the economics of graduate education, one can, however, examine the patterns of sources reported by the students in the sample in order to gain a rough idea of the major sources of stipend funds.

The data on sources consist of answers to the following question:

What is the source of the funds for your stipend? (Circle any which apply): University Funds_____, National Fellowship or Scholarship Program (Specify which one)_____, Research grant to the project director from (Specify source) _____, Other (Specify)_____.

Table 6.14 summarizes the results. Clearly the graduate schools carry the major load in providing stipend funds. Forty per cent of the graduate students receive money from their school (regardless of where the school ultimately gets the money), a little over 22 per cent receive money from the federal government (13 per cent receive veteran's benefits, 9 per cent other stipends) and the next most frequent source, private national scholarship and fellowship programs (Woodrow Wilson, Ford, SSRC, etc.) is reported by less than 5 per cent of the sample. If one excludes veteran's benefits, only 23 per cent of the sample received support from a source outside their own university. Because the data were collected prior to the National Defense Education Act and the expansion of other stipend programs, the current percentage is undoubtedly higher, but it is probably fair to say that, except to the degree that it provides general support for its institutions of higher education, the nation as a whole is hardly subsidizing the studies of graduate students in the arts and sciences.

Let us now consider the extent to which the differential distribution of stipends discussed above can be explained by the patterns of stipend granting by specific sources. Table 6.15 gives the source breakdown by division, stage, and control — the three key variables in stipend allocation. With two exceptions the differentials are small, the over-all pattern of stipend distribution being created by the summing of a number of tiny differentials. It is clear, however, that federal funds are far from evenly distributed by division, and that chances for receiving a stipend from one's own school are heavily influenced by control. Among natural scientists, 16 per cent received stipend funds only from Uncle Sam, as contrasted with 7 per cent in social sciences and 0 per cent in humanities. The absolute percentage difference is small, but the relative variation is considerable. Similarly, 41 per cent of the students in state schools receive a stipend only from their institutions, as contrasted with about a quarter in private schools.

A somewhat oversimplified but clearer picture of these differentials is given by excluding students with multiple sources and those with "other" sources and examining the distribution of university, federal, veteran's benefits, private national programs, and employers against the three academic characteristics — control, division, and stage.

Table 6.16 gives the percentage receiving a stipend from their universities for this simplified subsample. The table shows that regardless of stage or division, from half again to twice as many students in state schools receive a stipend from their school as do those in private institutions, and, in the social science and humanities groups (but not in natural sciences), advanced students are more likely to be supported by their institutions. This pattern is quite familiar and looks very much like the distribution of teaching assistantships. Is the control difference in university support explained by the heavier use of TA's in state universities and their lesser frequency in private schools, particularly for social science and humanities master's candidates? No, it is not. Table 6.16*b*, which excludes teaching assistants, still shows a considerable control difference, although the stage difference in social science and humanities disappears. (That is, the fact that in Table 6.16*a* there is a relationship between stage and university support for students not in natural science stems from the fact that, in both private and public schools, TA opportunities increase with stage in social science and humanities, but not in the "saturated" natural sciences.) Table 6.16*b* is of some importance in discussions of educational policy, since it suggests that there is more to the control differential than policy on the use of TA's. The private universities, whose tuition is much higher, also are unable to, or choose not to, provide other types of stipend as frequently. The bulk of this differential, of course, comes from the greater frequency of research assistantships from university funds in the state schools, not differential policy on fellowships and scholarships. In the humanities, where research assistantships are negligible, the control difference among non-TA's is quite small.

The patterning of federal (other than veteran's benefits) stipend support in the fall of 1958 is simple (see Table 6.17). Federal stipend support was heavily concentrated in the natural sciences, and is fairly heavy particularly at the Ph.D. level. Twenty-seven per cent of the natural science Ph.D. candidates in the simplified sample were receiving federal stipends, 10 per cent of the social science Ph.D. candidates had a federal stipend, and not a single humanities Ph.D. candidate in the sample reported one.

The remaining major sources — veteran's benefits, private national programs, and employers — show no marked association with stage, division, or control (see Table 6.18). Private university students do get a little more than public, but the difference is small. In addition, veterans are concentrated among the master's candidates in private schools, but these three sources taken together do not contribute much to the over-all allocation of stipends.

Reviewing these findings on sources, the important conclusions appear to be as follows:

1. Although stipends are offered by a number of sources, the major share of providing stipend funds falls to the students' own schools. In 1958, at least, neither the federal government, philanthropic organizations, or employers, taken individually, contributed to the support of more than 10 per cent of the students (excluding veteran's benefits from the federal percentage).

2. The major differential in university support lies in variations in use of teaching assistants. Public schools clearly hire many more in any division, and private schools seem particularly unwilling or unable to use TA's in the social sciences and humanities.

3. Even after TA's are excluded from the tabulations, public schools still provide more stipends per capita than do private institutions — research assistantships from university funds being the major factor here.

4. The federal government was a major source of stipend funds for natural scientists, particularly at the Ph.D. level, but students in other divisions rarely received federal money, except in the form of veteran's benefits, which are not associated with division of study.

5. Stipend support from the "private sector" (private national programs and employers) is small and neither accentuates nor compensates for the differentials in other sources.

OPINIONS ON DUTY STIPENDS

Remembering that 31 per cent of the sample cited "exploitation of its schools" as a valid criticism of American graduate students and also remembering that assistantships cut down course work as much as do part-time jobs, one is prepared to find seething indignation as the typical student's reaction to his assistantship.

The crude data, however, do not support this idea (see Table 6.19). A slight majority of the students (56 per cent) say they would like an assistantship even if they didn't need the money, 72 per cent of the assistants rate their job as a "good" or "unusual" opportunity for training in their field, and two-thirds (67 per cent) of the assistants say they have no complaints when asked a direct question on the matter.

The only important criticism is simply the amount of money received. Twenty-nine per cent of the assistants claimed to be underpaid, while only a handful raised any other criticisms. Fiction to the contrary notwithstanding, most professors apparently do not browbeat their assistants or pirate their discoveries.

Perhaps the strongest tribute to assistantships is that those who have them like them even better than those who do not (see Table 6.20). Fellows, those students with a non-duty stipend which nets them $1,000 a year or more after tuition, are clearly not chafing at the bit to go to work, but a third of them (36 per cent) would like an assistantship. Among full-time and part-time workers, a little over 60 per cent would prefer an assistantship, while among assistants themselves, slightly more than 60 per cent would prefer staying in harness. Research assistants appear to be a little more satisfied, 54 per cent preferring an RA, as compared to 42 per cent of the TA's who would keep their type of job if financial matters were of no concern.

Read this way, the bright side of the picture emerges. However, one should also note that, among all types of employed students, a third or more would prefer not to work, that 32 per cent of the TA's would prefer some other type of job, as would 25 per cent of the RA's. Clearly, the fit between desired and actual work situations is far from perfect in graduate school. Even in the happiest group, the RA's, 46 per cent — almost half — would (at least at the fantasy level) prefer a change of some sort.

Evaluations of the training value of stipends are fairly uniform (see Table 6.21). Regardless of control, stratum, or stage of study, around 70 per cent of the assistants rate their jobs as excellent or good in terms of training, and the difference between RA's and TA's is very slight. There does appear to be a slight divisional effect. In the humanities TA's give quite high ratings, while in natural sciences they consider their jobs somewhat less valuable (80 per cent versus 65 percent). The reason undoubtedly is that fewer natural scientists are interested in teaching and a greater percentage of them get TA's than in other divisions, so that their apprentice training is more often inappropriate for their professional futures. It would be interesting to have the reactions of RA's in the humanities, but, alas, there were only eight of them. For what it is worth, however, seven out of the eight gave high ratings to their jobs.

Financial complaints among assistants appear to be endemic, rather than concentrated (see Table 6.22). TA's, especially in the humanities, have slightly higher rates of financial complaints in most, but not all, comparisons, just as we have seen they make a little less money. The only systematic factor appears to be stage. The further along a student is the more likely he is to complain about his wages, strikingly so among RA's and to a lesser degree among TA's. We have no further tabulations to explain this trend, but possibly the nearer a student gets to the Ph.D. the more he expects professional rather than apprentice wages, particularly in research where the professionals can command fairly high salaries.

In sum, except for those students with fellowships, teaching and research assistantships are seen as quite desirable, aside from their vital economic importance. The bulk of assistants rate their jobs as good or excellent in training value, and less than a third have any complaint. That complaint, however, is almost always the money.

Summary

A large number of independent and unrelated decisions have the consequence that stipends — the most important source of income for American graduate students — are distributed far from randomly among students. Financial need plays little or no role in this distribution, and, although academic ability is related to stipend holding, students of distinctly lesser ability are quite likely to have stipends if they are in the "right" academic niche. In particular, students in public institutions, those in natural sciences, and those in advanced stages of graduate study tend to have disproportionate probabilities. There is, in fact, some indirect evidence that among advanced natural scientists in public schools and the larger private ones a saturation point has been reached, such that some 85 per cent have an assistantship or fellowship. When this is compared with the 36 per cent of *outstanding* beginners in private social science and humanities departments who have such stipends, it is fair to conclude that institutional characteristics are more important than ability in stipend allocation. The same differentials occur in the dollar value of stipends among those who receive one.

By and large, these discrepancies are built up from small but consistent differences over a range of stipend sources. However, the concentration (in 1958) of U.S. government funds in the natural sciences, and the greater tendency for public institutions to provide not only teaching assistantships but other types of aid play a considerable part in the pattern.

Attitudes toward assistantships are essentially favorable, a majority of the sample reporting that they would like an assistantship even if they didn't need the money. About 70 per cent of the assistants give a high rating to the training value of their stipends, but a fairly constant third complain that their wages are too low.

■ Chapter 7

The Pattern of Non-Stipend Income

ALTHOUGH STIPENDS are the single most important source of income for American graduate students, only 41 per cent get half or more of their income this way, only 24 per cent receive 80 per cent of their income from stipends, and a mere 11 per cent are totally supported by scholarships, fellowships, or assistantships. Almost all students have to supplement their stipend income, and the majority must raise the bulk of their incomes from other sources.

How this is done is a very important question. To the extent that the students rely on their own work, their studies must be slighted, yet, aside from employment and stipends, other sources are quite limited. Wives play a vital role in providing incomes for childless husbands, but children tend to come along soon. Parents and in-laws sometimes contribute, but family aid is not very common for graduate students. Savings and borrowings provide logical alternative possibilities, but savings must come from somewhere, and borrowings must be repaid.

In this chapter we shall review the patterns of access to selected types of non-stipend income in order to complete the picture of graduate students' income sources. Particular attention will be paid to employment because of its importance as a barrier to completion of graduate studies.

EMPLOYMENT

The most important characteristic of graduate student employment is its high over-all frequency. Lumping together assistantships, part-time jobs, and full-time jobs, it is clear that the typical graduate student expects to be employed during the academic year (see Table 7.1). The only strong deterrent to employment is the fellowship. Among students who do not have a fellowship, more than 80 per cent expected employment of some type during the year, and, even among the fellows, almost half (44 per cent) anticipated some gainful employment (often, of course, an assistantship). In the sample as a whole, three-quarters planned to work. Thus the working graduate student is not deviant, but typical. There are some variations in work, but in every school, stage, division, and social background group, workers outnumber non-workers more than two to one, except among fellowship holders. The one exception to this rule hardly undermines it. Among married women graduate students with children, a mere 55 per cent expected employment.

The differences that do appear are slight (see Table 7.2) and are generally limited to non-fellows. Employment is a little more common among natural scientists, students from low-status origins, advanced students, men, and among fathers. However, except for the mothers in the sample, there is no cell in the subtables of Table 7.2 which has less than 72 per cent expecting employment among the non-fellows, and no cell in which more than 55 per cent of the fellows expected employment. Graduate students who do not receive a fellowship typically will work during the school year.

The uniformity of work does not mean that there is a uniformity in types of work. We have already seen the factors related to holding an assistantship. Let us then look at the other two important types of employment, full-time and part-time employment in a non-stipend job.

FULL-TIME WORK

The group of students whose employment pattern is the most striking are the full-time workers (those expecting a regular non-stipend job which requires $37\frac{1}{2}$ or more hours per week). Although only 18 per cent of the sample fall into this category, they stand out as a special group in many ways. We have seen that they get the very least amount of academic work done during the year and that they have the very highest incomes. They are thus a striking illustration of the graduate students' continual dilemma between money and course work. Although they are the archetypal illustration of this dilemma, they are not archetypal graduate students by any means. In some ways they do accentuate the general characteristics of the sample, but in many others they stand out as a special subgroup with distinctive patterns.

In chapter iii we saw that one of the most important factors in understanding the students was a complex relationship between age, academic progress, and progress in the life cycle. For various reasons graduate students' academic progress does not proceed smoothly along the axis of age, but among the men progress in the family cycle does. Thus, a goodly number of students are men over 27 with wives, children, but only a few graduate credits. This pattern is clearly typical of the full-time workers (see Table 7.3).

Reading along the rows of Table 7.3, it is seen that controlling for age and stage of academic progress, fathers are much more likely to expect to be employed full-time. Thus, among master's candidates under 27, for example, one-fourth of the fathers will have full-time jobs, as contrasted with 12 per cent of the husbands and 7 per cent of the single men. Because the differences between single men and husbands are small and inconsistent, while the differences between fathers and husbands are fairly strong and consistent, and also because the difference holds in each age group, one may infer not merely that it is "natural" for students to take on full-time jobs when they get older but that the financial pressures on fathers lead many of them into full-time jobs.

When one scans the columns of the table, a second pattern is seen. At each age and in each life-cycle group, full-time workers are at an earlier academic stage, and, conversely, at each academic stage full-time workers are older. It could be that older students are enticed into full-time work, but in the context of previous findings it seems more probable that full-time workers are seriously delayed in their degree progress. Thus among the full-time workers one finds the greatest accentuation of progress in the family cycle and the greatest retardation in academic progress.

In other ways, however, the full-time workers do not accentuate the typical (see Table 7.4). Their distribution by type of school is a special one. The difference is not really one of control or stratum. Rather, full-time workers are heavily concentrated in the lower-stratum private institutions. In these schools 39 per cent of the students expect to work full-time, while in Private I and in the public institutions full-time workers amount to 9 per cent. Running the percentages the other way, Private II and III schools have 68 per cent of the full-time workers, but only 33 per cent of the students who will not work full time.

Although the survey data do not fully document the interpretation, some suggestions for understanding this disproportion arise when the following findings from Table 7.4 and previous chapters are noted:

1. In each type of institution lower-status students are a little more likely to be full-time workers (Table 7.4).

2. Tuition and fees in Private II and III are not much less than Private I, and much higher than in public schools.

3. Private schools are concentrated in the large urban centers, public schools in smaller cities.

4. Stipend aid is rather low in Private II and III.

5. Private I students tend to come from high class origins.

Taken together all of these things suggest that the small private schools serve a particular function in American graduate education. In the large urban metropolises of the nation are thousands of young men and women who are motivated for graduate study but limited in their choice of school. If they live in the eastern states there are few first-rank public institutions in their states, and, even if they are in the Middle West or Far West where the strongest public institutions are concentrated, the state school may be in a small town a hundred miles or so away. If, in addition, they come from lower-status origins or have expensive families to support, they may find it necessary to enter a graduate school in their own city so that they may continue work. This means a private institution. The biggest private schools, however, are highly selective and quite expensive. Given all of this, the smaller private graduate schools and the urban working student seem to strike a mutually advantageous "deal." The school provides these students with opportunities for graduate study on a part-time basis, and the higher incomes of the working students enable the schools to compete for students while maintaining high tuition and low stipend levels.

Whether or not such an interpretation—which admittedly goes far beyond the statistical data—is valid, type of school, family role, and age provide a good combination of predictors of full-time work (see Table 7.5). Among fathers age 27 or older, who are in Private II and III schools, 69 per cent expect full-time jobs, but among non-fathers, under 27, who are in public or Private I schools, 3 per cent will work full-time.

Before too many tears have been shed for the full-time workers, it should be noted that they are not characteristically slaving away in menial jobs (see Table 7.6). Only 8 per cent have clerical or blue collar jobs, the rest work in professional or managerial positions. The exact type of job varies by school type and division: (*a*) full-time workers in the humanities include a high proportion of schoolteachers; (*b*) natural scientists tend to have full-time jobs as professionals in the field in which they are studying; (*c*) outside of Private II and III, natural science and humanities full-time workers are often college teachers; (*d*) social science full-time workers tend to have executive positions in some other field (e.g., a business executive doing graduate work in economics or a social worker doing graduate work in psychology) but the general impression is that regardless of school and division they have good jobs, not stopgap positions. Table 7.7 underlines this point. Except in humanities (schoolteachers) the full-time workers tend to average $500 a month or more, and among natural scientists two-thirds or more are at or above the $6,000 a year level.

A brief look at their career plans and their academic ability as rated by the faculty will complete the portrait of the full-time workers (see Tables 7.8 and 7.9). In Private II and III the full-time workers are conspicuously less likely to expect academic careers when they finish, and, except in natural science, the same is true in other schools. Whether because of this or for other reasons, they are a little less likely to be considered top academic material (except among natural scientists outside of Private II and III). Thus, particularly in Private II and III, the full-time worker is less academically oriented and considered less promising academically.

Can we now pull all this together? One way of looking at these materials is that the proportion of full-time workers among graduate students is a result of two different processes; first, some, but not many, graduate students tend to become full-time workers; second, some, but not many, full-time workers tend to become graduate students. The questionnaire does not contain enough detailed material on job histories to document the interpretation but our speculations are as follows:

1. *Students who become full-time workers.* — Those male graduate students whose family cycle has gotten too far ahead of their academic progress may be impelled to take on full-time jobs when children arrive, since this is the only way to compensate for the increased costs and decreased income when their wives leave the labor force.

Possibly too, the student of lesser academic ability may take on a full-time job, since he probably receives less encouragement to stay in school full time.

2. *Full-time workers who become students.* — In the larger cities where smaller private graduate schools are adapted to his needs, the full-time worker who is in a field where advanced degrees are an asset may be likely to do some graduate work on the side to brush-up or to qualify for promotion, particularly if his salary is such that he can afford the tuition.

In addition, it may be that some lower-status students in larger cities who have not been able to amass enough savings or capital to free themselves from their jobs continue to aim for academic careers by doing part-time graduate work in a school within commuting distance.

Thus the data on full-time workers probably conceal three different types of students, only two of which represent financial problems. The graduate students who were forced into full-time work because of family responsibilities and the hard-pressed student who never got enough ahead to become a full-time student both represent a financial problem group. The unknown, but undoubtedly high, proportion of full-time workers who are actually well-paid people in good jobs picking up some graduate work to improve their skills on the job should not be counted among the problem groups.

Part-time Work

The remaining type of employment in the classification is part-time jobs, non-stipend employment amounting to less than 37½ hours per week. Such jobs are fairly common and present a distinct pattern in their distribution.

The myth of the impoverished graduate student putting himself through school by washing dishes in a beanery is somewhat sterotypical according to the survey data. Among the specific part-time jobs reported (a number of students who expected part-time jobs had not located a specific position when the questionnaires were administered) 36 per cent were classified as clerical or blue collar, the remaining 64 per cent falling into the professional and managerial positions typical of the full-time jobs. We tend to forget that except in the humanities, graduate students possess training and skills which are in high demand in our society.

The Pattern of Non-stipend Income

At the same time, it is clear that these jobs are supplementary and seldom provide the major source of income. Thus, while 29 per cent of the sample expected a part-time job, only 6 per cent expected half or more of their total income from a part-time job. Given these figures, the expectation is that the student with a part-time job is one with lesser access to more desirable income sources (see Table 7.10). Tabulation of part-time employment by other income sources tends to support this claim. The lowest rates of part-time employment, not surprisingly, are among those students with full-time jobs, although even among these busy students more than 10 per cent are "moonlighting." More interesting, however, is the strong negative relationship between stipend holding and part-time jobs.

Excluding the full-time workers, 25 per cent of the stipend holders expected a part-time job; among non-stipend holders who were receiving income from a spouse's job or parents, 45 per cent expected a part-time job; and among non-stipend holders with no income from family sources, two-thirds expected part-time work. Stipend holding tends to cut down part-time employment regardless of the availability of family sources, but among students with no stipend the availability of money from spouse or parents makes a big difference in part-time employment. The one group of students for whom part-time employment is "typical" are those who have no income from stipends, spouse, or parents.

The negative relationship between stipend holding and part-time work is strong enough to provide a sort of reversed signpost for locating part-time workers. The factors which are positively associated with stipend holding are negatively associated with part-time jobs (see Table 7.11). In chapter vi it was shown that natural scientists, advanced students, and students in public schools were considerably more likely to hold stipends. Table 7.11 shows that part-time jobs are more common among beginning students, social science and humanities students, and private school students who are not in natural science. When, however, stipend holding is controlled (Tables 7.11*b* and 7.11*c*) these relationships attenuate or disappear.

To some extent part-time work appears to be a sort of do-it-yourself stipend program, which has some implications for considerations of policy in graduate education. While there is considerable doubt that stipend levels could be increased sufficiently to eliminate full-time work, it would appear that part-time work could be cut considerably by an increase in stipend. Because the typical stipend is a part-time job itself, not a fellowship, expansion of current stipend levels would not cut down employment per se, but would tend to affect the character and presumably the educational value of the employment which is endemic among graduate students.

The major conclusions to be drawn from the analyses of student employment are:

1. Employment of some sort is characteristic of graduate students. Among

students with no fellowship, more than eight out of ten will work during the school year, and even among the fellows more than 40 per cent will have some sort of employment.

2. The students who expect full-time jobs tend to be characterized by: high-paying professional and managerial occupations, heavy family responsibilities, striking retardation in academic progress, and concentration in the smaller private schools.

3. It is hypothesized that there are really three kinds of full-time workers: graduate student fathers who have been forced into employment because of family responsibilities; students from modest economic backgrounds who have never been able to get enough ahead to afford full-time study; and full-time workers seeking brush-up or promotion certification training.

4. The smaller private graduate school in the large city appears to have adapted itself to serve full-time workers.

5. Part-time jobs, while often high level professional positions, appear to be supplementary income sources, which substitute for stipends in those schools, fields, and stages of study which are characterized by a small supply of stipends.

Family Sources: Spouse and Parents

In many ways, income from family sources appears to be a very desirable source of funds for graduate students. To the extent that the graduate student receives money from parents or spouse, he can be freed from the employment that drags out his studies and divides his attentions. Families have a strong interest in the student's training and are often — but not always — motivated to help make it possible for students to get an advanced degree.

In other ways family support presents problems and difficulties. To what extent should a 30-year-old be dependent on parents, and to what extent should parents be required to subsidize half a decade of studies in addition to four expensive years of college? Although it appears that most young wives are willing and able to work, how long should they be required to postpone the children which are so important to them? What are the effects on a family of requiring a young mother to work to support her husband? Is it fair for the larger society, which more and more considers these students as a vital natural resource, to saddle their families with the financial responsibilities for getting the students trained? Statistical data cannot answer the value questions, but an examination of the statistical facts can provide information for considering these questions. Without attempting to decide what families should do, we can describe in some detail what they do do.

Spouse's Employment

The high frequency of male graduate students with working wives has caused some wry reactions among educators, if not among the students and their wives. A noted educator remarks that graduate students work their way through "by the sweat of their fraus," and a West Coast school awards the wives of its doctorates the honorary degree of "P.H.T." for "putting hubby through."

In previous chapters it has been shown that childless male students have a very high proportion of working wives, that married women students have a very high proportion of working husbands, and that even among men students with children a surprising number of their wives are in the labor force. Nevertheless, in chapter iv it was shown that spouse's employment is seldom the predominant income source. Among those with income from spouse's employment, only half get half or more of their total income from this source. Thus, the graduate student family is typically a working team, in which total family income is a sum of contributions from both husband and wife.

The occupation of the spouse varies considerably with the sex of the student and the presence or absence of children (see Table 7.12).

1. *Among husbands.* — Of those who are full-time workers and non-students 59 per cent have wives; 77 per cent of their wives have some sort of employment; only 11 per cent are students only, but 22 per cent of the wives are studying; and 12 per cent are pure housewives (neither working nor studying). Thus, the typical wife in this group is a full-time worker.

2. *Among fathers.* — Two-thirds of the spouses are pure housewives, 28 per cent have some sort of job, and 5 per cent are students.

3. *Among wives.* — Two-thirds of the spouses have a full-time job, half have a full-time job and are not students; around a quarter are students only.

4. *Among mothers.* — Of their spouses 83 per cent have a full-time job; 8 per cent are students only.

The differences are sharp but quite understandable. First, it is clear that in this social group some sort of activity is almost inevitable for childless married women. The wives in the sample are all students by definition, and among the spouses of the husbands a mere 12 per cent are neither working nor studying. Second, there is some evidence of a double standard with the implication that the husband's studies have higher priority. Among both the childless and the parents, a woman student is much more likely to have a student husband than a man student a student wife. The evidence is indirect, but it would appear that if someone has to go to work it will be the wife. Third, one notes the strong effect of children. Among men the presence of children makes a 48 per cent difference in spouse's full-time work; and among women the mothers have a 20 per cent increase in employed spouses. When children come along, family patterns are radically restructured.

As in the case of full-time and part-time jobs, spouses' jobs tend to be much more desirable than folklore would have it — if only because it takes a pretty good job to support a student family (see Table 7.13). The ladies have done especially well. A little less than 60 per cent of their working husbands have jobs classified as high status on the index described in chapter iii, quite a number of them being married to college professors. Among the men, working wives are concentrated in the middle-status levels, the traditional women's professions of schoolteaching, nursing, library work, and so on. For all practical purposes the working wives of male students are divided as follows: half in the feminine profession, one-third secretaries, the remainder scattered over various jobs.

It should be stressed that spouses' jobs tend toward the professions with lower salary levels, very few of the students having husbands or wives in the lucrative executive and major professional positions, but it is also true that very few spouses are in the less desirable blue collar or service occupations. The midde-class style of life of the married graduate students is supported typically by a middle-class or upper-middle-class occupation for the breadwinner.

In capsule form: the typical childless male graduate student is married to a schoolteacher or secretary who brings in about half of the total family income; the typical graduate school father works full- or part-time himself, so that his wife can stay home with the children; the childless wife in graduate school is either married to a student or is supported by a husband in a full-time professional job; the typical mother in graduate school is married to a professional man whose job pays enough to make it possible for her to continue her studies.

The association between presence or absence of children and wife's employment is probably the strongest statistical relationship in this study ($Q = .79$), but it is not perfect. Among the husbands a quarter of the spouses are not working, and among the fathers about a quarter of the spouses are employed. While it could be that some young mothers are career-minded and some young brides are home-oriented, a suspicion arises that economics play a part in deviations from the socially defined family patterns.

To begin with, there is a slight relationship between class origins and wives' employment (see Table 7.14). Among the fathers, the lower the class origins, the higher is the proportion of spouses employed. Interestingly, the relationship if anything is reversed among the husbands. Since lower-status origins are generally associated with less comfortable finances, the implication is that, while the childless wives may work to satisfy career motivations, the working mother (more specifically, the working wife of married male graduate students with children) is reacting to economic pressures. More direct evidence for this interpretation comes from a cross-tabulation of income from stipends, income from full-time work, presence or absence of children, and employment of the students' wives (see Table 7.15). The greater the income from stipends and the greater the income from the student's own full-time work, the less likely it is that wives are working. For those fathers with no stipend and no full-time job, 42 per cent have a working wife; for those fathers with a stipend worth $2,000 a year or more and no full-time job, 26 per cent have working wives; and for those fathers with a full-time job paying $4,500 or more for the academic year but no stipend, 6 per cent have working wives. A similar pattern, but with less sharp differences, appears among the childless husbands. The same data can be rearranged to show the simultaneous effect of children and financial matters on wives' employment (see Table 7.16). The use of both factors improves the prediction considerably: At one end, 84 per cent of the childless wives in the tightest financial circumstances are working; at the other, only 6 per cent of the most comfortably fixed mothers are employed. At the "middle" the two factors appear in balance — just about the same percentage of most hard-pressed mothers are working as most comfortably fixed childless wives.

Thus, it appears that the employment of graduate students' wives reflects both the social patterns of family life in these groups and also the economic pressure on some students for an alternative or supplementary source of income.

While the economic importance of the working wife is apparent to readers of the statistics in this report and is apparent to the educators who make up the wry quips on the subject, there is some doubt that the student families see it this way. Unfortunately, there are no schedules from the students' wives, but, if their husbands' impressions are to be trusted, the spouses are not resentful of the burdens they carry. Married students were asked, "How would your spouse feel about *your* continuing in graduate school for another year after this one? For two or more years after this one?" If the percentage checking "Probably Disapprove" or "Definitely Disapprove" is taken as an index of spousal rebellion, the level of discontent is low and unrelated to spouse's employment and presence of children (see Table 7.17). While about one-fifth of the students report that their spouse would disapprove of two more years of study, disapproval is only slightly higher among working mothers than other groups, although the evidence is fairly clear that their employment is conditioned heavily by financial pressures.

Even more surprising is the relationship — or rather lack of relationship — between spouse's employment and fertility expectations. Throughout the report the evidence, while indirect, has been abundantly clear that the advent of offspring has dire consequences for the married male graduate student. Children add to expenses, subtract the wife's income, make it less possible for men to live on assistantships, make it more probable that men will take on full-time jobs and be greatly slowed up in their degree progress. With all this in mind, let us look at the fertility expectations of the male students (Table 7.18). In each comparison wife's employment has only a minimal deterrent power on fertility expectations, if any — *but*, if the wife is studying, fertility expectations are conspicuously lower. Although age and religious difference might be at work here, the suspicion arises that graduate students are willing to postpone their families in order for their wives to complete school, but, except for those with two or more children already, economic dependence on wives' employment does not play much role in fertility plans.

To summarize:

1. The spouses of women students tend to have quite good jobs, the spouses of the men tend to have fairly good jobs.

2. The rate of employment of students' wives is a joint function of family situations and economic pressures.

3. There is no evidence that the working wives are rebellious about their lot, and no evidence that male students weigh the economic importance of working wives in their fertility plans, even though, if the wife is a student, fertility expectations are lowered considerably.

It would appear that the working wife is a highly strategic, but somewhat unappreciated economic resource for the male graduate student.

Parental Aid

In theory parental aid should be a major and benign form of financial support for students. To the extent that parents can and will aid students, their sons and daughters can finish graduate study sooner; because graduate students come from relatively high class origins, their parents should have more funds available than the general population; and almost all students have living parents, while only a minority have wives but no children.

In practice, however, less than a quarter of the students expected to receive any help from home (this figure excludes loans from parents which are included in the debt data). While one is tempted to speculate that there is some cultural barrier against parental aid for graduate study, detailed examination of the data suggests that the probability of receiving help from parents is primarily a function of the financial circumstances of the parties involved. Among students who need aid and whose parents are relatively able to provide it, a majority do receive help from home.

Thus the low levels of parental support actually stem from low levels of need and the fact that, while graduate students come from *relatively* prosperous homes, in *absolute* terms most of them come from families of rather modest means.

A direct question on parental aid (Table 7.19) gives the following results:

a) Twenty-three per cent expected some help from parents

b) Four per cent had no living parent

c) Of the remaining 73 per cent, six out of ten said, "I don't need any support from them." Only 3 per cent said, "They are unwilling to support my graduate education."

Putting it another way, while only 23 per cent receive aid, of those with

The Pattern of Non-stipend Income 85

a living parent who did *not* check, "I don't need any" — that is, among the 52 per cent of the sample who have a parent and who "need" help — half are receiving aid.

Thus the most common reason for not receiving parental help is lack of need for it. Answers to such opinion questions may be misleading and "I don't need any" may be checked out of stubborn pride or may actually mean "I don't need it enough to ask my parents to make such a sacrifice," but the characteristics of students who checked this item suggest that there is a degree of realism in the answer.

In terms of background characteristics the most important correlates of perceived need are age and family situation (Table 7.20a). The older the student the less needy he feels; married women feel less needy than married men; and the married, but childless students are particularly optimistic. These patterns are congruent with the analysis of income situations, which showed higher working levels among older students, good jobs for the husbands of married women students, and particularly felicitous finances for the married, but childless student.

When the non-needy are subtracted from the table (Table 7.20b) family situations seem to make little difference in receipt of parental largess. Within an age group, needy students (regardless of marital status and presence or absence of children) seem to have about the same probabilities, although for men the young husbands may be a little low in support levels. Age, however, makes considerable difference. The older needy student is considerably less likely to receive help from home. Perhaps parents feel that a child pushing thirty should be independent, but, perhaps also, a child pushing thirty has parents pushing sixty and experiencing the lowered incomes of the later working years. It is ironic that in modern America it does not seem possible to launch the younger generation of professionals during the normal working life of the parental generation.

Because married students have two sets of parents, the data in Table 7.20 may have overestimated the propensity to support them (Table 7.21). Examining support from parents and spouse's parents separately does not change the picture much. Regardless of sex and presence of children, married students are more likely to receive support from their own parents than from their in-laws. Subtracting in-law support from the data in Table 7.20b does not change the general conclusion that need and age are the major factors, marital status and children playing a negligible role. Parents do not seem to cut support much when their children marry or raise it conspicuously when they become grandparents.

The inference from all of this is that parental aid is more affected by the student's economic situation than by any particular prescriptions or proscriptions associated with kin relations in middle-class America. This can be seen more directly when parental aid is tabulated against the key income sources (Table 7.22).

In Table 7.22 students are classified by the presence or absence of full-time work and non-full-time workers are categorized in terms of receipt of income from spouse's employment and the more lucrative stipends (assistantships and fellowships). The percentage checking "I don't need any" increases up the columns of this index for both men and women; in each comparison holders of large stipends report themselves as less needy; and those with a working spouse (particularly among the women, whose husbands tend to have good jobs) see themselves as less needy, as do the full-time workers. For full-time workers and women with an employed husband, two-thirds say they don't need any help from home; but, among students with no breadwinner and no major stipend, the needy are in a majority. Just as need decreases down the columns, the percentage receiving parental aid increases up the columns. About half of those with no breadwinner and no stipend are receiving help from home, as contrasted with less than 10 per cent among the full-time workers. The third column, which gives the percentage "needy," but not receiving aid, shows no relationship with the income classification.

By and large it appears that one can trust the students' claim that the major reason for lack of parental support is lack of perceived need, which is heavily affected by the availability of a breadwinner and the allocation of stipends.

While student affluence is a major factor in depressing parental aid, half of the self-defined needy are receiving no help from home. In order to understand these situations, it is necessary to shift from characteristics of the students to characteristics of their parents. Although other factors undoubtedly influence the relationship, two variables come pretty close to telling us whether a needy student will receive parental support in graduate school. The first is father's occupation — considered here as an index of the socioeconomic status of the parental family. The second is a question about the value climate of the parental home, as follows:

Which of the following best describes the situation in your family when you were in high school?
1. It was "naturally assumed" that the children would go to college.
2. Children who wanted to go to college were encouraged to do so by one or both parents, but it wasn't assumed that all would go.
3. It was not assumed that any of the children would go to college.

Considered simultaneously, the two items provide a measure of two important dimensions of socioeconomic status: first, the orientation of the family toward higher education and, second, economic resources. Variation by father's occupation within an orientation group will be considered as a measure of economic factors, variation in orientation within an occupational group will be considered as a measure of family value climates.

The Pattern of Non-stipend Income 87

Both variables affect parental aid among the "needy" (see Table 7.23). Within each orientation group the higher the father's occupational level, the higher the proportion aided, and, within each occupational group, the more college oriented the family, the greater the proportion aided. Among needy children from elite, college-oriented families around two-thirds are receiving help from home, while among those from non-college-oriented low-status families 18 per cent of the needy have parental aid for graduate studies.

The results can be summarized in a single table showing the simultaneous contribution of the student's financial situation and characteristics of the parental family in affecting parental aid (see Table 7.24). Down the columns students are grouped according to income sources, and across the rows they are grouped according to parental family characteristics. Number of siblings has been added to the parental family data because there is a tendency for those from large families to be lower on receipt of aid from home.

In each column the proportion receiving help from home decreases with the availability of other income sources, and for each financial group there is a steady progression from the low-status, non-college-oriented, larger families to the high-status, college-oriented, small families. Among students with a full-time job, who come from low-status, non-college-oriented families, 2 per cent receive parental aid; among students with no stipend or breadwinner from small, high-status, college-oriented families two-thirds receive help from their parents.

What is perhaps the most interesting aspect of the table is the small proportion of students who fall in the groups where parental aid is probable. Only a fifth of the sample are in the no breadwinner, no stipend group, and among them 40 per cent are from family types with low support potential. Of the cases in the table, only 12 per cent are in the combination of situations which makes parental aid more probable than improbable.

The findings do cast doubt on the idea that parents "won't" aid graduate students. In certain categories two-thirds are receiving help from home. At the same time, some doubt is cast on the possibilities for increasing reliance on this source. Because perceived need for parental aid is less common for students with breadwinners or stipends and since so many students have one or both, perceived need for aid is low. Although graduate students come from relatively high status origins, absolutely speaking most come from moderate and low income families with other children to support; hence the ability to pay and motivation of their parents is limited. When, in addition, the low level of support for older students and high proportion of older students in graduate school is considered, it seems that the possibilities for increased support from parental families are slight.

Of the two sources of family support—parents and spouse—it is clear that the more important economic resource for the graduate student is the spouse and that economically, at least, the students are independent of their parental families.

Borrowing and Savings

In terms of understanding the economic problems of graduate students, saving and borrowing can be treated together as positive and negative signs of net financial positions. The existence of savings will be treated as a sign of net gain, and the existence of borrowing will be treated as a sign of net losses during the academic year. From this point of view, an analysis of these two income sources serves not only to complete the description of non-stipend income but also to indicate the net financial positions for various types of graduate students.

On the whole, the net position of the students appears favorable (Table 7.25). Nine per cent expected to borrow money during the year, while 47 per cent had savings of $500 or more at the beginning of the term. Debt, however, is cumulative, and the best predictor of future borrowing is present debt (see Table 7.25b). Among the students with less than $100 in non-durable debts (debts for expenditures with no resale value, as opposed to mortgages, instalment payments, etc.) 5 per cent expected to borrow, but, among those with $100 or more in debts, 27 per cent expected some form of loan. Using the debt data another way (Table 7.25b) a less conservative figure can be derived. If students who either (1) have an existing debt or (2) expect to incur one during the year are called debtors, 23 per cent of the sample are debtors, 77 per cent are debt free. Examining the cells of the table one sees that 4 per cent are new debtors, 14 per cent are old debtors who did not plan to borrow more in 1958–59, and 5 per cent were recidivists, old debtors who expected new debts.

Even under this less conservative definition of debt, about the same proportion (22 per cent) had savings of $1,500 or more as were debtors (23 per cent).

The generally rosy picture could, however, mask dire economic situations for particular groups of students. However, it turns out that the distribution of net positions is essentially unrelated to the variables which have been important for other financial analyses.

Type of school and division of study are very important for the distribution of stipends, part-time work, and full-time work, but debtors and savers are fairly evenly distributed by division and school. Social scientists may be a little higher on debt, humanities students may be a little lower on savings, private school students are a little more likely to be savers, but the similarities are more striking than the differences. While division and school make important differences in the sources of income, they are not related to net financial positions.

Family role has been shown to be strongly associated with total income, full-time work, spouse's employment, and slightly associated with assistantships, but there is no consistent difference in debt and savings by family role (see Table 7.27). The hard-pressed fathers have a little more debt than single men, but they also are more likely to have high savings. While family role makes important differences in the source and level of income, it is not related to net financial position.

Similarly, age and stage play no consistent part in debt or savings (Table 7.28). Beginning and advanced students, younger and older students, accelerated and retarded students have essentially similar savings and debt proportions. While age and stage are strongly related to stipend holding, employment, and income, they are not related to net financial position.

In fact, there is only one variable which appears to have a relationship to savings and debt. The relationship is not terribly strong, but debts increase and savings decrease as one moves from the highest socioeconomic origins to the lowest (Table 7.29). It has already been reported that graduate students from low status backgrounds take longer to get their undergraduate degrees, are more likely to be working full-time, and less likely to receive parental help, all of which is indicative of chronic economic problems. Even so, more students from the lowest status level have $500 or more in savings than are debtors. Although the students may not view it in this optimistic fashion, perhaps the deficit position of the lower-class student can be considered a personal investment in social mobility which is a substitute for the family support of the higher-status students.

While it will be shown in the next chapter that, for the small proportion of students with high debts and low savings, financial worries are very high, the general run of negative findings here perhaps tells more than could have been gained from discovering some correlations.

The implication is that in terms of the factors which explain how students are supported, net position is a random variable. While students in different schools, divisions, family situations, and stages have quite different ways of financing their studies, they do not differ much in the degree to which they can balance their books. The debtor and saver appear to be people who differ in their ability to manage their resources, or people subject to fortuitous troubles (operations, medical bills, family crises) rather than people with differential access to sources of income which guarantee solvency or promote destitution. Except for the students from particularly high or low class origins, we have been unable to locate any particular groups of graduate students for whom continued study means increasing wealth or increasing indebtedness. While this nice balance may be achieved by adapting scholastic progress to economic needs, rather than by adapting economic situations to the necessity for scholastic progress (suggested by chapter v) the analysis has been unable to pinpoint any danger spots in terms of disproportionate debt among the graduate students in the sample.

SUMMARY

In this chapter we have reviewed the major sources of non-stipend income for graduate students: full-time work, part-time work, spouse's employment, aid from parents, debt and savings. Rather than review the specific findings which are summarized at the end of the particular sections of the chapter, let us attempt to provide a more general summary of the financial situation of the graduate students. While the chicken-egg problem is a serious one in such data, the themes are as follows:

1. It appears that graduate students (at least in 1958 before the advent of National Defense Education Act loans) place a high premium on remaining debt free. Savings are high, borrowing is low, and the levels of each are fairly constant among all types of students. Interpreting this in another way, it appears that the students "decide" how much money they need to keep even in a given year and then raise it, even if this means cutting down seriously on academic progress. While a rational case can be made in favor of borrowing for graduate study (and a rational case against it) the argument appears to have fallen on deaf ears.

2. In raising the money needed, it is almost inevitable that the student will work during the year. The differences are almost entirely in the type of work. If assistantships are available they are almost universally preferred, but when they are not (and they are not very common among non-natural scientists in private schools and among master's candidates) part-time work is the next alternative. For the fathers, however, and for some lower-status students in private universities, full-time employment is the only solution which provides sufficient funds. A large proportion of the full-time workers, however, are genuine "part-time" students who happen to be taking a few courses, not graduate students who happen to be working full-time.

3. Support from families really does not modify the picture much. While spouse's employment is an important source of income, the added return is probably offset by the added expenses of a larger family and, except for some of the "husbands," married students have much higher incomes but are not much "better off." Parental aid is apparently turned to only when other sources are lacking and is generally available only from the parents of those students from high-status origins.

4. Graduate students tend to support themselves. Their university situation may make it possible for them to support themselves with an assistantship rather than part-time or full-time work; their spouse may add enough additional income to offset an increased budget of a family; and parents help when they can and when there is no other alternative; but by and large the graduate student (except for the small proportion of fellows) has no access to financial resources which give him enough margin to retire from the labor force and enjoy the cerebral delights of the ivory tower.

The Pattern of Non-stipend Income

Thus the self-sufficient, thrifty graduate student, while apparently in a much more advantageous financial position (in terms of income, savings, debt, etc.) than had been thought at the beginning of this research, can be thought of as a man handicapped by a late start but busily at work, keeping his ship afloat by patient labors and throwing the cargo of academic credits over the side, while being relentlessly pursued by an invisible stork.

■ Chapter 8

Concerns About Money:
Worry and Expectations

As WITH ANY important human value, there is a subjective side to money. A vast body of social science literature supports the claim that there are important relationships between finances and attitudes. A recent national survey shows that there is a positive relationship between income and happiness.[1] Among respondents with incomes of $15,000 a year or more 53 per cent reported themselves as "very happy," while among those with annual incomes of under $1,000, 20 per cent gave this answer. At the same time there is evidence that perceptions of finances are not totally objective and that perceptual mechanisms influence our beliefs. Thus Bruner and his colleagues have shown that when children are asked to estimate the *physical* size of coins, they tend to distort them in terms of the *monetary* relationships.[2] Although graduate students are highly intelligent, there is no reason to believe that they are immune to attitudinal and perceptual influences. In this chapter we shall treat one attitudinal variable — worry about finances — and one perceptual variable — estimates of future income — to gain understanding of the subjective dimension of finances among the graduate students.

[1] Gerald Gurin, Joseph Veroff, and Shiela Feld, "Tabular Supplement to *Americans View Their Mental Health*" (Ann Arbor: Survey Research Center, University of Michigan, 1960) (Processed), Table B-1.

[2] J. S. Bruner and C. C. Goodman, "Value and Need as Organizing Factors in Perception," *Journal of Abnormal and Social Psychology*, XLII (1947), 33–44. Subsequent studies have led to some modifications of the interpretation, but not to the general "point" of perceptual variation.

Worry about Money

What proportion of American graduate students are worried about their financial situations? Not a very high one, if answers to the question, "How much do you worry about your *immediate* financial situation?" are taken at face value (see Table 8.1). Eight per cent say that finances are their most serious problem right now; 23 per cent report that they worry but that it isn't their most serious problem, while 69 per cent are either not worried or pleased.

It is possible to get some rough idea how the rate of worry for the sample compares with that of the United States as a whole. The following question has been asked by a variety of opinion researchers: "What would you say is YOUR biggest worry these days — the thing that disturbs you MOST?"[3] We shall report two sources, the Gallup Poll already cited and Samuel Stouffer's *Communism, Conformity, and Civil Liberties*.[4] Stouffer set out to find, at the behest of the Fund for the Republic, the extent to which the American public was worried or concerned about either the threats to civil liberties concomitant to the McCarthy era or the threats of subversion used to justify restrictions on civil liberties. He found that the populace as a whole was concerned about neither. Instead, most people tended to worry about much more immediate matters, particularly money and health, and also the potential effect of war on sons in the armed forces. The question which he used to tap the most general dimension of concern was quite similar to Gallup's, as were his results.

Gallup found that the largest single group of worriers consisted of people who worried about money — 45 per cent of his sample. Stouffer found almost exactly the same percentage — 43. The threat of war was second in 1951, naturally enough, closely followed by health, whereas, in 1954, Stouffer found that health was the second most pressing concern for the population at large.

Clearly the kind of free answer questions used by Gallup and Stouffer are not comparable with our closed question. However, it was our suggestion to our respondents that finances might be a pressing concern — not only by asking directly about financial worry, but by devoting more space to financial matters than to any other topic in the entire questionnaire. Despite this fact, only 31 per cent of our sample responded that they were seriously worried about finances; and only 8 per cent reported that they were most worried about money. From these considerations one may tentatively conclude that the sample is less worried about money than the American population. In light of our emphasis on finances, this conclusion would seem to be rather conservative, but the differences in question wording will not allow us to say more.

While the absolute level of financial worry may be low among the stu-

[3] American Institute of Public Opinion, September 22, 1951.
[4] Samuel A. Stouffer, *Communism, Conformity and Civil Liberties* (Garden City, N.Y.: Doubleday & Co., 1955), pp. 58–69.

dents, it is possible that, relative to their other problems, financial worries are the most frequent and have the most serious consequences. One way of assessing this possibility is to compare financial worry with other problems which affect student morale. In chapter iii it was shown that using *esprit* items originally constructed for surveys of the American army, graduate students' *esprit* compares favorably with the highest levels of morale among enlisted men in the Second World War (although it is lower than for officers promoted from the ranks). An index of morale was constructed from answers to the questions: *a*) In general, how would you say you feel most of the time, in good spirits, or in low spirits? (I am usually in good spirits, I am in good spirits some of the time and in low spirits some of the time, I am usually in low spirits), and *b*) In general what sort of a time do you have in graduate school? (I have a very good time, I have a pretty good time, It's about fifty-fifty, I have a pretty bad time, and I have a rotten time.) Low morale was defined as giving less than the most positive response ("I have a very good time" or "I am usually in good spirits") to both items; high morale was defined as giving the most positive response to one or both items.

Morale varies with financial worries, academic worries, and social relationships. Academic worry was measured by answers to the question, "How satisfied are you with your academic standing in the department?" worriers being defined as those who checked "Fairly dissatisfied" or "Very dissatisfied." Social integration also contributes to morale, married students having higher scores on the index than single students; those who report that they belong to an informal student group having higher morale than those who do not. Considering all these variables at once, it is seen that each contributes to morale (see Table 8.2).

Holding constant the other factors; on the average:

1. Financial worries produce a 17 per cent difference.
2. Academic worries produce a 13 per cent difference.
3. Marital status produces a 10 per cent difference.
4. Peer-group membership produces a 6 per cent difference.

Because financial worries and academic worries produce about the same effect and because their incidence is about the same, one can conclude that they are about equally important as factors in morale. Neither, however, is decisive, nor are the four variables considered in the table. Among those worried about grades and money who are single and not members of student groups, 29 per cent still have relatively high morale; while among those who are married, members of student groups, and worried about neither finances nor grades, 23 per cent are low on the index.

The conclusions to be drawn are: Financial worries are about as important as academic worries in producing low morale, but student morale levels are also influenced by social integration and other factors which have not been identified. While financial worries have a demonstrable deleterious effect, their elimination would not affect the over-all morale level of graduate students (as measured here) more than a few percentage points.

While the evidence so far would lead to the inference that financial worries are not an overwhelming problem among graduate students, it is still true that about one-third are concerned to some degree. Who are these students, and what are the factors which affect their worry?

On the whole, financial worry shows little relationship with the variables and characteristics which have been used to analyze the students' financial situations. There are differences, of course, but generally speaking financial worry is not strongly associated with family role, age, academic stage, division, stratum, control, or stipend holding.

Family role is strongly related to financial problems, but weakly related to financial worries(see Table 8.3). While there is considerable evidence that fathers are subject to heavy financial pressures and that husbands have relatively favorable circumstances, fathers are only nine percentage points higher in worry, and husbands are about the same, when compared with single men. Fathers worry more, but "less more" than would have been predicted.

Advanced students have many advantages in stipends and in total income, but their worry is no less than that of beginners. Similarly, older students have higher incomes, higher levels of employment, but no difference in worry when compared with younger students (see Table 8.4).

Division, a prime factor in stipend allocation and an important factor in salary differences among full-time workers, makes little or no difference in worry. Students in the humanities have only an 8 per cent edge in worry, when compared with students in natural science (see Table 8.5), the difference only approaching statistical significance.

Type of school does show some relationship, but not of a kind which makes sense in terms of the previous analysis (see Table 8.6). Students in lower-stratum public schools are more worried, but no aspect of their financial situation which has turned up in the analysis can account for this difference.

Stipend holding, in itself, is not consistently related to financial worries (see Table 8.7). Fellows are indeed prone to be worry free, but assistants and those with scholarships appear no more or less worried than those with no aid.

One background factor which does show some relationship is father's occupation (Table 8.8). The association is moderate at best, but the lower the class origins, the greater the worry.

The relationships which have been turned up are what one would expect. The higher degree of worry among fathers, lower-status students, those who do not have a fellowship, and those in humanities fit into the mosaic of relationships which has been reported in previous chapters, although the worry levels in low-stratum public institutions do not.

A more important question, however, is why are these associations so low? If fathers are so hard-pressed, why don't they worry much more rather than a little more? If stipends are so financially advantageous, why doesn't possession of one lower worry levels perceptibly? These questions cannot be answered fully, but three lines of evidence give us some promising leads. The first concerns the relationship between net position and worry, the second concerns the social psychological concept of relative deprivation, and the third involves work levels.

At the end of the previous chapter, it was shown that, although the major background variables are strongly related to how students are supported, except for father's occupation, they tend to be unrelated to savings and debt — that is, these factors do not predict whether students will come out even. Since this is the same pattern shown by the relationships with worry, the suggestion is that worry is caused by problems in balancing the books, not the structure of income sources. To a considerable degree this appears to be the case (see Table 8.9). When worry is tabulated against perceived adequacy of income, savings, non-durable debt, and durable debt, fairly strong associations appear. Those students who anticipate a deficit are much higher in worry, as are those with lower savings, greater durable debt, and great non-durable debt. Among those who believe they will have enough to get through the year, who have $500 or more in savings, and relatively low debt levels, 15 per cent are worried. Conversely, among those expecting a deficit and who also have low savings and high debts, more than 80 per cent are worried about their immediate financial situation.

While it is hardly astounding that debtors and potential debtors are more worried about money, the point is important, for it helps to explain the low levels of worry among the students. Because financial worries are strongly affected by anticipated and existing debts, the persistent tendency to avoid debt, documented in the survey, goes some distance in explaining the low level of worry among the students. In addition, the fact that debt appears to be a function of idiosyncratic circumstances means that such things as variation in stipend levels, marital situations, and children are not much related to levels of financial worry.

A second mechanism involved here is that of relative deprivation. The concept was developed in the *American Soldier* studies when a similar problem arose — the lack of association between objective circumstances and subjective reactions.[5] The authors of the military studies concluded that subjective reactions are heavily affected not only by the realistic circumstances but also by people's tendency to evaluate their circumstances by comparison

---

[5] The theory is described in detail in Robert K. Merton and Alice S. Kitt, "Contributions to the Theory of Reference Group Behavior," in Robert K. Merton and Paul F. Lazarsfeld (eds.), *Continuities in Social Research, Studies in the Scope and Method of 'The American Soldier'* (Glencoe, Ill.: Free Press, 1950), pp. 40–105; and in James A. Davis, "A Formal Interpretation of the Theory of Relative Deprivation," *Sociometry*, XXII (1959), 280–96.

with the situations of others. Thus, although the air force had higher promotion rates than the military police, attitudinal differences regarding promotion, if anything, were inverse to unit promotion rates among soldiers with similar promotion statuses. The conclusion was that non-promoted soldiers in the military police were not so frustrated because few of the people they knew had been promoted, while in the air force the non-promoted felt *relatively* deprived in comparison with soldiers they knew and used for a standard.

The same sort of mechanism can be seen among the graduate students (see Table 8.10). Students were asked, "Compared with other graduate students you know, would you say that your financial situation is — Much Better, Slightly Better, About the Same, Slightly Worse, or **Much Worse?**" Relative deprivation affects worry regardless of perceived income adequacy. Among the students who expect a surplus but feel they are worse off than their friends, *more* are worried than among those who only expect to come out even but feel their situation is much better or slightly better than that of their friends.[6]

To the extent that worry is affected by relative deprivation within student groups, there will be a dampening of any correlations between worry and student characteristics. Among groups of students with difficult financial situations, relative deprivation will make them less worried, and among groups of students in very good circumstances relative deprivation will tend to make them more worried. While the mechanism can be either euphoric or disphoric in its effects, the net result will tend to be a homogeneity in attitudes across schools, fields of study, living units, and other factors which affect student groupings.

The third major factor in worry involves work. The effects are complicated but in the end appear to be rather easy to understand. To begin with, there is a U-shaped relationship between worry and work (see Table 8.11). Full-time workers and non-workers are considerably less worried than part-time workers and assistants. Thus those with the least work and those with the most are relatively low on financial worry.

Perhaps, of course, these differences merely reflect differences in income adequacy and/or relative deprivation. Indeed there are clear differences (see Table 8.12). The assistant or part-time worker is much less likely to expect a

[6] Logically, of course, the causal direction could run the other way. It is possible that worried students misperceive their friends' financial situations, rather than perceptions of financial situations affecting worry. To settle the issue it would be necessary to show that perceptions of relative standing vary with the financial situations of other students. In analysis to be reported elsewhere this problem is being considered in detail. At this preliminary stage, it is fair, however, to conclude that there is variation in students' perception of relative financial standing in departments with different kinds of students. Thus, students from lower status origins are more likely to report that they are relatively less well off in departments where majorities of the students come from high status origins.

surplus and much less likely to feel he is relatively better off than his friends. However, this is not all there is to it. The non-worker when compared with the full-time worker is lower on perceived adequacy and relative advantage, but he is less worried, rather than more. Putting it another way, the full-time workers are somewhat more worried than one would predict from their perceived adequacy and relative standing.

Simultaneous comparisons in terms of employment, perceived adequacy of income, and relative deprivation help to untangle the situation (see Table 8.13). Let us begin by comparing the worry levels of part-time workers plus assistants with the worry levels of full-time workers. Over-all there is a fair association ($Q = -.236$). When, however, relative deprivation or perceived adequacy is controlled, the position association disappears, and, among those students who do not expect a surplus, the relationship becomes positive ($Q = +.320$ among those relatively better off, $+.199$ among those defining themselves as same or worse). The low worry levels of the full-time workers can be explained entirely by their greater perceived adequacy of income and perceived relative advantage. Among students with similar adequacy levels, full-time work either makes no difference or has a negative effect. The full-time worker who does not expect a surplus is *more* worried than the part-time worker in similar circumstances.

A similar analysis of the difference between non-workers and part-time workers or assistants shows that, while the advantage in worry levels of the non-employed is reduced when perceived adequacy and relative deprivation are controlled, the effect does not disappear. Regardless of adequacy and relative deprivation the part-time worker or assistant is more worried (see Table 8.13*b*).

This analysis enables us to draw the following inference: Income from employment and employment per se have opposite effects on worry. To the extent that employment brings in income which allows the student to balance his budget and to feel his circumstances are relatively better than his peers, work lowers worry levels. However, for students in the same net and relative position, work adds to worry. The economic effect of work is to lower worry, but its intrinsic effect is to raise it (see Table 8.14). This generalization enables us to understand the U-shaped relationship between work and worry. The relatively high worry levels of those students with part-time jobs or assistantships appear to stem from the following: That they must work at all makes them more worried than those students with fellowships or other sources which keep them free of employment; that they work only part-time, however, makes them more worried than the full-time workers who earn a considerable amount of money. Because a little more than half of the students fall into the part-time job or assistantship classification, this effect is fairly important. While over-all about one third of the students are worried about money, all other things equal, if the part-time workers and assistantship holders could be kept from working at all, the worry proportion would drop to 23 per cent. The possibility is remote, but it does illustrate that, beneath the surface, the American system for financing graduate education by means of duty stipends and part-time jobs does add to the fianancial worries of the students.

In summary:

1. In absolute proportions and by rough comparison with the general population, financial worries are low among American graduate students.

2. Differences in financial worry by age, stage, family role, division, control, and stratum of school are not very great.

3. The student from parental families of lower socioeconomic status is somewhat more likely to be worried.

4. Worry appears to be heavily influenced by three factors:

a) Anticipated deficits, low savings, and high debts are strongly related to worry. Debtors are rare in graduate school, but the minority with deficits do suffer from heavy financial worries.

b) Worry is greater for students who feel their situation is worse than that of their friends; worry is less for students who feel better off than their friends, regardless of perceived income adequacy.

c) Employment per se adds to worry, unless its financial return is very high. The result is that the students with part-time jobs or assistantships are more worried than those with full-time jobs or those with no job at all.

ANTICIPATED INCOME

While graduate students, as a group, are not highly mercenary, they are not oblivious to the importance of money. When asked to rate the importance of various job characeristics, two-thirds check "A chance to earn enough money to live comfortably" as very important or extremely important. While it is true that altruistic and self-expressive values [7] are rated higher than money, it is also true that financial values have about the same rank among graduate students as they do in a national sample of undergraduates analyzed by Morris Rosenberg.[8] (See Table 8.15). At the same time, it would appear that the graduate students have considerably lower income expectations than do college undergraduates. In Rosenberg's data collected in the early 1950's, about half of the undergraduates expected an annual income of $10,000 a year or more "in ten years."[9] In our sample, however, from data collected in 1958, only 17 per cent anticipated $10,000 or more per year at a comparable date (five years

---

[7] The factors associated with occupational values in the sample have been analyzed in detail in Joe L. Spaeth, "Value Orientations and Academic Career Plans: Structural Effects on the Careers of Graduate Students" (Ph.D. diss., University of Chicago, 1961).

[8] Cf. Morris Rosenberg, *Occupations and Values* (Glencoe, Ill.: Free Press, 1957).

[9] Calculated from *ibid*., Table 30, p. 54.

after starting full-time work after graduate school) and the proportion anticipating $10,000 or more only reaches 50 per cent for predictions for "age 45." Although the samples are not fully comparable, the suggestion is that the average graduate student expects at the peak of his career about the same salary which the typical undergraduate expects in his early thirties. What each will actually get is, of course, another matter, but, because behavior is influenced by expectations as well as reality, it is of some importance to examine the income expectations of the graduate students.

The following question was asked:

Please give the amount of annual income (from all sources and before taxes) which you would guess . . .

A. would be your actual starting salary when you start full-time work in your field . . .

B. You will be making five years after you have started full-time work in your field . . .

C. You would be making at age 45 if you had an *academic* job (minimum and maximum) . . .

D. You would be making at age 45 if you had a *non-academic* job (minimum and maximum) . . .

E. You *will* be making at age 45.

Considering that the students are highly trained and not-so-youngish adults, their expected starting salaries are not staggering (see Table 8.16). Ninety-five per cent expect to start at less than $9,000 a year, 62 per cent expect to start at less than $6,000 a year, and 34 per cent anticipate less than $5,000 per year. Considering that their median income from all sources at the moment is equivalent to $5,000 a year, the students do not seem to expect a great increase in total income when they finish graduate work.

As usual, the average figure is somewhat deceptive, for there is wide variation in salary expectations. Among some groups of students $5,000 a year is considered the bottom starting salary, among others only a handful aspire to the munificence of $100 a week. Division, sex, career plans, and stage of study each contribute independently to variation in expected starting salaries (see Table 8.17).

Natural science students have higher income expectations than humanities students, and social scientists tend to fall in the middle. This is true regardless of sex, stage, or career plans.

In ten out of 13 comparisons in Table 8.17, students who expect academic jobs have lower starting salary expectations. The exceptions occur among the humanities where non-academic and academic jobs are seen as offering about equally low starting salaries. It is perhaps interesting to note that the divisional and career differences are independent, and natural science students aiming for academic careers have higher expected starting salaries than humanities students aiming for either type of job.

Regardless of division, stage, or career plans, women expect lower starting salaries.

Finally, academic progress and plans to gain the Ph.D. are related to salary expectations. It is not surprising that terminal M.A.'s (master's students who say they do not "definitely plan" to get the Ph.D.) have lower expectations, but something more interesting turns up when Ph.D. candidates are compared with master's candidates who say they *will* get a doctorate. Among those anticipating non-academic jobs there is little difference in salary expectations, but among those who plan to become academics the Ph.D. students have higher expectations. The implication is that beginning students aiming for academic careers have rather low income expectations, but after being in graduate school for a while they become convinced that the financial opportunities are not as dim as they had originally thought. Thus, rather than becoming disillusioned about academic salaries as they get closer to the Ph.D., graduate students appear somewhat more optimistic.

When the prediction period is extended to five years after starting work and to age 45, the sex, division, and career differences remain essentially constant (see Table 8.18). At age 45 the average expectation for men in natural science who anticipate non-academic jobs is $13,175 per year, as compared with $6,552 for non-academically oriented women in humanities. Proportional increases are seen as essentially similar. In each division, sex, and career group, the students expect about a one-third increase in salary after five years (see Table 8.18*b*). By age 45, however, there are some differences: social scientists and humanities students expect a greater proportional increase in comparison with natural scientists; non-academics expect a somewhat greater rate of increase than do academics; men expect a considerably greater rate of increase than do women. Putting it another way, the students see sex and career differentials increasing over the work life, while the divisional difference is seen as somewhat less at age 45 than in terms of starting salaries.

At a more abstract level, these differences have a number of implications.

First, if graduate study is viewed solely as an economic investment the return is highly variable. The costs of graduate study are essentially the same by division, sex, and anticipated career. The male scientist aiming for a $13,000-a-year job in industry incurs about the same costs in obtaining his degree as does the female humanities student who hopes to become a $7,000-a-year college professor (the terminal master's student, of course, invests less than the Ph.D. student). In addition, support in the form of stipends tends to be proportional to the future income rather than a compensation for low salaries in the future. While there is little sex and career plan difference in stipends, natural scientists and Ph. D. students have a distinct advantage in the academic here and in the postgraduate school hereafter. Thus, if universities were to follow a ruthlessly rational pricing policy, they could justify wide differences in tuition by field of study. That they do not means that, although costs are similar, the economic return is very different for different types of graduate students.

A second implication of these differences is that they create rather different "opportunity structures" for different kinds of graduate students. The concept was developed in studies of juvenile delinquency but seems applicable here. David Matza puts it this way: [10]

> The lack of opportunity for legitimate advancement and the dire effects thereof have been a recurrent theme of sociological theory and research. It would not be unfair to say that restriction of social mobility is the *bête noire* of American sociology, particularly when coupled with an ideology that invokes high aspirations.

The idea can be translated into the problems of this research in the following way. Because the factors which affect the current income of graduate students are different from the ones which affect their income expectations, a cross-tabulation of present and expected incomes shows little or no relationship. Consequently, some students foresee a sharp rise in total income when they begin full-time work, some students foresee no change, and some foresee a drop in income. The degree of discrepancy between present and expected income can be viewed as a measure of the purely financial advantage or disadvantage to the student in hurrying to finish his degree.

Considering Ph.D. candidates only, and cross-tabulating current income, expected starting salary, and the student's prediction of how long it will take him to complete his Ph.D., the "dire effect" turns up (see Table 8.19). The higher the student's income and the lower his expected salary, that is, the less the economic incentive to finish, the lower the proportion of students who expect to finish within five years. Among Ph.D. candidates whose current income is less than $300 a month and who foresee an income of $580 a month or more when they finish, 74 per cent expect to complete their work within five years; among students whose current income (from all sources) is $500 a month or more and who anticipate an income of less than $400 a month when they begin full-time work, 31 per cent expect to finish in five years.

The suggestion is that the rate of progress toward the Ph.D. is a function of the degree of economic incentive for finishing and that the low income expectations of graduate students constitute an opportunity structure which retards their progress by lowering their motivation.

Many other factors are associated with speed in completing the Ph.D., and opportunity structures are not a total explanation, but regardless of the other characteristics introduced as control variables, the same pattern remains.

The more able the student, as measured by faculty ratings, the faster his progress, but within each ability group, perceived financial incentive makes a big difference (see Table 8.20).

[10] David Matza, review of Richard A. Cloward and Lloyd E. Ohlin, *Delinquency and Opportunity: A Theory of Delinquent Gangs*, in *American Journal of Sociology*, LXVI (May, 1961), 632.

Natural scientists anticipate faster progress, and humanities students anticipate the slowest progress, but within each division opportunity structures make a sharp difference (see Table 8.21).

Similarly, the relationship cannot be explained by holding constant expected job, although 16 per cent of the academics are classified as having negative incentive, as compared with 7 per cent of those expecting non-academic jobs (see Table 8.22); stratum (see Table 8.23); family role (see Table 8.24); employment status (see Table 8.25); or any other control variable which was introduced into the tabulations.

Before further consideration of this relationship, however, it is important to give some more detailed consideration to the relationship between employment status and predicted speed for attaining the Ph.D. In chapter v it was shown that there was a strong negative relationship between employment and course completion, and it was suggested that the high rates of employment for graduate students play a part in stretching out their studies. In Table 8.25, however, although full-time workers are much slower than the other groups, the non-workers are not any faster than those with a part-time job or duty stipend. The introduction of transfer status clarifies the matter somewhat. Ph.D. students who have changed schools appear greatly retarded in their degree progress (see Table 8.26). Although both opportunity structure and transfer status affect speed, the non-transfers with the bleakest expectations are faster than the transfer students with the greatest economic incentive.

When transfer status is introduced into the relationship between employment and speed, and stipends are treated separately in the employment index, the following pattern emerges (see Table 8.27). Among non-transfer students, work slows them up and stipends speed them on. Among those with no fellowship or assistantship, 32 per cent of the full-time workers expect to finish in five years, 59 per cent of the part-time workers, and 68 per cent of the non-workers. In addition, duty stipends, although they lower course loads, appear to provide other advantages, for assistants are much faster than part-time workers, though fellows are the fastest of all.

Among transfer students, the same relationships hold among workers. Full-time workers have 9 per cent expecting to finish in five years, part-time workers have 31 per cent, and assistants have 41 per cent. However, among the transfer students the non-workers are slower than the part-time workers! Why? We have no idea at all. Because, however, for the typical graduate student the question is not whether to work, but what kind of work is available, the following generalizations can be drawn:

1. Among students who are employed, assistants expect to finish the fastest; part-time workers are slower than assistants; and full-time workers are the slowest of all.

2. Fellowships or other factors which keep the student from working at all add to his degree progress, but only for students who have not transferred schools.

Among transfer students, for some unknown reason, non-workers are characterized by high rates of delay.

To return to the question of expected income as a factor in the rate of progress, it must be admitted that the evidence is far from conclusive. For one thing, the causal relationship could go the other way — students who have been unavoidably detained may rationalize their situations by a sour grapes mechanism of anticipating low salaries. For another, we do not know how accurate the students are in predicting their degree progress.

Even though doubts may arise about the importance of financial opportunity structures as a genuine causal mechanism, the data still underline a psychological theme which is of some importance in understanding American graduate schools. Remembering that to a surprising degree graduate students are not recruited directly from undergraduate studies, that the students appear reluctant to borrow money to finish, that the higher the income the lower the course completions regardless of work situations, that the male students do not postpone children in order to complete their studies, remembering all of these findings in addition to the relationship between financial incentive and speed, one is led to speculate that part of the problem of graduate study is the lack of "pull" from professional futures. It should be remembered that, unlike physicians or lawyers, the arts and science graduate student may practice his profession while in school. Teaching and research, the major functions of the Ph.D., are available to the student, and in many cases research opportunities for graduate students in major universities are more desirable (in terms of libraries, equipment, financial support) and teaching loads are lighter than those available to junior faculty in the beginning years of their jobs. Thus the intrinsic incentives for completing the Ph.D. come down to status, money, and the feeling of "being grown up." To the extent that student mythology creates the impression that academic salaries are low, and the graduate faculties suggest through informal conversations that the schools to which the neophytes will be sent for their first jobs are "second rate" in comparison with the major graduate institutions, it may well be that a climate has been created which lowers the incentive of the graduate student to hurry through to completion.

While a case may be made that the students are wrong, that academic salaries are comfortable and rising, that delay in completion is very expensive when viewed in terms of lifetime earnings and pensions; it may be that one of the major financial factors in graduate school is not the current financial situation of the students but their pessimistic images of their financial futures. It is thus neither their present nor their future, but the degree of push or pull created by the discrepancy between the two which is one of the prime "financial" problems of graduate students.

Summary

In this chapter we have explored the subjective side of finances present and finances future.

In examining present worry about financial matters, we found it to be fairly infrequent and evenly distributed across the categories of students used in other analyses. Part of this situation stems from the objective fact that many of the students are fairly well off; part comes from the fact that worry is more related to debt and expected debt than to absolute amounts of income or income sources; part appears to stem from the fact that students tend to evaluate their situations by comparison with others they know; and part stems from the fact that although part-time employment adds somewhat to worry, part-time employment is the norm for most groups of students.

In examining predictions of future income, a more negative tone developed. Many graduate students have fairly low income expectations, and a discouraging pattern of relationships appears when current income is compared with expected starting salaries and then related to speed of graduate study among Ph.D. candidates. The suggestion is that the students' (perhaps unrealistic) pessimism about their financial futures, in combination with their rather high current incomes, result in a lessening of incentive to complete the Ph.D. with unseemly haste.

■ Chapter 9

The Outcome One Year Later

AN IMPORTANT issue in the study of graduate student finances are the reputed effects of different financial situations, and attitudes toward such situations, on the abilities of students to remain on in graduate school and make progress toward attaining their degrees. Are those students who are relatively well supported through stipends and work more likely to remain on working for their degrees or obtaining them? What is the effect of worry over financial matters: Is the worried student more likely to abandon his career track for full-time employment?

To assess these effects properly would involve following our sample of graduate students over a period of time until they had either achieved the degrees for which they were working or had definitely abandoned these aims. Graduate study being so loosely organized (compared to the relatively rigid curriculum and time-span of undergraduate education), such a follow-up study might take more than a decade to reach the point where every one of our respondents had reached his academic destination or abandoned this career line. Such an extended research program was beyond the scope of our present study.

We are able, however, to extend our study a short distance into the future beyond the fall of 1958 by returning one year later to the schools in our sample to obtain information on the 1959 situations of our respondents. Our field representatives were asked in the fall of 1959 to determine the status of each student in our sample and at the same time to collect various ratings from the faculty and to copy grade records.

We did not contact the students themselves in the fall of 1959 but rather had our field representatives search records of enrolment, interview faculty members, or use other sources to obtain firm information on whether our respondents were still enrolled, and, if not, what they were doing.

Although these data are relatively simple, they nevertheless provide important information on the outcomes of a time segment in the educational lives of this group of graduate students. These data provide information on degrees awarded, shifts in field of study, transfers between institutions, dropping out of graduate school, and type of employment for students who left school. Because graduate students do not "graduate with their class" as undergraduates do, there has been little information available on attrition in arts and science graduate work, much less on the factors involved. By correlating student characteristics from the 1958 schedules with outcomes in 1959, one can make some progress in understanding the reasons for various outcomes. Most important, these materials make it possible to determine whether the financial factors discussed previously play a part in attrition from graduate studies.

Our field representatives were able to obtain some information about 99 per cent of the sample (see Table 9.1a). Two-thirds (66 per cent) were still in school, 59 per cent in the same school and field, 7 per cent had shifted field or institution. A third (34 per cent) were no longer registered at their 1958 institution. Most of these (28 per cent) were known to be non-students. However, 6 per cent of the sample had "disappeared." That is, although they were known to have left their institution and some member of the faculty knew they had dropped out, no one knew whether they were studying elsewhere or were working. Inspection of the follow-up materials suggested that many of the students who disappeared were first-year students who found graduate work unrewarding and left before the end of the first term without consulting faculty members for advice or help, or informing them of their future plans. It was very rare for an advanced student to "disappear," and, despite the alleged impersonality of graduate study, the advanced students for whom no information was available were almost always those whose faculty sponsors had disappeared themselves or where the faculty or institution refused to cooperate in the follow-up.

Of the students still in school, 90 per cent were in the same institution and field of study (see Table 9.1b). Six per cent had transferred to another institution, 3 per cent had shifted their field of study at the same institution, and 1 per cent had done both. Although the rate appears small, because (a) so many students leave school completely, (b) transfer students tend to be advanced master's candidates who shift to another institution for their Ph.D., and (c) many students come to the large graduate institutions for Ph.D.'s from schools which only offer the M.A., among advanced students in the sample, 47 per cent have studied in two or more graduate institutions.

Among the students who leave school, the largest single group (39 per cent of those on whom we had firm information) have academic jobs in colleges and universities (see Table 9.1c). However, a considerable proportion of graduate school alumni do not go into the standard fields of college level teaching and academic or non-academic research. Forty-six per cent of those who left school (with or without a degree) were in primary or secondary teaching, not in the labor force, or in a non-academic job which did not involve research. Thus, only a little more than half of the products of the graduate school begin their postgraduate school employment in academic or research jobs. As we shall see, however, the better the student and the further along he was in his studies when he left, the more likely it is that he ended up in an academic job.

To complete the overview of the follow-up results, outcome is cross-tabulated against stage of study in 1958 (see Table 9.2). Each of the four stages has its particular pattern. Among first-year students (Stage I), 60 per cent continued in the same school and field, and 30 per cent left school (assuming that those who disappeared did not transfer). Among advanced master's candidates (Stage II) 50 per cent continued in the same school and field, 38 per cent left school. Among those in Stage III (advanced Ph.D. students who had not started their theses) stability is the highest: 73 per cent remained in the same school and field, 21 per cent left school. Among those in Stage IV (advanced Ph.D. students working on their dissertations) 17 per cent got their Ph.D.'s, 53 per cent continued in the same school and field, and 26 per cent left without a degree, although undoubtedly a number have all but the formalities completed for their degree.

Despite the differences among the stages, several themes appear at all stages. First, it is clear that leaving without a degree is more common than leaving with one. Second, since between a fifth and a third of the students in each stage leave school without a degree, the attrition rates in graduate school are not low. Presumably only a small handful of graduate students survive straight through to the Ph.D. with no break in their studies. Third, at any stage, shifts in school or field of study are rather uncommon.

Probably the most interesting group to consider in detail are the students who dropped out. Graduate study being loosely organized, it is actually rather difficult to specify what is meant by the phrase. We shall consider as a dropout any student who left school (other than transfers) without being awarded a final degree.[1] For Ph.D. students the degree is, of course, the Ph.D. For master's candidates, however, degrees were treated as final only for those students who had told us that they did not plan to get a Ph.D. That is, a dropout is any student who in 1958 was aiming for a Ph.D. and in 1959 left school without one. The group thus defined is actually quite heterogeneous. It includes a handful who were asked to leave because of their poor performance, some who terminated with no intention of ever finishing, some who hope to return to school in the future, and some who plan to complete their studies *in absentia*. At the same time the entire group shares the fate of being Ph.D. aspirants no longer studying for the degree in a graduate school.

[1] Students who disappeared are excluded, although probably most of them are dropouts.

Let us then see what characteristics from the 1958 schedules are associated with 1959 outcomes.

Dropout

The best predictor of drop-out is academic ability. Using the faculty rating of native ability to do Ph.D. work (defined in chapter vi) it is seen that the students rated "low" had twice the probability of dropping out as did students rated high (see Table 9.3). In fact, the difference between drop-out rates among beginning and advanced students is almost totally due to a pruning of the less able. When ability is held constant there is no stage difference in drop-out, but a considerable stage difference in ability ratings.

Although the ability rating divides the students into about equal thirds, the big difference is between the top two groups and the lows. This suggests not that very best students are enticed to remain, but that the demonstrably inadequate are discouraged.

The relationship between grades and dropout is a curious one (see Table 9.4). When faculty ability ratings are controlled, it appears that among high- and middle-rated students dropout goes with high grades, while among low-rated students dropout is associated with low grades. Because of the narrow range in grades and because of the strong association between grades and ratings, most of the "effect" comes from cells with small numbers of cases. Thus, while it appears that among the "A" students the lows have a lesser drop-out rate, the difference would vanish if three cases were reversed. In the key cells, students with "B" and "C" averages, it is seen that ability makes a difference in dropout, but grades do not. Because of this, and because a separate analysis indicates that the effect of grades is no stronger when the averages are rescored in terms of school rank, we shall conclude that except for the 2 per cent of the sample who got grade averages of less than "C" (and, of course, have a very high drop-out rate) that the faculty rating is a better predictor, "B" students rated low having a higher dropout rate than "C" students rated middle or high.

Other dimensions of faculty ratings do show an effect. The higher the rating of research potential (see Table 9.5) and the higher the rating of teaching ability (see Table 9.6), the lower the drop-out rate, holding constant ratings of general ability.

Even more surprising — the student's own rating of his academic ability has little to do with dropout when faculty ratings are controlled (see Table 9.7). Among students rated high or middle by the faculty, self-ratings of academic standing make no difference, although the self-confident lows do have a lesser drop-out rate than those who are more realistic in their self-evaluations. The student given a high rating by his faculty but who places himself in the bottom 40 per cent of his class is *less* likely to drop out than the student rated low by the faculty but who sees himself in the top fifth.

Although the actual mechanism is unknown — whether the less able students are counseled to leave, whether they are forced to leave, whether they find outside opportunities more attractive than staying in school, etc. — the general trend is for the dropout to be a student of lesser academic potential.

Although the association between academic ability and dropout could be further improved by pooling our available measures, academic ability is only one of many factors involved. Thus, although students rated low in ability were much more likely to drop out, 25 per cent of the dropouts were rated as high on ability. The loss of the more able students can be considered as a challenge to graduate education. Hence we turn now to the non-intellectual correlates of dropout.

We can begin with a set of negative findings. One of the most consistent patterns of these data is the lack of any relationship between subjective states — morale, personality problems, criticisms of graduate school, and financial worry — and dropout. One would certainly expect that the unhappy, the maladjusted, the hostile critics, and the financially anxious would have higher drop-out rates, but such is not the case.

Considering personal adjustment first, morale in 1958 has no association with dropout in 1959, when ability rating is controlled (see Table 9.8a). Nor does the faculty rating of personality problems contribute independently when faculty rating of ability is controlled (see Table 9.8b). It is not that the maladjusted tend to stay in the ivory tower, either. Neither measure of personal adjustments has any relationship with the outcome.

Just as the general measures fail to predict, so do specific complaints. In chapter iii it was shown that the students accepted as valid a number of specific criticisms of graduate school. It would be perfectly reasonable to expect that those who were more critical would be more likely to leave, but such is not the case (see Table 9.9). For most items the critics do have a 1 or 2 per cent higher drop-out rate, but none of the individual item relationships is statistically reliable, and for each item the high-ability critic is considerably more likely to be present the next year than the low-ability student who approves.

Because this research was commissioned to study the financial problems of graduate students, the relationship between financial worry and dropout is of some importance (see Table 9.10). Although the worriers are slightly higher on dropout than the non-worriers, it is clear that the relationship is unreliable and of negligible importance. Shifting to the financial situations which were shown in chapter viii to affect worry, it is equally clear that debt, savings, and perceived adequacy of income show no consistent association with dropout, although there is a slight tendency for those low on adequacy to have higher drop out rates.

The evidence from our research is that there is no significant relationship between worry about financial problems and dropout from graduate school.

It is possible that morale and financial worry changed radically between the fall of 1958 and the spring of 1959 and that measures taken late in the year would have shown some effect. Remembering that past debt was predictive of future borrowing, our assumption is that general financial pressures do not fluctuate so rapidly. Putting it another way, the student who in the fall of 1958 anticipated going to school despite financial difficulties was no more or less optimistic when he came to reach a decision about 1959.

None of this means that *financial factors* (sources of income, stipends, employment, etc.) were unimportant, but it seems that financial *pressures and worries* are not associated with outcomes, just as outcomes are unrelated to personal adjustment and criticisms of graduate school.

So far one would be tempted to conclude that questionnaire data are not predictive, regardless of the content area. However a number of variables in the schedule are related to dropout. In many cases it is not clear what interpretation is to be given to the findings, but several factors do show a relationship. We shall consider in turn professional motivations, division, employment, age, and family role, each of which is related to outcome.

A consistent difference, albeit a slight one, turns up when professional values and preferences are considered. Students were asked to rank various activities (research, university teaching, liberal arts college teaching, academic administration, etc.) in terms of their career preference, and, when answers are divided into research, college or university teaching, and other, it is seen that researchers have somewhat lower drop-out rates, "others" have somewhat higher drop-out rates, and teachers are in the middle (see Table 9.12). In addition, in most comparisons the student who considers himself as an intellectual has a lower drop-out probability than a less cerebral student, regardless of ability rating or preferred future activity. Because it is fair to say that graduate schools give the highest priority to research, the next highest to teaching, and little stress to other occupational possibilities, and that intellectualism is given high value in graduate school, the conclusion is that, regardless of native ability, the student whose professional values and aims are in line with the values of graduate school is less likely to leave it. The joint effect of intellectualism and preferred activity can be seen by combining them into a motivational index (see Table 9.12*b*). The highs are researchers or teachers who are high on intellectualism, the lows are "others" and less intellectual teachers. In both ability levels, but particularly among the less able, low scores on the index are associated with higher drop-out rates.

Division of study along with motivation and ability affects dropout. Natural scientists have low drop-out rates, humanities students have high drop-out rates, and social scientists are in the middle, regardless of scores on the motivation index or ability levels (see Table 9.13). The divisional effect is an interesting and puzzling one. It cannot be explained by other variables and hence is not due to ability, motivation, employment, age, or family role. While there are divisional differences in stipends, career plans, salary anticipations, age, etc., none of these, when introduced as a control variable, explains the divisional effects. Perhaps there are divisional differences in the custom of finishing graduate study while out of residence; perhaps the curriculum in the sciences has more continuity; perhaps the Ph.D. is more often a prerequisite for employment in the sciences; and perhaps there are numerous other reasons. The fact that the divisional difference holds regardless of other control variables makes it an important statistical predictor, but it gives us little understanding of the mechanism involved. However it does justify the conclusion that just as the different divisions vary in their financial situations, they vary systematically in the degree to which dropout is a problem.

The burden of the previous chapters has been that financial pressures and financial situations are essentially independent aspects of graduate study. Thus the conclusion that financial worry is not related to dropout does not mean that the other dimension of finances is not a factor. As a matter of fact, employment and stipend holding have a rather striking relationship with dropout (see Table 9.14). When the students are classified in terms of employment and stipend holding, some fairly complex but sharp differences appear:

a) Full-time workers have quite high drop-out rates, particularly among the more able students.

b) Students with a duty stipend have quite low drop-out rates, regardless of ability.

c) Other students (fellows, those with part-time jobs, those with no stipend or job) tend to have drop-out rates between assistants and full-time workers.

The higher drop-out rates for the full-time workers appear intuitively reasonable, partly because many of them never were "really" in school to begin with and partly because of the intrinsic difficulties of carrying on graduate study while employed full time. The low drop-out rates of the assistants — other analyses showing this is true for both research and teaching assistants — are more of a puzzle. One can point to a number of factors which do *not* explain the difference. It is not because of their lower work loads, for part-time workers other than assistants have high drop-out rates. It is not stipend holding per se, for, oddly enough, the fellows have slightly higher drop-out rates than assistants or unemployed students with no stipend. It is not ability, for ability has been controlled in the table. Neither is it financial worry, for financial worry is unrelated to dropout.

Perhaps the advantage of the assistants comes from the social relationships which they develop. William Erbe in a detailed analysis to be reported elsewhere has shown that assistantship holding is strongly related to membership in student peer groups. More than 60 per cent of the assistants report membership in an informal student group, as contrasted with around a fifth of the full-time workers, and 44 per cent of the remaining students. However introducing membership in student groups as a control does not eliminate the effect, although among the lower ability students group membership is associated with staying in school (see Table 9.15). Similarly, one might hypothesize that assistants develop closer relationships with the faculty and that this bond tends to keep them in school. The students were asked whether "anyone on the faculty in your department (has) told you: 'You seem to have a flair for teaching,' 'You should definitely strive for a Ph.D.,' 'You are one of the best students in the department,' 'You might do better in a different department,' 'You should NOT plan to go ahead for a Ph.D.,' etc., etc." Anyone who checked one of the "positive" items in the list is scored as high on faculty encouragement. Assistants and students who are rated higher in ability are likely to report encouragement, but when this variable is introduced into the tabulations (see Table 9.16) it does not explain the lower drop-out rates for the assistants and in fact is unrelated to dropout when ability rating and assistantship holding are held constant.

In short, as in the case of division, the research has been unable to pinpoint the reasons, but students who hold a duty stipend had a lower attrition rate. The duty stipend is not only a major source of financial support for the students, but it is also associated with keeping them in school.

The factors considered so far — ability, motivations, division, and employment — are fairly closely related to academic life itself. By and large, background variables such as class origins and religion are not associated with dropout. However, the now familiar indexes of life-cycle progress — age and family role — do appear to play some part in the process. Although stage of study is unrelated to dropout, chronological age makes a difference. The older the student, the more likely he is to leave school, regardless of ability rating (see Table 9.17) or employment status (see Table 9.18).

Because age is strongly associated with marital status and because both life-cycle characteristics are associated with other predictor variables, it is necessary to consider a complex set of variables simultaneously in order to draw any conclusion (see Table 9.19). Because of the small number of cases available in a given cell, it was necessary to dichotomize the family role index in terms of fathers (married men with one or more children) versus all others. The simplification is justified by the fact that inspection of the more detailed data shows no difference by sex or between the single and the married but childless.

When ability and employment status are controlled and the students are arranged by age and family role, it appears that both characteristics are related to dropout (see Table 9.19a). There are 11 comparisons involving age, and in ten of these the older students have higher drop-out rates. Similarly, in the eight out of 11 comparisons between fathers and others, fathers have a higher drop-out rate. The joint effect of these two characteristics may be seen by constructing a joint index based on both variables. The highs are fathers over 27, the lows are non-fathers under 27, and the middles are young fathers or older non-fathers. With the exception of the low-ability full-time workers, this index produces a regular progression in drop-out rates (see Table 9.19c). Similarly, the tables show that ability and employment status contribute to drop-out rates (with one slight exception) in each family-age group.

Again, it is not possible to specify the mechanism involved in this relationship except negatively. It is not due to differences in ability, employment status, division, or professional motivation. Although there is no statistical proof for the interpretation, the predictor characteristics, except for division, may be thought of at an abstract level as measures of involvement and commitment to the world of graduate school, and thus the probability of leaving may be thought of as a function of the degree of involvement in graduate school and the degree of involvement in the outside world.

The students whose interests and motivations coincide with the motivations given high value in graduate school will undoubtedly find it a more attractive place, while the student who is less intellectual and more interested in an occupation other than research and teaching will find the outside world more attractive.

Students working full-time have a heavy involvement in the extra-graduate school world, while the assistants are physically (in terms of offices) and socially (in terms of quasi-faculty status) involved in school. Thus, the fellows, although given high status, do not have the degree of involvement in graduate school that assistants have.

Similarly, the father has the extra-academic world of his family and the older student probably has more "outside" involvements and feels less comfortable in the student role. If one thinks of employment, life cycle, and motivation as indexes of involvement one can combine them into a single index. By giving arbitrary weights to (*a*) the employment characteristics, (*b*) age, and (*c*) the question on intellectualism, and cross-tabulating the results against dropout, the joint effect of ability, division and "involvement" can be seen (see Table 9.20).

Each of the three classes of characteristics appears to contribute to dropout, division and "involvement" producing a range from 10 per cent to over 40 per cent dropout among the higher ability students, and a range from 17 per cent to 58 per cent among the low-ability group.

The following will serve to summarize the findings on dropout:

1. Of the students who did not receive a Ph.D. or self-defined terminal master's degree, 30 per cent either "disappeared" or were known to be out of school one year after the original survey.

2. When "dropouts" are defined as students who did not receive a Ph.D. or self-defined terminal master's degree, the following characteristics were found to be unrelated to dropout:

a) Measures of personal adjustment.
b) Specific criticisms of graduate school.
c) Financial pressures and financial worry.

3. The following characteristics were shown to be predictive:

a) Low academic ability, as measured by faculty ratings.
b) Motivation and professional values: Students who defined themselves as intellectuals or who preferred research careers were less likely to drop out.
c) Division of study: Natural science students had the lowest drop-out rates, humanities students the highest drop-out rates, social science students were in-between.
d) Employment: Full-time workers had high drop-out rates; students with duty stipends had low drop-out rates; students with part-time jobs, fellowships, or no employment were in-between.
e) Life cycle: Older students and fathers had higher drop-out rates.

4. The characteristics listed above contribute independently and when taken together produce a range in dropouts from 10 per cent in the most favorable subgroup to 58 per cent in the least favorable.

5. The findings on motivation, life cycle, and employment were tentatively interpreted as indicative of variation in attachments to the world of graduate school as opposed to attachments to the "outside world."

Transfers

Transfers to new institutions were shown to be rather rare, although over time they have a cumulative effect such that a goodly proportion of the Ph.D. candidates have studied in two or more graduate schools. If transfers in school are taken as a proportion of students known to be in school in 1959 rather than as a proportion of all students, 10 per cent of the advanced master's candidates transferred, while 6 per cent of the students in other stages shifted institutions.

By and large, the variables in the 1958 questionnaire are not strongly associated with transfer status. Married students, particularly married women, are less likely to transfer (see Table 9.21*a*). Research assistants are less likely to transfer than students with other stipends or no aid at all (see Table 9.21*b*). Analyses of a number of characteristics indicate that the only group with a transfer rate of more than 10 per cent are those students who in 1958 reported that they were dissatisfied with their choice of school, and even here it is only those in the lowest 5 per cent on satisfaction who show such a rate (see Table 9.21*c*).

In themselves, neither faculty ratings of ability nor stratum of school in 1958 are associated with transferring (see Table 9.22*a*). Control too is unimportant (see Table 9.22*b*). Students who transfer tend to remain in the same private or public orbit, and the number shifting from public to private is essentially the same as the number moving the other way. That is, there is no trend toward or away from public institutions for transfers. However there is considerable shift in stratum (see Table 9.22c). Sixty-two per cent of the codable cases shifted stratum, 41 per cent moving up (from Stratum III to Stratum I or II, or from II to I) and 21 per cent moving down (from I to II or III, or from II to III). Thus, the net effect is for shifting up the stratum scale.

The direction of mobility, however, is associated with academic ability (see Table 9.22d). Highly rated students were more likely to move up, while students rated low in ability were relatively more likely to move down. The result necessarily is a sharp difference in the ability ratings of recruits to schools in different strata (see Table 9.22e). Of the transfers ending up in Stratum I schools, 83 per cent had been rated high or middle in their original institution, in comparison with 47 per cent of those transferring to a Stratum III school. It is, of course, possible that all of this is an artifact of the rating standards used by faculty in different strata (the students were rated vis-à-vis departmental standards rather than in absolute terms) but the suggestion is that this is not the case. Thus, of the transfers *from* Stratum II schools, 86 per cent of the 15 "upwardly mobile" were rated high or middle as compared with 64 per cent of the 22 stable or downwardly mobile students. Hence, at least by the standards of the school from which they came, ability is associated with direction of movement.

If it is assumed that there already was a correlation between stratum and ability levels for entering students, the relationships shown here corroborate the famous dictum, "Them as has, gets."

Academic Jobs

Of the approximately 700 students for whom 1959 employment information was available (88 per cent of the students known to have left school), 39 per cent entered academic jobs, defined as teaching or research positions in a college or university. Although it turns out that 1958 financial situations are unrelated to type of job, the general importance of understanding recruitment to the academic profession justifies some attention to the differences between students who enter academia and those who get other jobs.

Current expansion in higher education, increased demands for trained professionals in industry and government, and publicized complaints about academic salaries have created considerable concern about the future supply of college staffs, and the question has been raised as to whether colleges and universities can compete with others for the graduate students they train.

In general, the students' own preferences and expectations are the best predictor of jobs (see Table 9.23). Of the students who expected and preferred academic jobs, 66 per cent got one, while among those who neither preferred nor expected such jobs, 14 per cent ended up in academia. Since a questionnaire filled out one year ahead is a pretty good predictor of the outcome, it appears that not much happens during the actual job search to change people's plans.

The figures in Table 9.23 are suggestive, however, of some shortage of academic positions, rather than a shortage of applicants. Among students who left school, 67 per cent said they preferred academic jobs, 55 per cent realistically expected one, but only 43 per cent got them. Thus, the academically oriented student is more likely to be frustrated than the non-academic-minded one, which in turn suggests that academic jobs are not a dumping ground for students who cannot do better.

What acounts for this winnowing? Stage of study is a very important factor (see Table 9.24). Among students who preferred academic jobs, 72 per cent of those who were Ph.D. candidates landed one, in contrast with 31 per cent of those working for a master's degree. The reason appears to be obvious — academic institutions demand that their novice employees be either Ph.D.'s or near enough to the final degree that it appears probable.

Another factor of importance is the ability rating (see Table 9.25). Regardless of preference and regardless of stage of study among those who prefer academic jobs, the student rated high in native ability is more likely to get an academic job when he leaves school. Thus, among Ph.D. candidates who preferred academic jobs, 76 per cent of the highly rated got one, in contrast with 56 per cent of those rated low in ability. However, it should be noted that the low-rated Ph.D. candidate had a better chance than the high-rated master's candidate among those who preferred academic positions.

It would appear that fears about academic recruitment are unwarranted and that colleges and universities get only a small proportion of the graduate school alumni only because they are so choosy. However two less sanguine conclusions should be drawn. First, the data compare academic jobs in general with non-academic jobs in general. Although there are too few cases to justify formal tabulations, for those students who went into non-academic research jobs (as compared with secondary teaching, business, etc.) the ability advantage of the academics is almost nil. More extensive research may show that for jobs with comparable requirements, the academic world may not be getting the better students. Second, it should be noted in Table 9.24 that the "breakage" goes to the non-academic world. Among those with the highest probabilities — the advanced, highly rated students who preferred academic jobs — 24 per cent did not get to academia, while, at the other end, among less qualified students who did not want academic jobs only 9 per cent were diverted to the academy. Because of the small number of cases available it is difficult to go much further, but the introduction of other variables into the tabulation leads to some suggestive differences, when the predictor variables are controlled by dividing the cases into three groups: A. advanced-, high- and middle-ability students who prefer academic jobs; C. low-ability students who do not prefer academic jobs; and B. all other combinations. Group A has a high academic probability, Group B a middle one, and Group C is so low that further tabulations cannot make any difference for it.

Control and division seem to make some difference, although the case bases in the cells are quite small (see Table 9.26). It would appear that Stratum III students have a lesser chance of getting academic jobs, and there is a slight tendency for public school students to be more academic in their outcomes.

There are, of course, strong divisional differences in preference and slight divisional differences in stage of study. When the predictor variables are controlled, however, divisional differences are not consistent (see Table 9.27). Among the "eligibles" (advanced, high-ability students who prefer academic jobs) humanities students have the highest proportion entering college and university positions — nine out of ten as compared with 66 per cent in the other two divisions combined. Among the less eligible, however, divisional differences are small. The suggestion here is that among the non-humanistic eligibles, non-academic competition is stronger, and a number of qualified students who prefer academic jobs are wooed away. Since, however, academic eligibility qualifications are similar in all three divisions, Group B shows no difference, since none of them have much of a chance for an academic job.

Two other, more subjective, variables show some relationship to outcome. Because of the shrinkage in the case base and difficulties in interpreting the findings, they should be considered merely suggestive, but other people — teachers and spouses — seem to play a part in this decision.

Students who are high on our faculty encouragement index are more likely to get academic jobs, even controlling for the major predictor variables (see Table 9.28). Whether such students are more highly motivated or whether the professors who encouraged them hustled around to get them jobs, we do not know.

A shred of evidence — but a suggestive one — comes from a question asked of married students about the value they place on material comforts. They were asked "How important is it eventually to have a comfortable home, nice furniture, etc.?" and were to reply for themselves and for their spouse. Their own answers show little relationship to outcome, but the more materialistic the spouse (or rather the more materialistic they perceive their spouses to be) the less likely they are to get an academic job (see Table 9.29). The student's own perception of starting salaries, job availability, etc., is not related to type of job, but the suggestion is that the long-suffering spouse, who was shown to be so willing to put her husband through graduate school (almost all of the spouses in Table 9.29 are women) may be less eager to put him through life if she has her eye on material comfort . . . but that is the beginning of a separate research study.

In general, graduate students get the kind of jobs they prefer and expect. Academic jobs are highly selective, though, and even among students who prefer them only advanced students who are rated as potential Ph.D. material can be fairly sure of achieving their preferences. The variables that appear to intervene between preference and outcome for students otherwise qualified for academic jobs include: some slight stratum differences, non-academic competition for students in natural and social science, relationships with faculty members, and spouse's resistance against entering a low-paid career. Most of these findings are to be highly qualified, but, taken together, they suggest that the academic world is subject to powerful competition for its progeny.

SUMMARY

One year after the administration of the questionnaires, the status of a large proportion of the sample was determined by inquiries to university registrars and departmental faculty. Most of the students (59 per cent) were studying in the same field in the same institution, 7 per cent had shifted school or field of study, 5 per cent had left school with a Ph.D. or self-defined terminal master's, and the remainder (36 per cent) had dropped out of school or disappeared.

Analysis of dropouts, transfers, and type of employment for those who left school led to the following findings.

Regarding dropout: Academic ability seems to be the most important variable, low-ability students having quite high drop-out rates, even though failing grades are very rare in graduate school. Subjective states such as morale, personal adjustment, and criticisms of graduate school are not associated with dropout. Neither financial worry nor financial pressures in 1958 were associated with dropout in 1959. The characteristics which are predictive of dropout are: motivation (researchers have low drop-out rates, students who don't prefer either teaching or research have high rates, self-defined intellectuals have lower rates); division (natural science students have low drop-out rates, humanities students have high rates, social scientists are in the middle); employment (full-time workers have high drop-out rates, assistants have low rates, fellows, part-time workers, and those with no employment or fellowship generally are in the middle); age and family role (older students and fathers have high drop-out rates). Except for the divisional difference, most of these findings can be loosely interpreted as indexes of involvement in graduate school versus involvement in the world outside it. The more the student is involved in school, the more likely he is to stay an additional year.

Transfers are fairly rare and are not strongly associated with the personal characteristics measured in the study. Married students and research assistants are a little less likely to shift schools. Among the transfers, however, there is a distinct difference in the school of destination for students who differ in academic ability. Better students tend to move up in stratum of school, poorer students tend to stay at the same level or to move down.

Among the students who were known to be working, 39 per cent received academic jobs. The best predictors of academic jobs are the student's own preference, his ability rating, and his stage of study. However, even among advanced students of high ability who preferred academic jobs, a quarter went into non-academic employment. Part of this "loss" is explained by non-academic opportunities for natural and social scientists as compared with humanities, relationships with faculty members, and a lesser rate of academic employment for students whose spouses were reported to be more materialistic.

Chapter 10

Summary

THE LAST CHAPTER of a report, by tradition, is devoted to summary and conclusions. We shall leave to others, better qualified to make recommendations, the drawing of conclusions. Whether the data are indicative of a healthy situation or of pressing needs for reform is a very important question but one which is beyond the scope of our commission, which was to describe the financial situations of American arts and science graduate students.

We shall conclude by summarizing the major findings of the study. The chapter is designed to summarize the detailed and often complex inferences drawn from the data and to provide the reader who wishes a quick review of the findings with a capsule version of the report. Needless to say, numerous qualifications and details of documentation have been ignored in this summary.

THE STUDY

In the fall of 1958 detailed self-administered schedules were collected from 92 per cent of 3,000 arts and science students drawn as a national sample of master's degree and Ph.D. candidates in natural (physical and biological) sciences, social sciences, and humanities in residence in American graduate schools. Twenty-five graduate institutions were sampled proportionately to their enrolments, and within schools systematic probability samples were taken.

One year later the academic status of 99 per cent of the sample and the employment status of most of those who had left school were ascertained, along with grade point averages and faculty ratings of aptitudes and personality characteristics.

Summary

Chapter i: Seven Graduate Students

In this chapter, seven case studies are reconstructed from questionnaires. The students are described in terms of the variables which are later shown to be important in the statistical analyses, in order to provide some concrete examples of the generalizations drawn in later chapters.

Chapter ii: The Academic World of the Graduate Students: A Composite Portrait

The sample is described in terms of five measures of academic environments: (*a*) stratum classification of universities, (*b*) control of university, (*c*) division of study, (*d*) academic stage, (*e*) career expectations. In considering the interrelationships of these variables and data on evaluations of school, the following conclusions were drawn:

1. High-prestige graduate schools tend to have more students and to offer work in the same fields of study as smaller schools, plus offerings in additional rare fields. Consequently, graduate students are heavily concentrated in the large, diverse, high-prestige institutions.

2. Private versus public control is unrelated to the stratum dimension of size-offerings-prestige, but private universities are concentrated in the urban East, large public universities in the less urbanized areas of the Midwest and Far West, and small public universities in the less urbanized areas of the South and Mountain states. The result is that America has two geographically differentiated systems of graduate training of about the same size and stratum level.

3. A little less than half of the graduate students are in the natural sciences, a little less than one-quarter are in the social sciences, and a little more than one-quarter are in the humanities. Divisional differences by control and stratum are small.

4. About half of the students are in the beginning or master's degree stages, about half are in the advanced or Ph.D. stages of training. Students in humanities and in lower-stratum schools tend to be at earlier stages, which is suggestive of problems of speed and retention in these groups.

5. Very few of the students eschew the Ph.D., although a number are not certain that they will get one.

6. A clear majority of the students prefer academic jobs, and a slight majority expect them, the discrepancy being accounted for by 16 per cent of the sample who prefer academic jobs but do not expect them, often because of their sex or academic record.

7. Although often critical of specific aspects of graduate school, the students tend to be pleased with their choice of school and optimistic about their vocational futures. Their personal *esprit* compares favorably with the highest morale groups of enlisted men in the World War II army.

8. There is no relationship between a student's location in the academic world described here and his morale.

Chapter iii: The Life Histories of the Graduate Students: A Composite Portrait

Chapter iii describes the sample in terms of father's occupation, age, family role, and the interrelationships of these characteristics.

The general conclusions are: Absolutely speaking, graduate students are considerably older than is necessary. Relatively speaking, their progress in the life cycle tends to keep up with their age, while their progress in academic stage does not.

The specific conclusions are:

1. From the viewpoint of the society as a whole, graduate students are disproportionately recruited from the higher class levels, but in absolute terms they come from families of modest economic circumstances.

2. About half of the students were over 22 years of age when they received their bachelor's degree, delay of this type being associated with undergraduate self-support, being a male, and lower status origins.

3. A little more than 40 per cent of the students were out of college a year or more before they began graduate work.

4. Delay in starting graduate school after receiving the A.B. is only partly due to military service and economic difficulties. More commonly it seems to be due to late development of motivation for graduate studies, particularly in the humanities and social sciences.

5. Because delay in receipt of the A.B. and gaps between the bachelor's degree and graduate study are statistically independent, their additive effect comes close to explaining the high age levels of the students. All other things equal, if all graduate students received their A.B.'s at 22 and went to graduate school immediately, only 17 per cent of the students in residence would be over 26 years of age, as contrasted with half of the sample who are 27 or older.

6. Overage students are disproportionately concentrated in lower-stratum schools and in the social sciences and humanities.

7. Regardless of his academic progress, the *typical* male graduate student marries around age 26, is fairly likely to have a child by the time he has been married three years, and expect a child within the next two years unless he has two children already or has been married seven or more years without any children.

8. The only social characteristic which affects fertility and fertility plans among the married men is that Roman Catholics have and expect more children.

9. Women students have a lower proportion married and a higher proportion expecting to be married than men, which suggests that women tend to drop out of graduate school when they get married.

10. Because progress in the family cycle is strongly related to age and progress in academic stage is loosely related to age, at every stage of academic progress there is considerable variation in family situations.

Chapter iv: Graduate Students' Incomes: Sources, Totals, and Perceived Adequacy

Student incomes are analyzed in terms of three dimensions: (*a*) sources of income, (*b*) total income for the student's spending unit during the academic year, and (*c*) students' estimates of whether their incomes will be adequate. The major conclusions are:

1. Graduate students tend to have multiple and diverse income sources. The only source which is characteristic of the majority of students is stipends (scholarships, fellowships, and assistantships). Over 70 per cent receive stipend income, half receive $150 a month or more in stipend income, and 41 per cent receive half or more of their total income from stipends.

2. For about a quarter of the students, income from spouse's employment is an important source; for a small minority, full-time employment is the major source of income; and for a considerable minority withdrawals from savings, part-time work, and aid from parents are important supplementary sources. Investments, borrowing, veteran's benefits, and other sources are relatively unimportant.

3. The sample reported a median income of approximately $400 a month during the academic year, which appears to be fairly high, but needs to be qualified by the fact that (*a*) half of the sample are married, (*b*) on the average 15 per cent of this income must be spent on graduate school, and (*c*) incomes for comparable people in the general population are probably higher.

4. High incomes are concentrated among married students, low incomes among single students. Part of the high income levels of the married comes from their access to income from full-time jobs and income from spouse's employment, but, even among those with no income from these sources, total incomes run high for married students.

5. Eighty-four per cent of the students believe that they have enough income to cover their expenses; 53 per cent believe that they have enough for their expenses plus a surplus for emergencies.

6. Whether incomes are seen as adequate or not depends on the size of the income and the size of the family it must support. On the average, it takes an income of $300 a month to put married men with no children in the same financial position as single students receiving $200–$299 a month, and it takes over $500 a month for the fathers to achieve the same proportion who believe their incomes are adequate.

7. Because students with larger families tend to have larger incomes, perceived adequacy of income does not vary much with family situations or

with other major variables, although married women are a little more comfortably fixed and fathers somewhat less so than the others.

8. Family role position is the major determinant of financial situations:

a) Single students have low incomes, low income needs, and seldom work full-time.

b) Married women tend to have high incomes and to be supported by working husbands.

c) Childless married men tend to have high incomes, fairly high income needs, and working wives to supplement their other income sources.

d) Fathers have higher income needs than married men with no children, about the same income receipts, and appear to compensate for the loss of spouses' employment by taking up full-time work.

e) Of all the groups, only the fathers seem to have financial troubles, and these are not due to low incomes but to income sources which divert them from their studies.

Chapter v: Graduate Students as Consumers of Education: Expenditures, Prices, and Demand

This chapter is divided into two parts, first an analysis of 1958–1959 expenditures for graduate study as anticipated by the respondents in the 1958 questionnaire, second an analysis (based on data from the 1959 follow-up) of the actual course completions for the sample.

Regarding expenditures:

1. Median total expenditures for graduate education amount to about $450 a year, the bulk of this going for tuition. Viewed as a proportion of total income, the average student expected to spend about 15 per cent of his total income on academic expenses.

2. Academic expenses are highly variable: One-fifth of the students expected to spend $900 or more and 23 per cent expected to spend 30 per cent or more of their total income on graduate studies. At the opposite extreme, 16 per cent expected to spend less than $225 a year and 34 per cent expected to spend less than a tenth of their total income on school.

3. Variations in academic expenditures are essentially due to two factors: tuition differences between public and private schools and highly variable course loads in both types of institutions.

4. Although for some students (e.g., single students with high course loads in private institutions) academic costs consume a large fraction of their total income, the proportion of total income which must be spent for education shows no relationship with financial adequacy. That is, students with higher educational bills are no more likely to expect ending up in the red at the end of the year.

Regarding course loads:

1. Of the students in the sample who were registered for the entire 1958–59 academic year, 12 per cent received credit for what their school's catalogue defines as a full-time load, and about 40 per cent received credit for more than two-thirds of a full year's load.

2. There is a strong negative relationship between amount of employment (including assistantships) and course loads completed.

3. Regardless of employment or stage of study, older students and those with higher incomes carried lower academic loads.

4. The findings, along with the previous data on the low level of debt and borrowings among the students, are interpreted as suggesting that rather than adjusting their employment to their course loads, graduate students adjust their course loads to allow for a level of employment that will get them through the year without incurring debt.

Chapter vi: Stipends

Stipends, the major source of income for graduate students, are described and analyzed in terms of distribution, source, and student opinions.

For the sample as a whole:

1. Seventy-one per cent received some sort of stipend.

2. About half had a non-duty stipend, about one-fourth had a non-duty stipend worth $1,000 or more per year over and above tuition costs.

3. Four out of ten students had a duty stipend. Teaching assistantships were twice as common as research assistantships, a little more than one out of four students holding a teaching assistantship.

In terms of distribution:

1. Natural science students had a distinct advantage over social science and humanities students in terms of: (*a*) probability of holding a stipend of any type, and (*b*) amount of money received from non-duty stipends among holders of such aid.

2. Humanities students have more teaching assistantships than do social science students, the reverse is true for research assistantships. For duty stipends in general, there is no difference between humanities and social sciences.

3. Ph.D. candidates have an advantage over master's candidates in terms of: (*a*) probability of holding a stipend of almost any type, and (*b*) amount of money received from non-duty stipends among holders of such stipends.

4. Public school students have a distinct advantage over private school students for both teaching and research assistantships, but there is little control difference in: (*a*) non-duty stipends worth $1,000 or more after tuition, (*b*) net value (after subtraction of tuition and fees) of non-duty stipends, among holders of such stipends.

5. Hourly pay rates for assistants do not vary much by division, stage, or control.

6. Three combinations of these variables stand out:

a) Among advanced natural science students, except possibly in lower-stratum private schools, stipend levels are so high as to have approached something like a saturation point.

b) Advanced humanities and social science students in public institutions have very high proportions with teaching assistantships.

c) Beginning social science and humanities students in private schools have very low rates of support.

7. Financial need is not associated with stipend holding, and, although ability is related to stipend holding, it plays a less important role than division, stage, and control. Low ability students in the "right" circumstances have a better chance of getting a stipend than outstanding students in less fortunate academic niches.

In terms of sources:

1. The major proportion of stipends are provided by the students' own schools.

2. The major differential in university support lies in variation in the use of teaching assistants. Public schools use many more, regardless of division, and private schools seem particularly unwilling or unable to use TA's in the social sciences and humanities. Even after TA's are excluded from the tabulations, public schools still provide stipends for more of their students than do private schools (not counting lower tuition as a stipend), research assistantships from university funds being a major factor here.

3. The federal government in 1958 was an important source of stipend funds for natural science students, particularly at the Ph.D. level, but students in other divisions seldom received federal money, except in the form of veteran's benefits which are not associated with division of study.

4. Stipend support from the "private sector" (private national programs and employers) is small and neither accentuates nor compensates for the differentials in other sources.

In terms of opinions on duty stipends:

1. Except for those students who hold non-duty stipends worth $1,000 or more a year after tuition, teaching and research assistantships are seen as quite desirable by all students, aside from their vital economic importance.

2. The bulk of assistants rate their jobs as good or excellent in training value, and less than one-third have any complaint. If there is a complaint, it is almost always about the amount of money.

Chapter vii: The Pattern of Non-Stipend Income

Chapter vii describes and analyzes the major sources of non-stipend income: full-time jobs, part-time jobs, spouse's employment, aid from parents, and borrowing.

Concerning employment:

1. Employment of some sort (assistantships, part-time jobs, full-time jobs) is characteristic of graduate students. Among students with no fellowship, more than eight out of ten work during the year.

2. The students who have full-time jobs tend to be characterized by high-paying professional and managerial occupations, heavy family responsibilities, retardation in academic progress, and concentration in the lower-stratum private schools, which are adapted to their needs.

3. Part-time jobs, while often high level professional positions, appear to be supplementary income sources, which substitute for stipends in those schools, divisions, and stages where stipends are rare.

Concerning family sources of income:

1. The spouses of women students tend to have quite good jobs, the spouses of men students tend to have fairly good jobs.

2. The rate of employment of the students' wives is a joint function of fertility and economic pressures.

3. There is no evidence that the working wives are rebellious about their lot, and no evidence that male students weigh the economic importance of working wives in their fertility plans, although, if the wife is a *student*, fertility expectations are conspicuously lowered.

4. Less than a quarter of the students were receiving help from parents and/or in-laws.

5. The major reason reported for not receiving parental aid is "I don't need any."

6. Among students who "need" parental aid, the proportion receiving it varies directly with the class level of the parental family and the family's orientation toward higher education.

Concerning borrowing and savings:

1. Borrowing is rare, savings are common in the sample.

2. The best predictor of borrowing is extant indebtedness.

3. Except for slightly higher debt levels among students from lower-status origins, there is no particular group of students (in terms of academic variables, family situations, employment, stipends, etc., etc.,) which is either amassing savings or running into debt while in graduate school.

Chapter viii: Concerns About Money: Worry and Expectations

Two subjective aspects of finances are considered in this chapter, worry about financial problems and anticipated salaries after finishing graduate school.

Concerning financial worries:

1. In absolute proportions and by rough comparison with the general population, financial worries are low among American graduate students.

2. Differences in financial worry by age, stage of study, family role, division, control, and stratum of school are not very great.

3. The student from parental families of lower socioeconomic status is (justifiably) more likely to be worried.

4. Worry appears to be heavily influenced by three factors:

a) Anticipated deficits, low savings, and high debts. Debtors are rare in graduate school, but they do suffer from heavy financial worries.

b) Worry is greater for students who feel their situation is worse than that of their friends, regardless of perceived adequacy of income. This is interpreted as "relative deprivation."

c) Employment per se adds to worry, unless its financial return is high. The result is that students with part-time jobs or assistantships are more worried than those with full-time jobs or those with no job at all.

Concerning anticipated income:

1. Men, students in natural sciences, Ph.D. candidates, and those expecting non-academic jobs (except among humanities students) have higher salary expectations.

2. Because anticipated salaries are uncorrelated with current incomes, some students expect a big increase in income when they complete their studies, some anticipate a lowered annual income.

3. The higher the current income and the lower the expected starting salary for Ph.D. candidates, the greater the proportion of students who expect to take more than five years for their Ph.D.

4. The suggestion is that the students' (perhaps unrealistic) pessimism about their financial futures, in combination with their rather high current incomes, result in a lessening of incentive to complete the Ph.D. with unseemly haste.

Chapter ix: The Outcome One Year Later

One year after the questionnaires were administered, the current status of most of the students in the sample was established. Fifty-nine per cent were found to be studying in the same field at the same institution, 7 per cent had shifted school or field of study, 5 per cent had left school with a Ph.D. or a self-defined terminal master's degree, and the remainder (36 per cent) had dropped out of school or disappeared.

Concerning dropout:

1. Academic ability appears to be the most important variable in retention, low ability students having a high loss rate, even though failing grades were rare.

2. Subjective states such as morale, personal adjustment, aad criticisms of graduate school are not predictive of dropout.

3. Neither financial worries nor financial pressures in 1958 were predictive of dropout in 1959.

4. Characteristics which are associated with dropout are:

a) Motivation: Students interested in research have low drop-out rates;

students interested in neither teaching nor research have high drop-out rates. Self-defined intellectuals have low drop-out rates.

b) Division: Natural science students have low drop-out rates, humanities students have high drop-out rates, social science students tend to be in the middle.

c) Employment: Full-time workers have high drop-out rates, assistants have low drop-out rates, other students (those with fellowships, part-time jobs, or no employment) are in the middle.

d) Age and Family Role: Older students and fathers have higher drop-out rates.

Concerning transfers:

1. Transfers are fairly rare, although there is a cumulation such that a goodly proportion of Ph.D. students have done graduate work in more than one school.

2. Transfer status is not strongly associated with the variables in this study.

3. Better students transfer to schools higher in the stratum classification, less able students stay at the same level or move down.

Concerning academic employment among students who left school:

1. The student's preference and expectations from the 1958 schedule are predictive of his type of job in 1959.

2. High-ability students and students in advanced stages of study were more likely to get academic jobs, regardless of their preference.

3. Even among advanced, high- and middle-ability students who preferred academic jobs, about one-quarter went into non-academic work.

4. Part of the "loss" of academics is explained by non-academic competition for natural and social scientists, by personal relations with faculty members, and a lesser rate of academic employment for those students whose spouses were reported to be more materialistic in their concerns.

Appendix I

The Sample

The design of the sample[1] involved two stages: (1) a stratified systematic sample of universities, and (2) a simple systematic sample of students within each of the 25 universities chosen in Stage I.

STAGE I: UNIVERSITIES

The universe was defined in two ways. To be eligible, a university had to offer the Ph.D. degree in at least one TAS (traditional arts and sciences) field. The problem of defining a TAS field is not an easy one, however. The organization of different universities gives different functions to departments bearing the same title and similar functions to departments bearing different titles.

Definition of a TAS field was determined primarily by exclusion. The first step was to exclude clearly professional or technical fields such as law, business, education, architecture, pharmacy, the specialties in clinical fields of medicine, purely agricultural fields, psychiatry, engineering, etc.

A number of remaining fields were ambiguous as to their TAS status. In the humanities, the performing arts were excluded. Although art historians were included, musicologists were not. Similarly, pharmacology in the biological sciences, and rural sociology in the social sciences were excluded. Decisions on departments like these were more difficult than the first ones — and in many instances were somewhat arbitrary. Generally, we were guided by a tendency in the direction of exclusion rather than inclusion, so that if we had a reasonable doubt about the "TAS-ness" of a field, we excluded it.

[1] Jacob J. Feldman, director of research at NORC, was primarily responsible for the sample design and is the coauthor of Appendix I and Appendix II.

132 *Appendix I*

There was, however, a countertendency. In universities where a non-TAS-type department offered a TAS-type program — biochemistry in a medical school, for example — we included that department. Table 2.8, page 150, gives the fields which finally fell in the sample. The reader should note that this list encompasses only TAS fields in the sample. There are more TAS fields than these in American universities, but they did not happen to fall into the sample: either because universities offering Ph.D.'s in other fields did not fall into the university sample or because students in some of the fields in sample universities did not fall into the sample of students.

For a department to be eligible it must have offered the Ph.D. This decision both simplified the sampling problem, since about one-fifth as many universities offer the Ph.D. as the M.A., and it limited the students in the universe more narrowly to those who might be likely to pursue the doctorate.

PROCEDURES

The procedures for constructing the universe were:
1. A list was compiled of institutions which awarded the Ph.D. or its equivalent.[2]
2. Institutions were dropped from the list which, by reference to the *Education Directory* and/or their latest catalogue, proved to:
    a) offer no Ph.D.,
    b) offer the Ph.D. in professional, applied, or technical fields only,
    c) be not locatable (i.e., Institutum Divi Thomae, somewhere in Ohio, listed in DPIUSU but not in *Ed. Dir.*, for which no catalogue could be found).
3. Questionnaires about offerings and enrolments were sent to institutions still on the list. Institutions were dropped from the universe when their replies to the questionnaire fell under categories 2a and 2b above.
4. Telephone calls were made to registrars or graduate deans of the institutions which did not reply to the questionnaire if inclusion of their university was doubtful. If the calls indicated that these universities fell under category 2a or 2b, they were also excluded. One hundred and forty universities remained.

These 140 universities were stratified on two criteria: "stratum" (defined in chapter ii) and public vs. private control. This yielded six strata:

Stratum 0 — privately controlled institutions which ranked 1 through 10,

[2] The following sources were used: *Education Directory, 1957–58*, Part 3, "Higher Education" (Washington, D.C.: U.S. Department of Health, Education, and Welfare, Office of Education, 1957); *Doctorate Production in United States Universities, 1936–1956* (Washington, D.C.: National Academy of Sciences — National Research Council, Publication 582, 1958); Frederick W. Ness, *A Guide to Graduate Study* (Washington, D.C.: Association of American Colleges, 1957).

over-all, in the then unpublished "Educational Survey, Standing of American Graduate Departments,"[3] plus M.I.T. and Cal. Tech. There were eight such universities.

Stratum 1 — publicly controlled institutions which ranked 1 through 10, over-all, in the Keniston survey. There were four of these.

Stratum 2 — privately controlled institutions which are not in Stratum 0 or 1 but which were members of the Association of Graduate Schools of the Association of American Universities, Fall 1958, or which awarded 400 or more Ph.D.'s in TAS fields between 1936 and 1956.[4]

Stratum 3 — publicly controlled universities meeting the same criteria as for Stratum 2.

Stratum 4 — all other privately controlled institutions in the universe.

Stratum 5 — all other publicly controlled institutions in the universe.

Procedures for drawing the sample of universities were as follows:

1. The total number of graduate students in Ph.D.-granting TAS departments was obtained either from registrar's estimates or from our own projections from previous enrolments. When the actual enrolments for the schools which fell into the sample were compared with the estimates, it was found that both the registrar's prediction and the NORC projections were quite accurate. Hence, it is assumed that for the total universe these enrolment estimates were essentially satisfactory.

2. The total sample size was set at 3,000.

3. The total enrolments for each of the six strata were obtained by summing the results of Step 1.

4. The middle two strata had more graduate students than any of the other strata. We therefore decided to take four universities from each of the first and last two strata and five from each of the middle strata.

5. The total sample size of 3,000 was divided among the strata in proportion to the stratum enrolments, and the resulting stratum quota, when divided by the number of schools selected in the stratum, gave the school quota for each institution in the stratum.

6. Within each stratum the universities were ordered according to their eligible enrolments. Institutions with enrolments smaller than the school quota for their stratum were combined into clusters roughly twice as large as the quota. None of these was drawn in the sample.

7. A sampling interval was computed for each stratum. This was the number of students in the population of each stratum divided by the number of schools to be sampled in that stratum.

[3] Hayward Keniston, *Graduate Study and Research in the Arts and Sciences at the University of Pennsylvania* (Philadelphia: University of Pennsylvania Press, 1959).
[4] *Doctorate Production, op. cit.*

134 *Appendix 1*

8. Each school was assigned a hypothetical serial number for each of its eligible graduate students; e.g., in Stratum 1, Columbia was given numbers 00001 through 03525.

9. For each stratum a random start was obtained from a table of random numbers. This number could range from 0 to the total number of students in the stratum.

10. A systematic sample of universities was drawn starting from the random start and continuing through all serial numbers, taking the universities corresponding to the serial numbers drawn and adding the sampling interval at each step. Thus each university had a probability of being drawn equal to the proportion of its eligible graduate students to all eligible graduate students in the stratum. The University of California, at Berkeley, was drawn twice. Its quota therefore was 172, rather than 86.

Following this procedure 25 institutions were selected to fill the 26 quotas. Each of the sample schools agreed to participate in the study.

It should be noted that Step 10 allowed us to draw a sample representative of all graduate students in the universe — because each had the same probability of being drawn.

The logic of our sampling procedures is very simply demonstrated. The probability that an individual will fall in the sample is the product of the probability that his university will be chosen and the probability that he will be chosen if his university falls in the sample.

Let $x =$ enrolment in university, $n =$ the sample size per university per stratum, and $y =$ the sampling interval.

P (U being chosen) $= x/y$
P (Student being chosen if his university is chosen) $= n/x$
P (Student falling in sample) $= n/y$, by multiplication.

The use of quotas at the second stage of selecting undoubtedly introduced a slight bias into the sampling scheme owing to the inaccuracy of some of the measures of size employed in the primary stage. This bias could have been avoided by assigning each school a sampling fraction rather than a quota. Then, schools whose size had been underestimated would have had more than the expected number of students drawn from them while schools whose size had been overestimated would have contributed fewer students than expected. The biased procedure was adopted because it provided greater control over the total sample size, assured us nearly equal-sized samples from the various universities (a highly attractive feature given the interuniversity comparisons which were to be made), and materially reduced the sampling variance of estimates for particular strata, since they were based on returns from only four or five schools and could be seriously distorted by an extremely large number of cases from a single primary unit whose size had been underestimated. In fact, it seemed quite likely, given the limited number of primary units, that the mean-square error for most estimates would be less using the biased design than the unbiased one.

It would of course have been possible to eliminate the bias produced by the quota design by a compensatory weighting scheme, but the primary-stage measures of size appeared in general to be accurate enough to render the weighing operation superfluous for ratio estimates.

Stage II: The Sample of Graduate Students within Sample Institutions

Actual sampling procedures varied from university to university; however, they followed the following general patterns:

1. A list of eligible departments was constructed from registrars' reports and the university catalogue. Only students in these departments (TAS offering the Ph.D.) were eligible. Moreover they had to be working for either the master's or the doctor's degree. We were trying to exclude non-degree students by this criterion, but "part-time" students were eligible if they were working toward a master's or Ph.D.

2. Procedures varied from this point depending on the university's system for keeping records. The universities can be divided into those keeping records on IBM cards and those not doing so.

   a) For the former, our field representatives were provided with a sampling interval and requested to do the following:

   (1) Sort out the cards of all students registered in ineligible fields.

   (2) Have an IBM Collator (with counter) wired so that it would insert an "odd" card after every nth regular card.

   (3) Remove all regular cards preceding each "odd" card.

   b) In one institution with IBM facilities, the procedure was different. Here a ten-digit random number was punched into each eligible card, and the cards were serialized on these random numbers until the quota was reached. This is the only institution in which a systematic sample was not used. In a few schools with IBM equipment, the actual drawing of cards was done manually.

   c) In schools where the records were not kept on IBM cards, a different procedure was used.

   (1) First, it was impracticable to sort out the records of students who were ineligible. Therefore, the gross quota was inflated to provide enough cases so that the original quota could be obtained in the end.

   (2) Every nth card was then selected by hand. The field representative examined it to see if the student was in an eligible department. If he was, the field representative listed his

name; if he was not, the card was returned to the field, and the nth card after it was selected.

(3) Field representatives were instructed to continue this process until the pile of cards was exhausted. In other words, they were not to stop when they reached their quota.

d) Both the machine and the manual methods usually left a greater number of cards than the quota. Each name listed was assigned a consecutive serial number from 001 on. Names were eliminated from the list by reference to a table of random numbers until the quota was reached.

e) In a few cases, too few cards were drawn. The procedure for adding cases was somewhat more complicated than that for subtracting them. The field representative drew a random number corresponding to the number of a respondent on his list. He located this card in the file and took the card of the student half the sampling interval further on, listing the appropriate information if the student was eligible, but ignoring that card and repeating the whole process if he was not. This procedure was repeated until the quota was reached.

f) In two universities, all eligible graduate students were sampled. One of these was reduced to the quota in Chicago. The other did not have enough cases to reach its quota, falling short by 13 out of 92 cases. No attempt was made to replace these cases. In theory, these 79 cases should receive a weight to bring them in line with other universities but their contribution to the whole is negligible, and we therefore did not assign such a weight.

g) A copy of the sample list was sent to the Chicago office where the names of the students were checked as their questionnaires arrived.

RESULTS

A few words are in order about our system of conducting field operations in twenty-five widely scattered universities. The procedures were the same in all schools, with few exceptions. After the field representative was chosen, he got in touch with the dean of the graduate school in his university and arranged to draw the sample. He also arranged for the dean to sign a master letter to be sent to each graduate student in the sample for his university. This letter indicated the dean's general support for the study and his recommendation that the student participate.

The extent and difficulty of tracking down non-respondents varied from university to university, but, by and large, enough persistent contacts served to produce a high "take rate."

The variations in this procedure came basically at the beginning. In areas where NORC had a sampling unit, NORC field supervisors were given responsibility for the universities in their area. Seven NORC interviewers handled twelve universities, including three medical schools. On the other hand, fourteen field representatives were hired directly by the project staff. Each of these was responsible for one university, and the project staff handled the University of Chicago. Most of the field representatives were faculty members in the sociology department of the sample institution. One was a sociologist in a neighboring university, however; another was a psychologist in a sample school; and two were graduate students in sociology at sample schools.

Over-all, questionnaires were received from 92.4 per cent of the graduate students in the sample. The median response rate for schools was 94.5 per cent, and the mode fell in the 95-100 per cent category. The actual distribution of response rates is shown in Table 1.

TABLE 1
FREQUENCY DISTRIBUTION
OF RESPONSE RATES BY SCHOOL

Rate (in per cent)	Frequency
80– 85	1
85– 90	7
90– 95	6
95–100	11
Total	25

These figures indicate that, with one possible exception, response rates are high enough in all of our universities so that differential patterns of non-response should not affect the findings.

In the nature of probability samples, their justification comes from the logic of the design rather than from comparison of sample results with data on the universe. That is, even though the results of a sample may be close to the characteristics of the universe for selected items, this is no guarantee that this is true of all items, while to collect universe data for all items would defeat the purpose of probability sampling. At the same time departures from universe values are to be expected on the basis of sampling variability.

So far as we know, there are no important biases in the sample drawn for this study, and differences between the sample and other published data can be explained by definition of the universe (e.g., exclusion of professional schools, exclusion of departments offering only the master's degree, exclusion of students not in residence). For what it is worth, however, comparison of sample and universe characteristics in terms of division of study are presented below.

In each of the six strata three divisional distributions are given in Table 2. The first row gives the distribution of enrolments in the universe, based on the questionnaires returned by the registrars. The second row gives the distribution for the total enrolments in the sample schools. The third row gives

TABLE 2
PERCENTAGE DISTRIBUTION OF ENROLMENTS IN THE UNIVERSE, ENROLMENTS IN THE UNIVERSITY SAMPLE, AND RESPONDENTS IN THE SAMPLE OF STUDENTS BY STRATUM AND DIVISION

					TOTAL	
STRATUM	HUMANITIES	SOCIAL SCIENCES	PHYSICAL SCIENCES	BIOLOGICAL SCIENCES	Per cent	Number of Students
Universe 0........	24.61	35.53	31.65	8.20	99.99	(9,920)
Sample Schools 0........	27.87	40.60	22.98	8.55	99.99	(7,377)
Response 0........	26.56	31.74	28.42	13.28	100.00	(482)
Universe 1........	22.41	29.24	30.19	18.15	99.99	(7,273)
Sample Schools 1........	21.95	30.12	29.70	18.22	99.99	(6,063)
Response 1........	21.36	33.53	27.89	17.21	99.99	(337)
Universe 2........	24.95	34.63	29.51	10.91	100.00	(13,376)
Sample Schools 2........	27.23	32.45	30.22	10.11	100.01	(5,828)
Response 2........	23.59	37.32	30.46	8.63	100.00	(568)
Universe 3........	18.92	27.34	37.72	16.02	100.00	(16,011)
Sample Schools 3........	22.36	30.98	31.56	15.10	100.00	(5,419)
Response 3........	15.15	29.87	37.45	17.53	100.00	(713)
Universe 4........	18.14	38.68	33.92	9.25	99.99	(8,566)
Sample Schools 4........	14.25	45.30	33.29	7.16	100.00	(1,607)
Response 4........	3.66	55.35	34.72	6.27	100.00	(383)
Universe 5........	11.75	21.82	43.59	22.84	100.00	(8,037)
Sample Schools 5........	17.84	32.84	35.50	13.82	100.00	(1,093)
Response 5........	14.76	30.36	37.32	17.55	99.99	(359)
Totals:						
Universe	20.47	31.23	34.39	13.91	100.00	(63,183)
Sample Schools	24.13	34.61	28.81	12.45	100.00	(27,387)
Response	22.34	34.69	29.49	13.48	100.00	(2,842)

the distribution for questionnaires received in Chicago. Differences between the first and second rows reflect sampling error in the selection of schools; differences between the second and third rows reflect sampling error within schools and error due to non-response.

The only discrepancy of any importance is an over-representation of social science students and under-representation of humanities students in Stratum IV. Many institutions in Stratum IV do not offer a full range of departments or are overweighted in favor of one division. Our sample reflects this fact, particularly in the social sciences. In other words, there was greater variability in the universe for Stratum IV, and this fact is reflected in the sample of universities which we drew.

Inspection of Table 2 shows that, by and large, our sample is representative of graduate students in arts and sciences fields in Ph.D.-granting universities. The variability of the universe for Stratum IV has biased our sample of that stratum by underweighting the humanities and overweighting the social sciences. This is the only cell which is off by an appreciable amount, and since historians, who were treated as social scientists for purposes of sampling, will be treated as humanists for purposes of analyis, the deficiency of humanities students in this cell is not as serious as it first appears.

Appendix II

Sampling Error

Because the students selected for the study constitute a sample, rather than a census, of students in the universe of 1958 arts and science graduate students, the results of the survey are subject to sampling variation, as well as to other sources of error. However, as in any probability sample, it is possible to estimate the maximum size of discrepancies from the population values which are at all likely to occur in a sample of the design and size of the present one.

The two-stage sample described in Appendix I has two separate sources of sampling variation: (*a*) error due to the selection of sample schools unrepresentative of the universe of all schools, and (*b*) error due to the selection of samples of students within schools which are unrepresentative of the universe of all students in the sample schools. Since the students in any given school are almost certainly more homogeneous with respect to most relevant characteristics than would be expected by chance, estimates from the two-stage sample are subject to greater sampling error than estimates from a simple random sample composed of the same number of students. While the stratification employed in the selection of schools probably served to counteract at least part of the cluster effect, there undoubtedly still remained considerable variation on most relevant variables between schools in the same stratum. Thus, most of the estimates appearing in this report are subject to greater sampling error than estimates of similar magnitudes derived from a simple random sample of 2,842 cases. Nevertheless, it should be noted that the overall efficiency of a two-stage sample is generally superior to that of a simple random sample when the cost factor is taken into account. That is, a given amount of money spent on a multistage sample will usually produce more reliable figures than the same amount spent on simple random sampling. The imprecision of two-stage (cluster) samples is only in comparison with a much more expensive simple random sample of the same number of cases.

In order to assess the sampling error of our estimates, in comparison with those of estimates from a hypothetical simple random sample with the same number of cases, we proceeded as follows:

1. Twenty-four of the twenty-five schools in the sample were allocated to four subsamples by randomly allocating one school from each of the six strata to each subsample.

2. Selected data from the survey were tabulated separately for each subsample.

3. Variations among the four subsamples were used to estimate the sampling error of our design for two-stage samples consisting of one school per stratum.

4. These sampling error estimates were adjusted for the fact that our actual design consists of twenty-five schools rather than six.

The results appear in Table 1. Since they too are derived from a sample, these estimated sampling allowances are themselves subject to an extremely large sampling error. Thus, in three instances the clustered sample design is assessed as being subject to less sampling variability than a simple random design — for these particular estimates, such efficiency in a multistage sample design is hardly likely. At the other extreme, with respect to the estimates of certain proportions, the sample presumably is subject to the same magnitude of sampling error as a simple random sample with only 6 or 7 per cent the number of cases as the present one. It is practically inconceivable that the present sample design could be so inefficient with respect to the types of estimates involved in the present study. Thus, the extreme efficiency ratios must be viewed as aberrations resulting from the small number of degrees of freedom on which the sampling error estimates are based. Nevertheless, some reliance can be put on the more central values appearing in the table. In the absence of more precise estimates of the sampling errors, the present computations provide us with at least a rough idea of the effects of clustering on the precision of the survey results.

The more the school-to-school variation within strata, the higher will be the ratios in the right hand column of Table 1. Thus, it is interesting to note which variables give high ratios in Table 1, and, hence, are more strongly associated with school characteristics other than control and the size-prestige dimension.

Taking the ratios over 2.0, we see that the percentage completing a high academic load, the percentage with a full-time job, the percentage 28 or older, and the percentage fathers all give high ratios, which is consistent with our analysis suggesting that particular institutions "cater" to full-time employed, older students with families. The percentage with a duty stipend is highly variable, although the percentage with a non-duty stipend is not. We think

TABLE 1
Estimated Standard Errors of Percentage from Graduate Student Survey and from Simple Random Sample of Same Number of Cases

Characteristic	Standard Errors (in Per Cent) Survey	s.r.s. design with same n	Ratio Survey/s.r.s.
Completing a high academic load	4.30	1.11	3.9
With full-time job	2.84	0.76	3.7
28 or older	2.47	0.98	2.5
Fathers	2.12	0.85	2.5
Preferring academic jobs	2.43	0.98	2.5
With a duty stipend	2.35	0.97	2.4
With 9-month income of $3,600 or more	1.64	1.01	1.6
Father's occupation high status	1.62	1.05	1.5
Receiving income from spouse's job	1.29	0.86	1.5
With savings of $500 or more	1.43	0.95	1.5
In natural science	1.32	0.98	1.3
With a fellowship	1.01	0.76	1.3
In Stages III, IV	1.28	0.99	1.3
With any non-duty stipend	1.11	0.95	1.2
Expecting to borrow	0.64	0.57	1.1
Receiving income from veteran's benefits	0.76	0.71	1.1
Receiving income from investments	0.57	0.68	0.8
With part-time job	0.51	0.90	0.6
Receiving aid from parents	0.39	0.84	0.5

that much of this is due to the private-school strata, where one finds some schools which, because of their separate faculties for undergraduate instruction, stand out as very low in teaching assistantships and, hence, in duty stipends, while other private schools provide a substantial number of such positions. The high variability in percentage preferring academic jobs is the final variable with a ratio of 2.0 or over.

The information in Table 1 may be used to give rough approximations of the degree of correction necessary to use standard sampling error tables in evaluating the results of the survey. We shall give approximations for confidence limits on a proportion and for testing the null hypothesis of no-difference between proportions.

Table 2 gives upper and lower limits for 95 per cent confidence intervals for selected proportions for: (a) a simple random sample of 2,500 cases, determined by averaging the confidence limits for 2,000 and 3,000 cases;[1] (b) a characteristic whose survey/s.r.s. ratio in Table 1 was 1.5; (c) a characteristic with a ratio of 2.0; and (d) one with a ratio of 2.5.

At the worst, for an observed percentage near 50 with a survey/s.r.s. ratio of 2.5, our estimated confidence interval is 6 percentage points broader than it

[1] Cf. Donald Mainland, Lee Herrera, and Marion I. Sutcliffe, *Tables for Use with Binomial Samples* (New York University College of Medicine, 1956). While the linear interpolation method used here has led to a slight overstatement of the breadth of the confidence intervals, the exaggeration is so small as to render a more precise but arduous mode of interpolation unwarranted.

TABLE 2
Estimates of 95 Percent Confidence Intervals

	\multicolumn{8}{c}{Ratio of Survey Standard Error to s.r.s. Standard Error, $n = 2{,}500$}
Observed Percentage	1.0		1.5		2.0		2.5	
	L*	U*	L	U	L	U	L	U
50	2.01	2.01	3.01	3.01	4.02	4.02	5.02	5.02
40	1.96	1.98	2.94	2.97	3.92	3.96	4.90	4.95
30	1.82	1.87	2.73	2.80	3.64	3.74	4.55	4.68
20	1.58	1.65	2.37	2.48	3.16	3.30	3.95	4.12
10	1.17	1.26	1.76	1.89	2.34	2.52	2.92	3.15
5	.83	.94	1.24	1.41	1.66	1.88	2.08	2.35

* L = Amount to be subtracted from observed percentage to obtain lower limit; U = Amount to be added to obtain upper limit. If observed proportion is greater than 50, limits can be estimated for 1 minus the percentage from the table, and for the percentage by subtraction.

would have been for a simple random sample. For the more typical ratio of 1.5, the 95 per cent confidence interval runs about 2 percentage points wider than for simple random sampling.

For the variables reported in Table 1, more precise confidence limits may be estimated. However, no high degree of precision was sought in the analysis which typically considered estimates at the level of "about half of the sample" or "less than a fifth of the sample." As a rule of thumb, one may say that for percentages between 40 and 60 based on the total sample, 95 per cent confidence limits of 4 or 5 percentage points seem reasonable; for percentages less than 40 per cent and more than 60 per cent, 2 to 4 per cent confidence intervals are typical. Percentages based on smaller subsamples from the total sample are, of course, more variable.

Similar rough estimates may be made for the standard error of a difference, which is used to test the null hypothesis that two subgroups are sampled from universes where the proportions having the characteristic in question are equal. With simple random sampling, the size of the percentage difference to be accepted as "significant" varies simultaneously with: (a) the sizes of the two subsamples being contrasted, (b) the value of the null hypothesis about the universe, and (c) the significance level chosen. The situation becomes far more complex with a sample design like the present one. First of all, the variance of the estimate for each of the subgroups enters into the variance of the difference between the estimates. The variance of an estimate for a particular subgroup cannot be readily imputed from the efficiency ratios appearing in Table 1. For instance, consider the dependent variable as being the possession of a teaching assistantship. The standard error of the present estimate of the proportion of all graduate students holding such a position is far greater than the standard error of an estimate of this proportion based on a simple random sample of the same size. But, as was pointed out earlier, the imprecision of the over-all estimate appears to be due primarily to the high degree of variability among the private institutions. The public institutions tend to have approximately equal proportions of their students holding such assistantships. Now, if the comparison being considered is the proportion holding teaching assistantships among the "fathers" in attendance at public institutions versus the comparable proportion among the "non-fathers" at the same types of institutions, the standard error of the difference between the estimated proportions might be only slightly greater than if we had simple random samples of the two subgroups. This is due not only to the relatively low intraclass correlation of the assistantship variable over the public institutions; there is also a reduction in the standard error of the difference resulting from a positive correlation between the estimates for the two subgroups over samples. Since the "fathers" and "non-fathers" who are being compared are selected, in any given sample, from exactly the same universities and since the policy with regard to the assistantship-"fatherhood" relationship is likely to be uniform among the public institutions (in other words, there is only negligible second-order interaction), there is some reduction in the variability of the difference. Of course, this gain in efficiency must be quite small owing to the relatively small intraclass correlation by primary units.

A somewhat different type of situation would arise if one were contrasting the proportion of students with a full-time job among those receiving veteran's benefits with the comparable proportion among those not receiving such support. Owing to the high intraclass correlation of full-time job holders over schools, the standard error of the estimate of this proportion would be quite large for each of the two subgroups. But, assuming only moderate second-order interaction, the sampling error of the difference between the estimates might be only slightly larger than if they had been based on independent simple random samples, owing to the correlation of the estimates over successive samples.

The type of comparison for which the present sample design provides the least efficient estimate of the difference between proportions is exemplified by a contrast between Stratum III public institutions and Stratum III private institutions in the proportion of students holding a full-time job. Here we have a variable characterized by a substantial institutional intraclass correlation within strata, each of the two estimates is based on the returns from only four schools, and there is no correlation between the estimates. While none of the findings discussed in the present report involves comparisons of this degree of unreliability, the reader should exercise considerable caution in his interpretation of tabular material bearing on differences between subgroups composed of students from small numbers of non-overlapping institutions.

Table 3 gives the difference significant at the .05 level for selected n's[2] null

[2] Cf. Vernon Davies, *Tables Showing Significance of Differences between Percentages and between Means* (Washington State College, Stations Circular 151 [Revised], 1954).

TABLE 3

Difference, Significant at .05 Level, for Selected n's and Null Hypotheses s.r.s. and s.r.s. Estimate Multiplied by Factor of 1.5

	\multicolumn{4}{c}{n_1}			
n_2	1,000	800	300	100
	\multicolumn{4}{c}{Null hypothesis = 10 per cent or 90 per cent}
1,000	2.7(4.1)	2.8(4.2)	3.9(5.8)	6.2(9.3)
800		3.0(4.5)	4.1(6.2)	6.3(9.4)
300			4.8(7.2)	6.8(10.2)
100				8.5(12.8)
	\multicolumn{4}{c}{Null hypothesis = 50 per cent}
1,000	4.4(6.6)	4.6(6.9)	6.5(9.8)	10.3(15.4)
800		4.9(7.4)	6.7(10.0)	10.4(15.6)
300			8.0(12.0)	11.3(17.0)
100				14.1(21.2)

hypothesis proportions of 10 (or 90) per cent and 50 per cent under the assumption of independent simple random samples. Next to each is the same value multiplied by the value of 1.5, as a sort of "average" correction for the variability introduced by two-stage sampling.

There is considerable variation in the tables. At one extreme, if both subsamples have 1,000 or more cases, and the null hypothesis is an extreme proportion above 90 or below 10, a difference of 4.1 per cent is significant at the .05 level, even when the s.r.s. difference is multiplied by 1.5. At the other, for subsamples of 100 cases each and a null hypothesis of 50 per cent, a 22 per cent difference is estimated to be necessary.

As a rule of thumb, it would appear reasonably safe to conclude that differences of 10 per cent or more, when both subsamples have more than 300 cases, are worth considering seriously.

As a matter of fact, formal significance tests were not used as a mechanical criterion in the analysis. However, with few exceptions, those findings which are given considerable attention can usually be justified by arguments such as that presented above.

The specialist reader who wishes to make detailed estimates for particular tables can use the data in Table 1 of this appendix as a guide to estimating the errors. The non-specialist reader is advised to consider differences of 10 per cent or more when based on subsamples in which both groups have more than 300 cases as substantial enough to consider as "findings."

Appendix III

Tables

TABLE 2.1
DISTRIBUTION OF ARTS AND SCIENCE GRADUATE SCHOOLS
BY ESTIMATED ENROLLMENT, FALL, 1958

Enrollment*	Number of Schools	Per Cent of all Schools	Total Students**	Per Cent of Students	Cumulative Per Cent Schools	Cumulative Per Cent Students
1,500 or more	7	5	15,576	25	5	25
1,000-1,499	11	8	13,212	21	13	46
700-999	11	8	8,816	14	21	60
500-699	11	8	6,452	10	29	70
400-499	11	8	4,942	8	37	78
300-399	13	9	4,541	7	46	85
200-299	18	13	4,448	7	59	92
100-199	26	18	3,742	6	77	98
Less than 100	32	23	1,458	2	-	-
Total	140	100%	63,187	100%		

*Enrollment data are based on registrars' estimates of Fall 1958 enrollment made during the Summer of 1958 at NORC's request (61% of the schools) or NORC's estimate from previous enrollment figures (39% of the schools). For 15 schools where actual 1958 enrollment figures were later received, the rank correlation coefficient between the NORC estimate and actual enrollment was .98.

**These figures have a spurious appearance of precision. Actually, in the vast majority of schools the estimates were made to the nearest 10 or for larger schools nearest 50 students.

145

TABLE 2.2
PRESTIGE RATING AND GRADUATE ENROLLMENT

Number of Arts and Science Graduate Students	Per Cent Listed in Keniston	Per Cent of Keniston Schools in Top Ten	Number of Schools
1,000 or more	76	50 (16)	21
500-999	31	25 (8)	26
Less than 500	1	- (1)	92

N 139
NA* 1
140

*Throughout the report, the letters NA designate "No Answer" or "Not Ascertainable."

TABLE 2.3
NUMBER OF UNIVERSITIES OFFERING THE PH.D., BY SPECIFIC FIELD, 1958
(N = 140)

Field	Yes	No	No information	Field	Yes	No	No information
Chemistry	111	26	3	Anthropology	36	103	1
Modern languages (any)	89	51	-	Geography	33	107	-
				Classics	29	110	1
				Entomology	28	111	1
Physics	89	50	1	Musicology	27	113	-
				Biology, general	27	112	1
Psychology	83	56	1	Pathology	23	113	4
Mathematics	80	59	1	Genetics	21	118	1
History	79	60	1	Biophysics	20	117	3
English	76	62	2	Astronomy, astrophysics	20	119	1
Economics	65	75	-	Comparative literature	17	123	-
Zoology	63	76	1	Art history	17	121	2
Physiology	62	76	2	Linguistics	13	126	1
Political science	62	77	1	Meteorology	9	131	-
Bio-chemistry	61	76	3	International relations	9	131	-
Sociology	59	80	1	Geophysics	8	132	-
Botany	56	83	1	Oceanography	5	135	-
Geology	55	85	-	Biometrics	3	136	1
Anatomy	52	85	3	Archeology, other than classical	2	137	1
Philosophy	48	90	2	Geochemistry	2	138	-
Microbiology	47	91	2				
Bacteriology	44	93	3				

TABLE 2.4
GUTTMAN SCALE OF DEPARTMENTAL OFFERINGS

Chemistry	Modern Languages	Philosophy	Astronomy	N	Scale score
+	+	+	+	16	IV
+	+	+	−	20	III
+	+	−	−	9	II
+	−	−	−	53	I
−	−	−	−	24	0
				122	
+	−	+	−	8	II
+	−	−	+	2	I
−	−	+	−	1	0
+	−	+	+	1	IV
+	+	−	+	1	III
−	+	−	−	1	I
				14	
No answer on one or more				4	
				140	

TABLE 2.5
CORRELATES OF STRATUM CLASSIFICATION

Stratum	Per Cent in Keniston Top 25 Schools	Per Cent With 500 or More Graduate Students	Per Cent With Offerings Scale Score of III or IV*
I.	83 (12)	92 (12)	83 (12)
II.	42 (36)	80 (36)	66 (32)
III.	0 (92)	7 (91)	8 (92)

*Scale Scores are defined in Table 2.4

TABLE 2.6
DISTRIBUTION OF SCHOOLS AND STUDENTS BY STRATUM AND CONTROL

(a) Numbers

		Private Schools	Private Students	Public Schools	Public Students
I.	Keniston Ranks 1-10 + MIT, Cal. Tech	8	9,920	4	7,273
II.	Others AGS and/or High Producers	18	13,376	19	16,015
III.	Other	44	8,566	47	8,037

(b) Per Cent

	Of all Students (Universe) Private	Public	Total	Of all Schools Private	Public	Total
I.	16	11	27	6	3	9
II.	21	25	46	13	14	27
III.	14	13	27	31	33	64
Total	51	49	100%	50	50	100%

N = 63,187   N = 140

Of all Students (Sample)

	Private	Public	Total
I.	17	12	29
II.	20	25	45
III.	14	13	27
Total	51	50	101%

TABLE 2.7
GEOGRAPHICAL PATTERNING OF GRADUATE SCHOOLS

(a) Per Cent of Graduate Schools Located in the Central City of a Standard Metropolitan Area	Private	Public
Major Producers ...	69 (26)	35 (23)
Other	80 (44)	38 (47)

(b) Per Cent of Graduate Schools Located in...	I. The East*		II. Midwest or West Coast**		III. South or Mountain States***	
	Private	Public	Private	Public	Private	Public
Major Producers ...	62 (26)	13 (23)	27 (26)	70 (23)	12 (26)	17 (23)
Other	61 (44)	11 (47)	25 (44)	21 (47)	14 (44)	68 (47)

(c) Per Cent of Graduate Schools Located...	...In Central City of an Eastern Standard Metropolitan Area		...Outside of Central City of a Standard Metropolitan Area and Not in The East	
	Private	Public	Private	Public
Major Producers ...	42 (26)	0 (23)	12 (26)	52 (23)
Other	50 (44)	0 (47)	18 (44)	55 (47)

*East is defined as the Census regions, New England and Middle Atlantic plus Maryland, Delaware and the District of Columbia.

**Midwest is defined as the Census regions West North Central and East North Central. West Coast is defined as the Census region Pacific.

***South is defined as the Census Regions West South Central, East South Central, and South Atlantic other than Maryland, Delaware and the District of Columbia. Mountain is defined as the Census Region Mountain.

TABLE 2.8
DISTRIBUTION OF THE SAMPLE BY DEPARTMENT AND DIVISION

(a) Department

Physical Sciences

Chemistry, excluding biochemistry	(319)
Mathematics and mathematical statistics	(187)
Physics (and mechanics)	(289)
Astronomy	(11)
Astro-physics	(2)
Geology	(108)
Geochemistry	(4)
Geophysics	(9)
Meteorology	(7)
Chemical physics	(2)
Geography (physical sciences)	(10)
Total	**948**

Biological Sciences

Biophysics	(6)
Biochemistry and physiological chemistry	(74)
Bacteriology and microbiology	(47)
Botany and plant physiology	(53)
Zoology	(62)
Entomology	(39)
Genetics (plant and animal)	(18)
Biology, general	(27)
Physiology (except plant)	(32)
Anatomy	(13)
Human pathology	(11)
Total	**382**

Social Sciences

Anthropology	(37)
Archeology (except classical)	(3)
Economics	(163)
Government, Political Science, and International Relations	(136)
Psychology, clinical	(153)
Psychology, other	(65)
Sociology	(85)
Geography, human and urban	(12)
Social psychology	(9)
Total	**663**

Humanities

Philosophy	(66)
History	(306)
History of culture	(2)
American civilization and American studies	(26)
English	(273)
Comparative literature	(12)
Linguistics and philology	(12)
Romance Languages	(77)
German	(27)
Slavic languages	(11)
Near and Far Eastern languages	(9)
Other languages	(3)
Classics and classical archeology	(15)
New Testament	(2)
Total	**841**

Interdivisional

Asian Area Studies	(7)
Bio-psychology	(1)
Total	**8**

Total Students 2,842

(b) Division

Natural Science	47%
Social Science	23%
Humanities	30%
Interdivisional	*
Total	**100%**
N	**2,842**

* = Less than ½ per cent.

TABLE 2.9
DIVISION BY STRATUM AND CONTROL

Stratum	Private Natural Science	Private Social Science	Private Humanities	Private Total	Public Natural Science	Public Social Science	Public Humanities	Public Total
\multicolumn{9}{c}{(a) Universe (History Classified as a Social Science)}
I.	40	35	25	100%	48	29	23	100%
II.	40	35	25	100%	54	27	19	100%
III.	43	39	18	100%	66	22	12	100%
\multicolumn{9}{c}{(b) Sample (History Classified as a Social Science)}
I.	42	32	26	100% (480)	46	33	21	100% (337)
II.	40	37	23	100% (562)	55	30	15	100% (713)
III.	41	55	4	100% (383)	55	30	15	100% (359)
\multicolumn{9}{c}{(c) Sample (History Classified as a Humanity)}
I.	42	19	39	100% (480)	46	24	30	100% (337)
II.	40	26	34	100% (562)	55	22	23	100% (713)
III.	41	29	30	100% (383)	55	21	24	100% (359)

```
N for Tables b and c . . . . . . . . . 2,834
Interdivisional . . . . . . . . . .      8
                                     -------
                                      2,842
```

TABLE 2.10
DISTRIBUTION OF THE SAMPLE IN TERMS OF DEGREE PROGRESS

Degree Sought and Academic Work	Per Cent
Master's	
Courses or seminars only	31)
Preparing for comprehensives or thesis	18) - 49
Doctor's	
Courses or preparing for comprehensives	32) - 51
Thesis	19)
Total	100
N	2,777
NA	65
	2,842

TABLE 2.11
DEGREE PROGRESS AND YEARS OF GRADUATE STUDY COMPLETED

a) Distribution by Years of Graduate Study Completed*

Years Completed	Per cent
0	29
1	21
2	18
3 or more	32
Total	100
N =	2,817
NA =	25
	2,842

b) Degree Progress and Years of Graduate Study Completed

Degree Progress		Years of Graduate Study Completed*			
Degree Sought	Academic Work	0	1	2	3 or more
M.A.	courses-seminars	68	30	14	6
M.A.	comprehensives, thesis	17	33	20	9
Ph.D.	courses, comprehensives	14	32	50	40
Ph.D.	thesis	1	5	16	45
	Total	100	100	100	100
	N	804	599	475	874

Total N 2,752
NA on Years or Progress . . . 90
2,842

*Years of Graduate School Completed is defined as the total number of years prior to Fall, 1958 in which the student was studying in graduate school, regardless of field of study or course load carried. Periods of dropout were excluded, and for students in residence for only parts of one or more years, an estimate was made of the total semesters or quarters in which the student was in school, which was divided by two or three to yield an estimate in years.

TABLE 2.12
CONSTRUCTION OF STAGE INDEX

Stage	Years Completed	Degree Sought	Academic Work	%	N
I	0	Any	Any	30	823
II	1 or more	Master's	Any	24	672
III	1 or more	Ph.D.	Any, except thesis	28	792
IV	1 or more	Ph.D.	Thesis, with or without other requirements	18	507

```
Total . . . . . . . . . 100%
N . . . . . . . . . . . 2,794
NA . . . . . . . . . .    48
                        ─────
                        2,842
```

TABLE 2.13
STAGE BY STRATUM, DIVISION, AND CONTROL
(Per cent in Stages III and IV)

Stratum	Private Natural Science	Private Social Science	Private Humanities	Public Natural Science	Public Social Science	Public Humanities
I.	59 (199)	57 (88)	52 (190)	55 (154)	54 (79)	43 (100)
II.	56 (214)	45 (146)	48 (187)	51 (392)	43 (158)	42 (154)
III.	44 (155)	36 (110)	19 (107)	35 (195)	44 (73)	31 (85)

```
N . . . . . . . . . . . 2,786
Interdivisional . . . .     8
NA on Stage . . . . . .    48
                        ─────
                        2,842
```

TABLE 2.14

"TERMINAL MASTER'S" BY STRATUM, CONTROL,
AND DIVISION

(Per cent in Stages I and II checking "I do
not plan to get a doctorate")

Stratum	Private			Public		
	Natural Science	Social Science	Humanities	Natural Science	Social Science	Humanities
I.	14 (74)	3 (34)	16 (86)	8 (66)	18 (34)	16 (50)
II.	16 (81)	16 (70)	20 (89)	16 (172)	13 (83)	12 (81)
III.	30 (77)	22 (64)	30 (73)	23 (109)	16 (38)	18 (55)

```
N . . . . . . . . . . . . . 1,336
NA on Ph.D. Plans . . . . .  154
Interdivisional or
  Not Stages I-II . . . . . 1,352
                             2,842
```

TABLE 2.15

STAGE BY STRATUM, CONTROL, AND DIVISION, AMONG
NON-TERMINAL MASTER'S STUDENTS

(Per cent in Stages III-IV among students not checking "I do
not plan to get a doctorate")

Stratum	Private			Public		
	Natural Science	Social Science	Humanities	Natural Science	Social Science	Humanities
I.	62 (189)	57 (87)	56 (175)	57 (149)	59 (73)	47 (92)
II.	60 (200)	50 (133)	53 (169)	55 (364)	46 (147)	44 (144)
III.	52 (132)	42 (95)	24 (85)	41 (170)	48 (67)	35 (75)

```
N . . . . . . . . . . . . . 2,546
NA on Stage or Ph.D. Plans   53
"I Do Not Plan..." . . . .  235
Interdivisional . . . . . .   8
                            2,842
```

TABLE 2.16

DISTRIBUTION IN TERMS OF MOST PROBABLE JOB FIVE
YEARS AFTER COMPLETING GRADUATE WORK

Job	Per Cent
Academic	57
Non-Academic in field	33
Non-Academic in different field	3
Secondary or primary teaching or administration	5
Non-Labor force	2
Total	100%

N 2,784
NA 58
2,842

TABLE 2.17
CAREER PREFERENCE AND EXPECTATIONS

| Expectation | Academic Jobs are... | | | Total |
	Much More Desirable	Slightly More Desirable	No Difference or Less Desirable	
Academic	40	13	4	57
Other	8	8	27	43
Total	48	21	31	100%

N 2,693
NA on 1 or both . 149
2,842

TABLE 2.18

CAREER EXPECTATIONS BY STRATUM, CONTROL, DIVISION, AND STAGE

(Per cent expecting academic job five years after completing graduate study)

Stage	Stratum	Private Natural Science	Private Social Science	Private Humanities	Public Natural Science	Public Social Science	Public Humanities
Ph.D.	I.	68 (117)	72 (50)	89 (95)	67 (85)	83 (41)	95 (43)
	II.	56 (119)	55 (64)	89 (89)	58 (198)	60 (67)	95 (64)
	III.	37 (67)	52 (40)	72 (18)	53 (68)	44 (32)	96 (26)
M.A.	I.	54 (79)	66 (38)	70 (89)	35 (65)	60 (35)	76 (55)
	II.	44 (95)	40 (78)	52 (96)	40 (189)	48 (89)	69 (87)
	III.	21 (82)	22 (69)	45 (83)	34 (125)	39 (41)	76 (55)

NA on Stage + Interdivisional — 43% (51)

```
N . . . . . . . . . . . . 2,784
NA on expectations . .      58
                         ─────
                         2,842
```

TABLE 2.19

SATISFACTION WITH SCHOOL CHOICE

Answers to the question, "Looking back, do do you think you made the best decision by choosing this university for your graduate study?"

Answer	Per Cent
I definitely made the best decision by coming here	39
I'm pretty sure I made the best decision by coming here	35
This decision was no better and no worse than another I might have made	20
I'm pretty sure I should have gone elsewhere	5
I definitely made a bad decision	2
Total	101%

```
N . . . . . . . . . 2,795
NA . . . . . . . .    47
                   ─────
                   2,842
```

TABLE 2.20

EVALUATIONS OF JOB OPPORTUNITIES

(Per cent rating job opportunities in their field as "excellent" or "good" versus "fair" or "poor")

For a Person With...	Type of Job	
	Academic	Non-Academic
Bachelor's degree only	4 (2,700)	32 (2,620)
Master's degree only	31 (2,768)	72 (2,664)
Doctor's degree	95 (2,783)	88 (2,637)

TABLE 2.21

"GOOD TIME"

Answers to "In general, what sort of a time do you have in graduate school?"

Answer	Per Cent
I have a very good time	24
I have a pretty good time	45
It's about 50-50	26
I have a pretty bad time	4
I have a rotten time	1
	100%

N 2,803
NA . . .   39
          2,842

TABLE 2.22
CRITICISMS OF GRADUATE SCHOOL
(Per cent checking given criticisms as "valid" or "somewhat valid" versus "not valid" or "dead wrong")

Criticism	Per Cent
It has too many purely formal "hurdles" which are really initiation rituals, not genuine training	50
It doesn't provide enough training for teaching	49
It encourages over-specialization	43
It stifles the creativity of its students	37
Faculty members tend to become more involved in building research empires than in making creative contributions to the field	32
It exploits its students by using them as cheap labor	31
It rewards conformity and punishes individualism	28
The training has little or nothing to do with the jobs the students will eventually get	26
It doesn't provide enough training for research and scholarly activities	26
It discourages students who wish to apply their knowledge to practical problems	20

```
N  . . . . . . . . . . . 2,810
NA . . . . . . . . . .      32
                         ───────
                         2,842
```

TABLE 2.23
PERSONAL ESPRIT
Answers to "In general, how would you say you feel most of the time?"

Answer	Per Cent
I am usually in good spirits	58
I am in good spirits some of the time and low spirits some of the time	40
I am usually in low spirits	2
	100%

```
N  . . . . . 2,834
NA . . . .       8
              ──────
              2,842
```

TABLE 2.24
MORALE AMONG GRADUATE STUDENTS AND SOLDIERS

| | Esprit ||| Total | N |
Group	Usually Low	Sometimes Good Sometimes Low	Usually Good		
Company Grade Officers who were formerly enlisted men	2	24	74	100%	774
Graduate students . . .	2	40	58	100%	2,834
Noncoms	7	48	45	100%	1,332
Privates and PFC's . . .	13	55	32	100%	2,902
AWOL's	41	40	19	100%	638

Military data are from Samuel A. Stouffer, Edward A. Suchman, Leland C. DeVinney, Shirley A. Star, and Robin Williams, Jr., Studies in Social Psychology in World War II, Vol. I. Adjustment During Army Life (Princeton, New Jersey: Princeton University Press, 1949), p. 89.

TABLE 3.1
AGE DISTRIBUTION OF THE SAMPLE

Age	Per Cent	Cumulative Per Cent
20-23 . .	22	100
24-26 . .	27	78
27-29 . .	23	51
30-39 . .	23	28
40+ . . .	05	05
Total	100	
N =	2,835	
NA =	7	
	2,842	

TABLE 3.2
DISTRIBUTION IN TERMS OF PARENTAL EDUCATION

Highest Grade Completed	Father	Mother
Less than high school	40	37
High school	16	28
Part college	14	18
Bachelor's degree	12	12
Graduate work degree	18	5
Total	100%	100%
N	2,818	2,822
NA	24	20
	2,842	2,842

TABLE 3.3
DISTRIBUTION IN TERMS OF FATHER'S OCCUPATION: CENSUS CLASSIFICATION

Group	Per Cent	
Professional, technical, and kindred	27	
Managers, proprietors, officials, except farm	31	
Sales	6	
Clerical and kindred	6	
Total White Collar		70
Craftsmen, foremen, and kindred	11	
Operatives and kindred	7	
Private household and service	3	
Laborers, except farm	3	
Total Blue Collar		24
Farmers and farm managers	6	6
Farm laborers and foremen	*	
Total		100%

N 2,611
Uncodeable 47
NA (mostly fathers deceased before respondent was in high school) 184
        2,842

*Less than ½ per cent.

TABLE 3.4
FATHER'S OCCUPATIONAL PRESTIGE AND PERCEIVED RELATIVE STATUS

%	N	Prestige Rating	(Per Cent Saying Father's Type of Job is..) Much Lower or Slightly Lower Than Professor's	Same as Professor's	Much Higher or Slightly Higher Than Professor's	Total	N
18	(454)	Elite	7	37	56	100%	445
27	(664)	Middle-Middle	40	34	26	100%	653
32	(776)	Bottom-Middle Working Class Elite	82	13	5	100%	765
16	(395)	Working Class	94	5	1	100%	391
7	(167)	Low Status	99	0	1	100%	164
100%	(2,456)						2,418

			NA on Relative Status	
N	1,446	509	463	38	2,456
Uncodeable*	177	33	27	13	250
NA**	48	12	11	65	136
Total N	1,671	554	501	116	2,842

	Lower	Same	Higher	
Per Cent	61	20	19	100% = 2,726

*Most of the uncodeable are farmers.
**Most of the fathers of the "No Answers" died before the respondent was in high school.

TABLE 3.5
CORRELATES OF FATHER'S OCCUPATION
(In each table, the entry is the per cent of students whose fathers were coded middle-middle or elite)

(a) Age

Age	% High	N
20-23	51	564
24-26	50	668
27-29	41	562
30-39	41	540
40+	38	117
NA on age	–	5

(b) Stage

Stage	% High	N
I.	46	714
II.	43	578
III.	45	677
IV.	50	448
NA on stage	36	39

(c) Stratum and Control

Stratum	Private	Public
I.	60 (427)	48 (297)
II.	38 (487)	44 (611)
III.	47 (340)	43 (294)

(d) Division

Division	% High	N
Natural Science	44	1,133
Social Science	45	586
Humanities	48	730
Inter-divisional	–	7

(e) Career Expectations

Expectation	% High	N
Academic	48	1,351
Other	42	1,061
NA	43	44

In Tables (a), (b), (c), (d), (e):

N 2,456
NA on father's occupation . . . 386
                                  2,842

TABLE 3.6
ORIGINAL AND CURRENT RELIGION
AND CHURCH ATTENDANCE

Original Religion	Current Religion				
	Same		None	Convert	Total
	Regular Attender	Infrequent Attender			
Protestant	19.0	17.9	12.7	2.2	51.8
Catholic	18.5	1.8	2.9	.7	23.9
Jewish	.9	7.7	4.3	.3	13.2
None	-	-	4.9	2.0	6.9
Other	.7	2.4	1.0	.1	4.2
Total	39.1	29.8	25.8	5.3	100.0

N 2,820
NA   22
                2,842

TABLE 3.7
DISTRIBUTION BY AGE AT BACHELOR'S DEGREES

Age	Per Cent	Cumulative Per Cent
Under 20	1	1
20	3	4
21	12	16
22	35	51
23	18	69
24	8	77
25	6	83
26	5	88
27	3	91
28	3	94
29	2	96
30+	4	100
Total	100	

N 2,823
NA or no bachelor's degree .   19
                              2,842

TABLE 3.8

FATHER'S OCCUPATION, SEX, AND AGE AT BACHELOR'S DEGREE

(Per cent receiving Bachelor's Degree at 23 or older)

Father's Occupation	Sex Male	Sex Female
High*	44 (868)	25 (245)
Low*	56 (1137)	42 (194)
NA	63 (311)	41 (68)

```
N . . . . . . . . 2,823
NA on age at A.B.   19
                  -----
                  2,842
```

*Throughout the report, High Status = middle-middle or elite, Low Status = other, unless specifically stated otherwise.

TABLE 3.9

FATHER'S OCCUPATION, SEX, AND UNDERGRADUATE EMPLOYMENT

(Per cent reporting 50 per cent or more of undergraduate expenses from own earnings)

Father's Occupation	Sex Male	Sex Female
High	23 (857)	11 (246)
Low	42 (1,122)	26 (185)
NA	41 (302)	26 (62)

```
N . . . . . . . . 2,774
NA on Earnings  .   68
                  -----
                  2,842
```

TABLE 3.10
FATHER'S OCCUPATION, SEX, UNDERGRADUATE EMPLOYMENT AND AGE AT BACHELOR'S DEGREE
(Per cent receiving Bachelor's Degree at 23 or older)

	Per Cent of Undergraduate Expenses From Own Earnings			
Status	Less than Half		Half or More	
	Male	Female	Male	Female
High	41 (654)	22 (218)	57 (201)	56 (27)
Low	53 (645)	36 (135)	59 (475)	48 (48)
NA	59 (175)	33 (45)	67 (124)	62 (16)

```
              N . . . . . . . . . . . 2,763
              NA on Age at A. B. . . .   79
                                       ------
                                       2,842
```

TABLE 3.11
AGE BY AGE AT BACHELOR'S DEGREE

Age at Bachelor's Degree	Per Cent 27 Years or Older	N
22 years or younger .	32	1,435
23 years or older . .	71	1,380
Everyone	51	

```
                    N . . . . 2,815
                    NA . . . .   27
                             ------
                             2,842
```

TABLE 3.12
DELAY BETWEEN BACHELOR'S DEGREE AND FIRST REGISTRATION IN GRADUATE SCHOOL IN CURRENT FIELD OF STUDY

| Age at Bachelor's | Years Delay ||||| Total | N |
	0	1-2	3-4	5-6	7+		
Under 22 years .	56	17	10	04	13	100%	(438)
22 years	60	18	12	05	05	100%	(999)
23-25 years . .	52	18	14	08	08	100%	(918)
26+ years . . .	57	23	07	06	07	100%	(460)

```
                            N . . 2,815
                            NA. .    27
                                 ------
                                 2,842
```

TABLE 3.13

CLASSIFICATION OF ACTIVITIES DURING HIATUS BETWEEN BACHELOR'S AND FIRST ENROLLMENT IN GRADUATE WORK IN CURRENT FIELD

Category	Activity	Preferred School	Per Cent Among Those Reporting 1 or 2 Activities
Willing Work	Employment or Military	No	56
Field Switch	Study in another Field	—	23
Unwilling Work	Employment	Yes	21
Draft	Military	Yes	20
Willing Non-Labor Force	Not employed or studying	No	5
Unwilling Non-Labor Force	Not employed or studying	Yes	3

Percentages total over 100% because of multiple answers.

```
N . . . . . . . . . . . . .  915
3 or more activities . .     41
NA or uncodeable . . . .    265
NA on Hiatus . . . . . .     27
No Hiatus . . . . . . . .1,594
                          2,842
```

TABLE 3.14

PATTERNS OF ACTIVITIES DURING INTERRUPTION BETWEEN BACHELOR'S DEGREE AND FIRST ENROLLMENT IN GRADUATE STUDY IN CURRENT FIELD

(a) Major Patterns and Combinations Among Students Listing 1, 2, or 3

Pattern	Per Cent
Willing work only	36
Unwilling work only	11
"Draft" only	11
Willing work and study in different field	9
Study in different field only	8
Any combination of 3 or more activities	4
Total	79%*
N	956

*All other less frequent patterns and combinations equal 21%.

(b) Pattern of Preference for Being in School, Among Students Listing 1 or 2

Would Have Preferred School		Per Cent
No	Yes	
+	−	61
+	+	11
−	+	28
Total		100%
N		915

TABLE 3.15

FATHER'S OCCUPATION BY AGE AT BACHELOR'S DEGREE AND HIATUS BETWEEN A.B. AND FIRST ENROLLMENT IN GRADUATE STUDY IN CURRENT FIELD

(Per cent low status)

Age at A.B.	Hiatus Between A.B. and Graduate Study	
	No	Yes
22 years or younger	51 (775)	47 (505)
23 years or older	63 (641)	60 (517)

N 2,438
NA on Father's Occupation . . . 377
NA on age at A.B. 27

2,842

TABLE 3.16
FIELD OF STUDY AND DATE OF FIRST SERIOUS
CONSIDERATION OF GRADUATE STUDY
IN FIELD

Field	Sophomore Year in College or Before	Junior or Senior Years	After Graduation	Total	N
Sociology	26	42	32	100%	85
Philosophy	33	46	21	100%	66
Political Science	41	34	25	100%	134
Clinical Psychology	41	37	22	100%	153
History	47	31	22	100%	305
Other Psychology	49	37	14	100%	65
Economics	50	35	15	100%	163
Bio-Chemistry	52	32	16	100%	73
Foreign Languages	57	25	18	100%	126
English	58	28	14	100%	273
Mathematics	61	20	19	100%	186
Botany	61	28	11	100%	53
Zoology	68	22	10	100%	62
Physics	74	13	13	100%	289
Chemistry	75	19	6	100%	317
Geology	77	16	7	100%	107

N 2,457
NA 9
Fields with 50 or fewer
  cases 376
                              ─────
                              2,842

TABLE 3.17
DELAY IN BACHELOR'S DEGREE, HIATUS BETWEEN BACHELOR'S
DEGREE AND GRADUATE STUDY IN FIELD, AND AGE
(Per cent 27 or older)

Age at A.B.	Hiatus Between A.B. and Graduate Study	
	No	Yes
22 or younger	17 (849)	54 (586)
23 or older	56 (745)	88 (635)

N 2,815
NA on Age or Hiatus . 27
                       ─────
                       2,842

TABLE 3.18

DELAY IN BEGINNING GRADUATE SCHOOL BY STRATUM, CONTROL, AND DIVISION

Stratum	Private		Public	
	Natural Science	Social Science & Humanities	Natural Science	Social Science & Humanities

(a) Per Cent Receiving A.B. at 23 or Older

I.	38 (200)	37 (279)	52 (155)	47 (179)
II.	43 (218)	55 (339)	48 (393)	49 (313)
III.	46 (157)	61 (219)	58 (198)	58 (158)

(b) Per Cent Reporting a Year or More Between A.B. and First Enrollment for Graduate Study in Current Field

I.	28	42	30	39
II.	43	51	35	43
III.	54	63	45	49

(c) Per Cent Reporting A.B. at 23 or Older and/or Gap of One Year or More

I.	51	63	66	68
II.	66	76	66	70
III.	70	86	77	80

In Tables (a), (b), and (c):

```
N . . . . . . . . . . . . . . . 2,808
Interdivisional . . . . . . .      8
NA on Age . . . . . . . . .       26
                              ───────
                               2,842
```

TABLE 3.19
AGE BY STAGE, STRATUM, CONTROL, AND DIVISION
(Per cent 27 or older)

Stage	Stratum	Private Natural Science	Private Social Science & Humanities	Public Natural Science	Public Social Science & Humanities
Master's	I.	22 (81)	32 (130)	29 (69)	41 (92)
	II.	36 (95)	45 (178)	34 (193)	27 (179)
	III.	46 (87)	58 (156)	39 (126)	43 (100)
Ph.D.	I.	40 (118)	63 (148)	61 (85)	65 (86)
	II.	61 (118)	81 (155)	60 (198)	65 (132)
	III.	68 (68)	85 (60)	74 (69)	84 (58)

N 2,781
NA on age or stage . . . 53
Interdivisional 8
                          2,842

TABLE 3.20
PER CENT EVER MARRIED, BY AGE AND SEX

Age	Per Cent Ever Married Men	Per Cent Ever Married Women
20-21	08 (49)	10 (30)
22	23 (193)	15 (71)
23	37 (200)	21 (71)
24	44 (200)	38 (45)
25	46 (228)	24 (46)
26	49 (222)	35 (23)
27	58 (217)	48 (29)
28	61 (212)	37 (19)
29	66 (160)	43 (23)
30	70 (105)	41 (17)
31-35	69 (347)	46 (59)
Over 35 . . .	80 (179)	42 (90)
NA	- (2)	- (3)
Total per cent married . .	54	32
N	2,314	526
NA on Marital Status . . .	2	0
Total N . . .	2,316	526

TABLE 3.21

MARRIAGE PLANS OF SINGLE STUDENTS BY
AGE AND SEX

(Per cent checking "Definitely plan to be married"
or "Quite likely that I will be married")

Age	Sex	
	Male	Female
20-23	32 (317)	40 (141)
24-26	33 (342)	39 (75)
27-29	33 (230)	49 (39)
30-34	31 (122)	39 (33)
35-39	29 (35)	7 (28)
40+	7 (15)	0 (24)

```
              N . . . . . . . .  1,401
              NA on age, sex,
                marital status,
                or plans . . . . .   27
              Not among "single,
                never married"
                group . . . . .   1,414
                                  2,842
```

TABLE 3.22

CHILDREN BY DURATION OF MARRIAGE AND AGE AT MARRIAGE

(Per cent with one or more children among males married one or more years)

Age at Marriage	Duration of Marriage in Years						
	1	2	3	4	5	6	7 or more
21 or younger	16 (25)	28 (25)	50 (32)	57 (30)	62 (24)	90 (21)	87 (91)
22-23	15 (52)	28 (54)	58 (38)	68 (37)	68 (38)	83 (23)	83 (81)
24-25	18 (38)	44 (50)	60 (47)	69 (32)	72 (18)	81 (21)	94 (62)
26-28	23 (39)	42 (33)	61 (28)	78 (18)	73 (15)	93 (15)	89 (53)
29+	14 (22)	40 (15)	67 (15)	- (6)	63 (11)	- (6)	78 (36)

```
N . . . . . . . . . . . . .  1,151
NA on one or more items .      4
Not a Married Male . . .   1,619
Married less than one
    year . . . . . . . . .    68
                           ───────
                            2,842
```

TABLE 3.23
FERTILITY EXPECTATIONS BY DURATION OF MARRIAGE AND NUMBER OF CHILDREN, AMONG MARRIED MALES
(Per cent expecting a child within two years)

Duration of Marriage	0	1	2	3 or more
Less than 1 year	46 (63)	— (1)	— (0)	— (0)
1 year	53 (137)	56 (27)	— (3)	— (0)
2 years	54 (106)	57 (54)	— (9)	— (0)
3 years	67 (63)	73 (56)	25 (32)	— (1)
4 years	58 (38)	76 (45)	33 (30)	— (6)
5-6 years	67 (46)	68 (53)	42 (64)	46 (28)
7 or more	42 (40)	46 (56)	24 (94)	23 (116)
Total for respondents reporting on duration of marriage	55 (493)	63 (292)	31 (232)	28 (151)

```
N . . . . . . . . 1,168
NA on Duration or
  children now . .    5
NA on Expectation    50
Not a married
  male . . . . . 1,619
                 2,842
```

TABLE 3.24
RELIGION, DURATION OF MARRIAGE AND FERTILITY
(Per cent of married males with one or more children)

Religion (Original)	Religion (Current)	Less than 2 Years	3-5 Years	6+ Years
Catholic	Catholic	30 (59)	87 (54)	92 (87)
Protestant	Protestant	18 (172)	59 (166)	86 (173)
Jewish	Jewish	16 (44)	62 (24)	91 (22)
Catholic	None	12 (16)	62 (16)	- (9)
Protestant	None	28 (46)	64 (56)	78 (45)
Jewish	None	18 (28)	45 (11)	80 (10)
None	None	35 (20)	60 (20)	83 (12)
Other religions and combinations		36 (36)	57 (42)	82 (51)

```
N . . . . . . . . . . . . 1,219
NA on one or more items .      4
Not a married male  . . . 1,619
                              -----
                              2,842
```

TABLE 3.25
RELIGION, NUMBER OF CHILDREN AND FERTILITY EXPECTATIONS
(Per cent of married males expecting a child)

Religion (Original)	Religion (Current)	0	1	2 or more	
Catholic	Catholic	84 (51)	74 (43)	54 (94)	
Protestant	Protestant	58 (222)	59 (113)	20 (161)	
Jewish	Jewish	60 (43)	70 (23)	31 (16)	
Catholic	None	57 (21)	60 (10)	20 (10)	
Protestant	None	36 (59)	60 (45)	10 (39)	
Jewish	None	40 (30)	64 (11)	- (7)	
None	None	32 (22)	59 (17)	27 (11)	
Other religions and combinations		46 (46)	65 (31)	40 (45)	
NA on children now					- (3)

```
N . . . . . . . . . . . 1,173
NA on expectation . . .    50
Not a married male  . . 1,619
                            -----
                            2,842
```

TABLE 3.26
FAMILY ROLE INDEX

Marital Status	Children	Description	N	Per Cent Within Sex	Per Cent Total Sample
Female					
Single or ex-married	No	Single Women	364	71	13
Married	No	Wives	67	13	2
Married	Yes	Mothers	79	16	3
				100%	
Male					
Single or ex-married	No	Single Men	1,082	47	38
Married	No	Husbands	525	23	19
Married	Yes	Fathers	696	30	25
				100%	
		Totals	2,813		100%
		Other and insufficient information	29		
			2,842		

TABLE 3.27
AGE AND FAMILY ROLE INDEX

(a) Males

Age	Single	Husbands	Fathers	Total	N
20-23 ..	72	20	08	100%	(442)
24-26 ..	54	29	17	100%	(650)
27-29 ..	39	24	37	100%	(582)
30-39 ..	31	17	52	100%	(545)
40+ ...	19	16	65	100%	(83)
NA ...	-	-	-	-	(1)

Total 2,303
NA on Family Role . . . 13
2,316

(b) Females

Age	Single	Wives	Mothers	Total	N
20-23 ..	83	16	01	100%	(171)
24-26 ..	71	16	13	100%	(114)
27-29 ..	59	16	25	100%	(68)
30-39 ..	63	07	30	100%	(98)
40+ ...	63	07	30	100%	(56)
NA ...	-	-	-	-	(3)

Total 510
NA on Family Role . . . 16
526

TABLE 3.28
CHRONOLOGICAL AGE AND STAGE INDEX

Age	Stage I	Stage II	Stage III	Stage IV	Total	N
20-23 years ..	65	22	10	03	100%	(613)
24-26 years ..	24	27	30	19	100	(759)
27-29 years ..	19	25	34	22	100	(650)
30-39 years ..	15	20	37	28	100	(634)
40+ years ..	15	31	38	16	100	(133)
NA on Age ...	-	-	-	-	-	(5)

Total N 2,794
NA on Stage 48
2,842

TABLE 3.29
ACADEMIC STAGE AND FAMILY ROLE INDEX

(a) Males

Stage	Single	Husbands	Fathers	Total	N
I ..	60	20	20	100%	(632)
II ..	49	21	30	100%	(520)
III ..	40	24	36	100%	(680)
IV ..	38	28	34	100%	(440)
NA	29	10	61	100%	(31)

```
                    Total . . . . . . . . . 2,303
                    NA on Family Role . . .    13
                                            2,316
```

(b) Females

Stage	Single	Wives	Mothers	Total	N
I ..	79	10	11	100%	(183)
II ..	68	15	17	100%	(148)
III ..	63	19	18	100%	(103)
IV ..	68	11	21	100%	(62)
NA	86	-	14	100%	(14)

```
                    Total . . . . . . . . .  510
                    NA on Family Role . . .   16
                                             526
```

TABLE 4.1
EXPECTED INCOME FOR THE ACADEMIC YEAR 1958-1959 BY SOURCE

Cumulative Per cent of Students Receiving...

Source	Per Year	$1	$450	$900	$1,350	$1,800	$2,700	$3,600
	Per Month	-	$50	$100	$150	$200	$300	$400
Stipend		74	59	56	50	40	11	05
Withdrawals from savings		35	18	08	04	03	01	01
Part-time job		29	12	08	05	04	02	01
Spouse's job		25	16	15	14	12	08	06
Parents		22	12	07	04	03	01	*
Full-time Job		18	13	13	13	13	13	11
Veterans' Benefits		16	09	07	03	01	*	*
Investments		13	05	03	02	02	01	01
Loans		09	03	02	01	*	00	00
Spouse's parents		04	01	01	*	*	*	*
Other		03	01	01	*	*	*	*

N for $1 2,810
N for > $1: N Stipend . . . 2,776
All other sources 2,774

* Per cent < .5.

CHART 4.1
FREQUENCY AND INTENSITY OF INCOME SOURCES

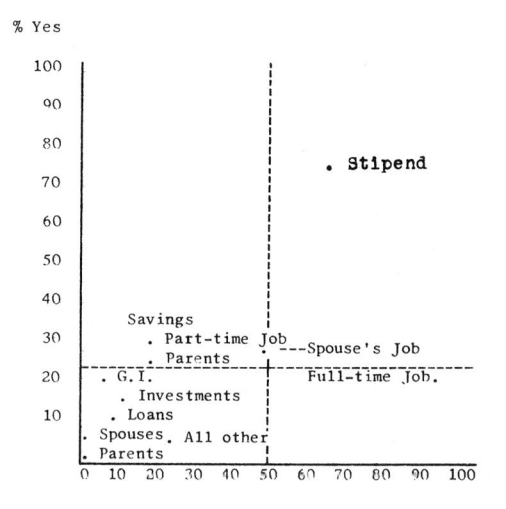

% Yes

- Stipend (approx 70, 70)
- Savings
- Part-time Job
- Parents
- Spouse's Job
- G.I.
- Investments
- Full-time Job
- Loans
- Spouses
- All other
- Parents

% ≥ 50% of Total Income Among Yeses

TABLE 4.2

EXPECTED INCOME FOR ACADEMIC YEAR 1958-59 BY SOURCE AS A PER CENT OF TOTAL INCOME

(Cumulative Per Cent of Students Reporting Sources as Contributing . . . Per Cent or More of Total Income)

Source	Any	20%	40%	50%	60%	80%	100%
Stipend	74	57	48	41	36	24	11
Savings	35	13	06	04	03	01	01
Part-time job	29	14	07	06	04	03	02
Spouse's job	25	21	17	12	08	03	01
Parents	22	11	06	04	04	02	01
Full-time Job	18	18	18	17	16	14	07
Veterans' Benefits	16	10	03	01	01	*	*
Investments	13	03	02	02	01	01	*
Loans	09	03	01	01	*	*	*
Spouse's parents	04	01	*	*	*	*	00
Other	03	01	01	*	*	*	*

N for 1% = 2,810
N for > 1% = 2,730, except Stipend which is - 2,731

* Per cent   .5.

Tables

CHART 4.2

INCOME, FAMILY ROLE, AND PERCEIVED ADEQUACY OF INCOME

(Per cent reporting enough or more than enough)

```
~~~~~~~~~~ : Fathers
---------- : Husbands
────────── : Single Men
‧‧‧‧‧‧‧‧‧‧ : Single Women
```

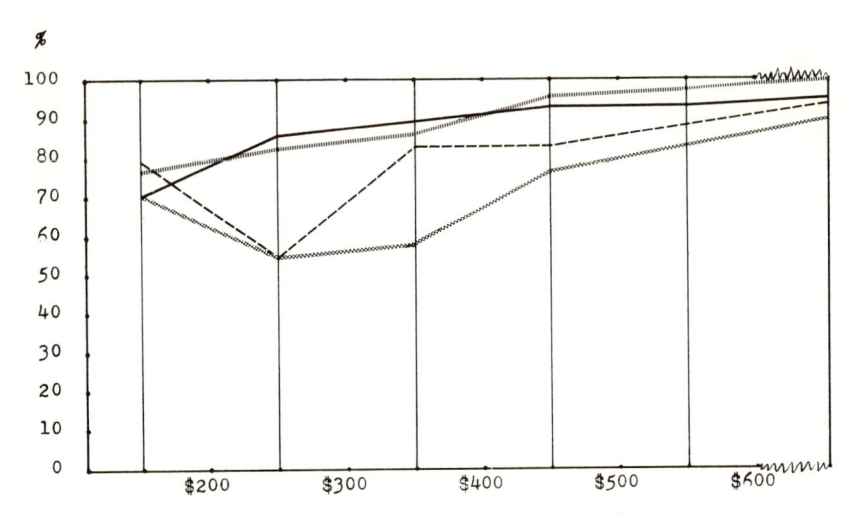

Income per month during academic year

TABLE 4.3
NUMBER OF SOURCES OF INCOME REPORTED

Number of Sources	Vis-a-vis Total Income					
	Any		10% or More		20% or More	
	%	Cum.	%	Cum.	%	Cum.
1	22	100	39	100	56	100
2	33	78	44	61	39	44
3	26	45	15	17	05	5
4	13	19	02	2	*	-
5	05	6	*	-	0	-
6	01	1	0	-	0	-
7	*	-	0	-	0	-
8+	0	-	0	-	0	-
Total N	(2,810)		(2,724)		(2,724)	

*Less than one-half of one per cent, but not zero.

TABLE 4.4
DISTRIBUTION OF EXPECTED TOTAL INCOME FROM ALL
SOURCES FOR THE ACADEMIC YEAR 1958-1959

Total Income Per Year*	Per Cent	Cumulative Per Cents		N
Under $1,800, or less than $200 per month	11.9	11.9	100.0	319
$1,800-2,699, or $200-299 per month	22.3	34.2	88.1	599
$2,700-3,599, or $300-399 per month	17.4	51.6	65.8	469
$3,600-4,499, or $400-499 per month	14.5	66.1	48.4	390
$4,500-5,399, or $500-599 per month	10.8	76.9	33.9	289
$5,400 or more, or $600 or more per month	23.1	100.0	23.1	621
Total	100.0	-	-	2,687

N 2,687
NA on Income . . 155
2,842

*Estimated on the basis of a nine month academic year.

TABLE 4.5
MEDIAN TOTAL INCOME, 1958

Population Group	Median
Persons 14 years of age and over	$ 2,474
Unrelated individuals, female, year round full-time worker	3,153
Unrelated individuals, male, year round full-time worker	3,878
Families, male head, year round full-time worker, wife _not_ in paid labor force	5,726
Families, male head, year round full-time worker, wife in paid labor force	7,034
Family income by age of family head, for families, in which head completed four or more years of college	
25-34	7,248
35-44	8,568
45-54	10,775
55-64	9,330
65 and over	4,940

Source: Current Population Reports: Consumer Income, Series P-60, No. 33, January 15, 1960. Washington, D.C., Bureau of the Census.

TABLE 4.6
TOTAL INCOME BY PRESENCE AND ABSENCE OF SPECIFIC SOURCES
(Per cent with total incomes of $3,600 or more for the academic year)

Source	Reporting Income from This Source	
	Yes	No
Full-time Job	87 (509)	39 (2,178)
Spouse's Employment	83 (693)	36 (1,994)
Spouse's parents	69 (121)	47 (2,566)
Investments	68 (368)	45 (2,319)
Veteran's Benefits	63 (436)	46 (2,251)
Other	51 (75)	48 (2,612)
Non-Duty stipend (scholarship, fellowship, etc.)	48 (878)	49 (1,809)
Part-time job	44 (789)	50 (1,898)
Duty stipend (assistantship)	42 (1,090)	52 (1,597)
Savings	40 (994)	53 (1,693)
Borrowing	37 (257)	50 (2,430)
Parents	31 (624)	54 (2,063)

```
              N in each category . . . . 2,687
              NA . . . . . . . . . . . .   155
                                         -------
                                          2,842
```

TABLE 4.7
FULL-TIME WORK, SPOUSE'S EMPLOYMENT, AND TOTAL INCOME
(Per cent reporting total income of $3,600 or more during the academic year)

Income from Full-time Work	Income from Spouse's Employment	
	Yes	No
Yes	99 (78)	85 (431)
No	81 (616)	23 (1,562)

```
              N . . . . . . . 2,687
              NA on Income  .   155
                              -------
                                2,842
```

TABLE 4.8
FAMILY ROLE, SPOUSE'S EMPLOYMENT, AND FULL-TIME WORK
(Per cent reporting income from . . .)

Full-Time Work	Spouse Employment	Females — Single	Wives	Mothers	Males — Single	Husbands	Fathers
Yes	Yes	0	12	8	0	6	5
Yes	No	16	6	4	10	7	33
No	Yes	1*	70	77	1*	70	20
No	No	83	12	11	89	17	42
		100%	100%	100%	100%	100%	100%
Total Yes, Full-time work..		16	18	12	10	13	38
Total Yes, Spouse Employed..		1*	82	85	1*	76	25
Total Yes, 1 or both		17	88	89	11	83	58
(N)		353	66	78	1,070	524	691

```
N . . . . . . . . . . 2,782
NA on Family Role
    or Sources . . .     60
                       ──────
                        2,842
```

*These apparently illogical per cents arise from 11 students who are ex-married and receiving support from their spouse, or single students expecting to be married during the year who reported anticipated income from spouse's job.

TABLE 4.9
TOTAL INCOME BY FAMILY ROLE

Income for Academic Year	Females — Single	Wives	Mothers	Males — Single	Husbands	Fathers
Under $1,000	05	03	05	03	01	*
$1,000- 2,999	67	17	13	64	11	12
$3,000- 4,999	23	17	21	25	42	38
$5,000- 6,999	04	30	19	05	32	32
$7,000- 8,999	*	14	07	02	10	11
$9,000 or more	01	19	35	01	04	07
N	(317)	(64)	(68)	(1,019)	(518)	(676)

```
N . . . . . . . . . . . . 2,662
NA on Income and
    Family Role . . . . . .  180
                            ──────
                             2,842
```

TABLE 4.10

FAMILY ROLE, FULL-TIME WORK, SPOUSE'S EMPLOYMENT, AND TOTAL INCOME

(Per cent reporting total incomes of $3,600 or more during the academic year)

Full-time Work or Spouse's Employment	Females			Males		
	Single	Wives	Mothers	Single	Husbands	Fathers
One or both	67 (55)	74 (58)	83 (60)	75 (118)	86 (432)	88 (396)
Neither	08 (262)	- (6)	- (8)	12 (901)	47 (86)	62 (280)

```
                N . . . . . . . . . . . . . . .  2,662
                NA on sources or family role       25
                NA on total income . . . . .      155
                                                 ─────
                                                 2,842
```

TABLE 4.11

TOTAL INCOME BY AGE, ACADEMIC STAGE, FAMILY ROLE, AND SOURCE OF INCOME

(Per cent with incomes of $3,600 or more for the academic year)

Family Role	Age	Full-Time Job or Spouse's Job	Stage	
			Beginning	Advanced
Married	27+	No	63 (95)	63 (170)
		Yes	87 (216)	90 (345)
	<27	No	38 (56)	52 (50)
		Yes	76 (217)	90 (154)
Single	27+	No	12 (144)	20 (229)
		Yes	75 (53)	88 (40)
	<27	No	07 (563)	12 (218)
		Yes	59 (58)	67 (18)

NA on Family Role, Age, Sources,
Stage 54 (61)

```
                              N . . . . . . . . . . . . . . .  2,687
                              NA on Income . . . . . . . .      155
                                                               ─────
                                                               2,842
```

TABLE 4.12

PERCEIVED ADEQUACY OF INCOME

(Answers to the question, "Which of the following best describes your financial situation this academic year?")

Response	Per Cent	Cumulative Per Cent
I'll have enough money for my necessary expenses, and enough left over for emergencies	53	53
I'll have enough money for my necessary expenses, but nothing left over for emergencies	31	84
I'm not sure whether I'll have enough money to cover my necessary expenses	10	94
It's doubtful that I'll have enough money to cover my necessary expenses	6	—

Total 100%
N 2,809
NA 33

2,842

TABLE 4.13

FAMILY ROLE AND PERCEIVED ADEQUACY OF INCOME

(Per cent not sure or doubtful about having enough money to cover necessary expenses)

Sex	Single	Married, No Children	Married, Child
Female	15 (348)	6 (67)	10 (77)
Male	15 (1,076)	13 (524)	21 (689)

N 2,781
NA on family role . 28
NA on adequacy . . 33

2,842

TABLE 4.14
STRATUM, CONTROL, AND PERCEIVED ADEQUACY OF INCOME
(Per cent reporting "Enough money for my necessary expenses")

Stratum	Total Income: Single Students			
	Less than $2,700		$2,700 or more	
	Private	Public	Private	Public
I.	78 (138)	79 (113)	89 (138)	85 (53)
II.	85 (109)	81 (246)	93 (149)	87 (75)
III.	77 (63)	78 (107)	94 (77)	87 (46)

	Married Men			
	Less than $4,500		$4,500 or more	
	Private	Public	Private	Public
I.	75 (55)	72 (71)	91 (92)	90 (78)
II.	66 (50)	70 (177)	90 (162)	90 (156)
III.	78 (37)	72 (107)	93 (141)	80 (65)

NA on Income and Family Role   93 (140)

```
N . . . . . . . . . . . . 2,665
NA on Adequacy . . . . .    31
Married Women  . . . . .   146
                         ─────
                         2,842
```

TABLE 5.1
DISTRIBUTIONS OF EXPENDITURES FOR SPECIFIC CATEGORIES OF ACADEMIC EXPENSES

	Per Cent
Total Professional Expenditures (expected in 1958-59)	
$ 0-225	16
$226-449	33
$450-899	31
$900+	20
	100
Total Professional Expenditures (as a per cent of total income from all sources)	
50% or more	6
40-49%	6
30-39%	10
20-29%	13
10-19%	29
Less than 10%	36
	100
Tuition and Fees	
$ 0-199	24
$200-349	26
$350-699	24
$700+	26
	100
Books	
None	8
$ 1-54	57
$ 55-99	15
$100+	20
	100
Journals	
None	54
$ 1-19	28
$ 20+	18
	100
Theses	
None	72
$ 1-39	9
$ 40-99	9
$100+	10
	100
Other Professional Expenditures	
None	79
$ 1-99	17
$100+	4
	100

N for Total Professional expenditures
(as a per cent of total income) 2,667
NA 175
                                         2,842

For Total Professional expenditures,
Tuition and Fees, Books, Journals,
Theses, and Other 2,821
NA   21
                                         2,842

TABLE 5.2
"NORMAL" TUITION AND FEE COSTS PER ACADEMIC YEAR FOR A FULL-TIME STUDENT

Stratum	Private Schools	Public Schools
I	N = 4 Range = $900-$1,250 Mean = $1,100	N = 3 Range = $90-$250 ($410-$600)* Mean = $155 ($512)
II	N = 5 Range = $572-$1,000 Mean = $860	N = 5 Range = $206-$350 ($306-$750)* Mean = $251 ($541)
III	N = 4 Range = $535-$1,080 Mean = $774	N = 4 Range = $74-$225 ($74-$525)* Mean = $146 ($312)

*In the Public School data, the figures in parentheses refer to non-residents, other figures to residents of the state.

TABLE 5.3
STRATUM, CONTROL, AND TUITION COSTS
(Mean Expected Expenditures for Tuition Plus Fees for Students Registered for the Entire Year)

Stratum	Private Schools	Public Schools
I	$822 (358)	$301 (297)
II	$614 (429)	$345 (623)
III	$599 (253)	$256 (301)

N 2,261
NA on Tuition and Fees   23
Not fully registered . 558

                       2,842

TABLE 5.4

STRATUM, CONTROL, COURSE LOAD COMPLETED, AND TUITION COSTS

(Mean Expected Expenditures for Tuition Plus Fees for Students Registered for the Entire Year)

Stratum	Private			Public		
	Course Load Completed*			Course Load Completed*		
	2/3 or Less	More than 2/3 but less than full	Full or more than full	2/3 or Less	More than 2/3 but less than full	Full or more than full
I	$779 (100)	$933 (90)	$1,024 (62)	$244 (129)	$354 (128)	$339 (33)
II	$476 (204)	$723 (184)	$936 (34)	$341 (356)	$348 (182)	$395 (70)
III	$507 (164)	$796 (55)	$765 (30)	$233 (138)	$270 (127)	$359 (26)

```
N . . . . . . . . . . . 2,112
NA on Tuition and Fees      22
NA or No Load or not
  fully registered . . .  708
                        ─────
                        2,842
```

*Course credits received as a fraction of the catalog statement of the course credits for a full year's work by a full-time student.

TABLE 5.5

CONTROL, STRATUM, COURSE LOAD, AND
PROPORTIONAL EXPENSES

(Per cent expecting to spend 30 per cent or more of
total income on professional expenses)

Course Load Completed	Private	Public
Two-thirds or less		
I	39 (113)	05 (131)
II	15 (236)	13 (351)
III	20 (162)	06 (180)
More than two-thirds		
I	65 (132)	18 (154)
II	47 (147)	20 (239)
III	59 (68)	10 (104)

```
N . . . . . . . . . . . . . . . . 2,017
NA on Expenses . . . . . . . . .   117
NA or No Load or Not Registered
    for Entire Year . . . . . . . . 708
                                  2,842
```

TABLE 5.6
CONTROL, STRATUM, COURSE LOAD, FAMILY ROLE, AND PROPORTIONAL EXPENSE
(Per cent expecting to spend 30 per cent or more of total income on professional expenses)

Course Load Completed	Private	Public
Single		
Two-thirds or less		
I	60 (58)	10 (62)
II	28 (106)	25 (166)
III	36 (75)	13 (78)
More than two-thirds		
I	81 (90)	26 (88)
II	68 (94)	37 (114)
III	79 (43)	19 (48)
Married		
Two-thirds or less		
I	13 (52)	00 (69)
II	04 (128)	02 (181)
III	06 (87)	01 (101)
More than two-thirds		
I	25 (40)	06 (64)
II	09 (53)	04 (122)
III	24 (25)	02 (56)

```
N . . . . . . . . . . . . . . . . 2,000
NA on Family Role and Expenses.   134
NA or No Load or Not Registered
    for Entire Year . . . . . .   708
                                 ─────
                                 2,842
```

TABLE 5.7

INCOME, FAMILY ROLE, PROFESSIONAL COSTS AS A PER CENT OF TOTAL INCOME, AND PERCEIVED INCOME ADEQUACY

(Per cent expecting enough income for necessary expenses)

Professional Expenses as Per Cent of Total Income	Income for Academic Year		
	Less than $2,700	$2,700–$4,499	$4,500 or more
Single			
Less than 10%	82 (60)	90 (101)	97 (73)
10–29%	82 (370)	86 (194)	95 (40)
30% or more	78 (356)	90 (118)	— (5)
Married			
Less than 10%	62 (29)	74 (185)	93 (509)
10–29%	60 (57)	76 (200)	87 (258)
30% or more	62 (24)	76 (38)	— (5)

NA on Family Role, Professional Expenses and Total Income 91 (187)

```
                     N . . . . . . . . . . . 2,809
                     NA on Adequacy . . . .    33
                                             2,842
```

TABLE 5.8
ACADEMIC WORK COMPLETED 1958-1959

(a) Registration Status	Per Cent
Registered both semesters or all three quarters	80
Registered one semester or one or two quarters	13
Withdrew, all audit, technical registration only, etc.	7
	100%

```
            N . . . . . 2,724
            NA . . . .   118
                       ───────
                        2,842
```

(b) Credit Received Among Students in Residence All Year

Type of Term	Credits as a Proportion of Catalogue Definition of Full-Time Load for a Year				
	Less than 1/3	1/3 to 2/3	More than 2/3 but less than full	Full or More	Total
Semester	2	57	29	12	100%
Quarter	*	61	27	12	100%

```
            N Semesters . . . . . . 1,692
            N Quarters . . . . . . .  474
            NA on Load . . . . . .    118
            Not fully registered . .  558
                                    ───────
                                     2,842
```

*Less than .5 per cent.

TABLE 5.9

COURSE LOAD COMPLETED AND EMPLOYMENT SITUATION

(Per cent completing ⅔ or more of a full year's load among students registered for the entire year)

Employment				Total
Full-time job			05	(287)
Other			40	(1,247)

		Part-time Job	
		Yes	No
Teaching or Research Assistantship	Yes	35 (250)	39 (671)
	No	47 (326)	

None				63	(579)
Fellowship for tuition, plus $1,000 or more				68	(259)
Other				59	(320)

N	2,113
NA on Sources	21
NA or Not fully registered on load	708
	2,842

TABLE 5.10
FAMILY ROLE, EMPLOYMENT STATUS, AND COURSE LOAD COMPLETED

(Per cent completing more than ⅔ of a full year's load among students registered for the entire year)

Sex	Single	Married, No Children	Married, Children	N
(a) Over-all			
Women	47 (273)	40 (53)	23 (61)	
Men	45 (829)	43 (414)	33 (484)	
				2,114

NA on Family Role, Load, or Not fully Registered . . 728
                                                                2,842

(b) Controlling for Employment Status
1. Full-Time Workers

Sex	Single	Married, No Children	Married, Children
Women	07 (28)	— (9)	— (6)
Men	09 (58)	00 (39)	05 (144)

2. Part-time Job or Assistantship

Sex	Single	Married, No Children	Married, Children
Women	40 (142)	37 (27)	13 (23)
Men	41 (546)	42 (259)	37 (241)

3. Not Employed

Sex	Single	Married, No Children	Married, Children
Women	72 (95)	62 (16)	35 (31)
Men	65 (217)	57 (115)	66 (98)

NA on Employment and Family Role . . . 38 (40)

N 2,134
NA on load or not fully registered 708
                                                        2,842

TABLE 5.11

STAGE, EMPLOYMENT STATUS, AND COURSE LOAD COMPLETED

(Per cent completing more than ⅔ of a full year's load among students registered for the entire year)

Employment Status	Stage I.	Stage II.	Stage III.	Stage IV.
(a) Over-all				
Any	60 (690)	25 (502)	38 (626)	34 (289)

```
N . . . . . . . . . . . . . . 2,107
NA on Stage . . . . . . . . .    27
NA on Load or not fully
   registered . . . . . . . .   708
                               -----
                               2,842
```

Employment Status	Stage I.	Stage II.	Stage III.	Stage IV.
(b) Controlling for employment status				
Full-time job	07 (57)	03 (98)	06 (101)	08 (26)
Part-time job or assistantship	56 (390)	24 (288)	41 (390)	31 (167)
Not employed	80 (236)	50 (109)	56 (131)	46 (95)

```
N . . . . . . . . . . . . . . 2,088
NA on Stage or Employment . .    46
NA on Load or not fully
   registered . . . . . . . .   708
                               -----
                               2,842
```

TABLE 5.12

EMPLOYMENT STATUS, STAGE, AGE, INCOME AND COURSE LOAD COMPLETED

(Per cent completing ⅔ or more of a full year's load among students registered for the entire year)

Stage and Age	Not Employed — Low Income*	Not Employed — High Income*	Part-time Job or Assistantship — Low Income*	Part-time Job or Assistantship — High Income*	Full-time Job — Low Income*	Full-time Job — High Income*
I						
Under 27	87 (119)	79 (39)	57 (243)	54 (59)	— (5)	11 (19)
27 or older	81 (32)	72 (29)	62 (40)	49 (35)	— (5)	00 (26)
II-IV						
Under 27	67 (82)	52 (44)	35 (272)	38 (149)	00 (15)	06 (33)
27 or older	43 (83)	46 (90)	33 (198)	28 (201)	03 (29)	06 (140)

No answer on Stage, Age, Employment or Income 34 (147)

```
                    N . . . . . . . . . . . . . . 2,134
                    NA or Zero Load or not
                        fully registered . . . . .   708
                                                   ─────
                                                   2,842
```

*For Income, Low: Less than $3,600 per year; Income, High: $3,600 or more.

TABLE 6.1
PERCENTAGE DISTRIBUTION OF STIPEND TYPOLOGY
(Per cent of all students, excluding trainees, interns, and those holding both research and teaching assistantships)*

Duty Stipend	Value of Non-Duty Stipend			Total
	None	Less than Tuition Plus $1,000 (Scholarship)	Tuition Plus $1,000 or more (Fellowship)	
None	32	12	16	60
Research Assistant . .	6	3	4	13
Teaching Assistant . .	14	9	4	27
Total	52	24	24	100%

```
N . . . . . . . . . . . . . . . 2,689
TA and RA . . . . . . . . . .     28
Internship or Traineeship . .     28
No answer or ambiguous answer     97
                                2,842
```

*Including the 56 cases which do not fit the stipend typology, the following percentages apply: Out of a total of 2,745 reporting, 71 per cent reported a stipend, 47 per cent a non-duty stipend, 23 per cent a high non-duty stipend, and 41 per cent a duty stipend.

TABLE 6.2
STAGE OF STUDY AND STIPEND HOLDING
(Per cent reporting . . .)

Type	Stage			
	I	II	III	IV
Any stipend	61 (790)	65 (651)	72 (769)	92 (489)
Non-duty stipend	45 (782)	45 (640)	49 (749)	58 (469)
Fellowship	22 (782)	15 (640)	23 (749)	37 (472)
Duty Stipend	31 (785)	36 (645)	47 (759)	49 (482)
Research Assistantship .	8 (785)	12 (645)	14 (759)	23 (482)
Teaching Assistantship .	23 (785)	25 (645)	34 (759)	28 (482)

```
For any Stipend, N . . . . . . 2,699
NA or ambiguous . . . . . . .     95
NA on Stage . . . . . . . . .     48
                                2,842
```

(N's for certain sub-types are smaller because of students who could be coded on a general category, but not on specific sub-types)

TABLE 6.3

DIVISION AND STIPEND HOLDING

(Per cent reporting . . .)

Type	Natural Science	Social Science	Humanities
Any Stipend	79 (1,291)	63 (627)	57 (820)
Non-Duty Stipend	54 (1,268)	45 (595)	43 (819)
Fellowship	29 (1,260)	21 (595)	18 (819)
Duty Stipend	51 (1,290)	31 (600)	29 (820)
Research Assistantship	21 (1,290)	12 (600)	1 (820)
Teaching Assistantship	31 (1,290)	19 (600)	28 (820)

```
For any Stipend, N . . . . . 2,738
NA or ambiguous . . . . . .    96
Interdivisional . . . . . .     8
                            ──────
                             2,842
```

(N's for certain sub-types are smaller because of students who could be coded on a general category, but not on specific sub-types)

TABLE 6.4
STRATUM, CONTROL AND STIPENDS

Stage	Private	Public
(a) Per Cent With a Non-Duty Stipend		
I....	53 (474)	47 (323)
II....	48 (532)	49 (658)
III....	42 (369)	50 (333)
(b) Per Cent Reporting a Fellowship		
I....	30 (474)	23 (323)
II....	25 (532)	24 (658)
III....	17 (369)	23 (333)
(c) Per Cent With an Assistantship		
I....	33 (479)	52 (326)
II....	25 (541)	57 (668)
III....	17 (369)	52 (334)
(d) Per Cent With a Teaching Assistantship		
I....	23 (479)	33 (326)
II....	16 (541)	39 (668)
III....	14 (369)	40 (334)
(e) Per Cent With a Research Assistantship		
I....	11 (479)	21 (326)
II....	10 (541)	19 (668)
III....	3 (369)	13 (334)
(f) Per Cent Reporting a Stipend)		
I....	70 (479)	76 (329)
II....	59 (550)	79 (674)
III....	52 (371)	75 (342)

```
N for Tables a and b . . . 2,689
Trainee or TA-RA . . . . .    56
NA or ambiguous on stipend   97
                           2,842

N for Tables c, d, e . . . 2,717
Trainees . . . . . . . . .    28
NA or ambiguous on stipend   97
                           2,842

N for Table f . . . . . . 2,745
NA or ambiguous on stipend   97
                           2,842
```

TABLE 6.5
STAGE, DIVISION, TYPE OF SCHOOL AND STIPEND HOLDING

School	Social Science & Humanities Beginning	Social Science & Humanities Advanced	Natural Science Beginning	Natural Science Advanced
(a) Fellowships (Per Cent With a Fellowship)				
Private I	20 (129)	21 (144)	35 (80)	47 (116)
Public	18 (348)	19 (251)	20 (367)	36 (330)
Private II-III . . .	14 (315)	24 (200)	19 (177)	30 (178)
(b) Research Assistantships (Per Cent With a Research Assistantship)				
Public	8 (348)	9 (253)	19 (371)	34 (338)
Private I	2 (129)	5 (147)	15 (81)	26 (117)
Private II-III . . .	3 (316)	6 (200)	7 (179)	17 (184)
(c) Teaching Assistantships (Per Cent With a Teaching Assistantship)				
Public	30 (347)	51 (253)	37 (371)	36 (338)
Private I	50 (127)	27 (146)	37 (81)	28 (117)
Private II-III . . .	9 (323)	16 (200)	21 (179)	22 (184)
(d) High Aid (Per Cent With a Fellowship and/or Assistantship)				
Public	51 (348)	71 (253)	69 (371)	84 (338)
All Private	24 (445)	43 (347)	53 (260)	68 (301)
Private I	26 (129)	48 (147)	80 (81)	85 (117)
Private II-III . . .	24 (316)	39 (200)	41 (179)	58 (184)

```
N for Table a . . . . . . . . 2,689
Trainee or RA-TA . . . . . . .   56
NA or ambiguous on stipend . .   97
                               -----
                               2,842

N for Tables b,c,d . . . . . . 2,717
Trainee . . . . . . . . . . .    28
NA or ambiguous on stipend . .   97
                               -----
                               2,842
```

TABLE 6.6

STIPEND TYPOLOGY AND POOLED ABILITY RATING

(Per cent rated "high" in native ability)

Duty Stipend	Value of Non-Duty Stipend		
	None	Less than Tuition Plus $1,000	Tuition Plus $1,000 or more
None	24 (704)	26 (293)	46 (355)
Research Assistant	51 (132)	51 (81)	46 (85)
Teaching Assistant	42 (320)	36 (213)	44 (85)

```
                N . . . . . . . . . . . . . . 2,272
                NA on Ability . . . . . . . .   417
                NA or Ambiguous or RA-TA or
                    Trainee on Stipends . . . .  153
                                               2,842
```

TABLE 6.7
STAGE, DIVISION, CONTROL, ABILITY, AND STIPEND HOLDING
(Per cent with a fellowship or assistantship)

Control	Division	Stage: Beginning Low Ability	Beginning Medium Ability	Beginning High Ability	Advanced Low Ability	Advanced Medium Ability	Advanced High Ability
		(a) Division					
Public	Natural Science	62 (130)	73 (94)	86 (87)	78 (41)	88 (106)	84 (147)
	Soc-Hum	38 (113)	50 (86)	70 (98)	45 (33)	73 (81)	88 (122)
Private	Natural Science	42 (109)	60 (58)	71 (45)	55 (55)	61 (84)	74 (113)
	Soc-Hum	18 (169)	36 (127)	36 (82)	32 (56)	33 (105)	48 (113)

(b) Same Data Rearranged to Show Effect of Control

Natural Science	Public	62	73	86	78	88	84
	Private	42	60	71	55	61	74
Soc-Hum	Public	38	50	70	48	72	80
	Private	18	36	36	32	33	48

(c) Same Date Rearranged to Show Effect of Stage

		Public	Public	Public	Private	Private	Private
Natural Science	Advanced	78	88	84	55	61	74
	Beginning	62	73	86	39	60	70
Soc-Hum	Advanced	45	73	88	32	33	48
	Beginning	38	50	70	18	36	36

For Table a:
N 2,254
Interdivisional, NA on Division,
Stage, Ability 463
NA, Ambiguous, or Trainee on Stipends. 125
2,842

TABLE 6.8
FATHER'S OCCUPATION AND STIPEND HOLDING
(a) Fellowships (Per Cent With a Fellowship)

	Father's Occupation	
	Low	High
Natural Science, Advanced	35 (286)	36 (240)
All Other	19 (934)	18 (817)

(b) Assistantships
(Per Cent With a Teaching or Research Assistantship)

Control	Division	Stage	Father's Occupation Low	Father's Occupation High
Public	Any	Advanced	62 (470)	60 (351)
Public	Natural Science	Beginning	36 (387)	43 (391)
All other, except as below				
Private	Soc. and Humanities	Any	14 (378)	22 (325)

```
N for Table a . . . . . . . . . . . . 2,777
NA on Division, Stage, Father's
  Occupation . . . . . . . . . . . . . .  412
NA or Ambiguous or Trainee or RA-TA
  on Stipends . . . . . . . . . . . .    153
                                        2,842

N for Table b . . . . . . . . . . . . 2,302
NA on Division, Stage, or Father's
  Occupation . . . . . . . . . . . .     415
NA or ambiguous or TA-RA on Stipends.    125
                                        2,842
```

TABLE 6.9
FAMILY ROLE AND STIPEND HOLDING

Control	Division	Stage	Sex	Single	Married, No Children	Married, Children
\multicolumn{7}{c}{(a) (Per Cent With a Fellowship)}					
Any	Natural Science	Advanced	Female	33 (30)	45 (11)	30 (10)
			Male	37 (214)	32 (164)	39 (189)
All Other			Female	23 (297)	12 (51)	11 (66)
			Male	17 (799)	19 (329)	24 (450)

N 2,610
NA on Division or Stage or Family Role 79
NA or Ambiguous or RA-TA or Trainee 153
                                                     2,842

(b) (Per Cent With a Teaching or Research Assistantship)

Control	Division	Stage	Sex	Single	Married, No Children	Married, Children
Public	Any (or)	Advanced	Female	53 (62)	54 (11)	47 (17)
Public	Natural Science	Beginning	Male	64 (359)	71 (231)	49 (280)
Any other, except as below or NA			Female	31 (154)	27 (37)	17 (36)
			Male	46 (434)	43 (209)	22 (244)
Private	Soc. (or)	Any	Female	14 (118)	22 (18)	17 (24)
Private	Hum.	Beginning	Male	14 (235)	19 (69)	8 (128)

N 2,666
NA on Division or Stage or Family Role 79
NA or Ambiguous on Stipend . . 97
                                                     2,842

TABLE 6.10

GROSS VALUE OF STIPEND BY CONTROL, DIVISION, STAGE, AND TYPE OF STIPEND

(Per cent receiving $2,000 or more a year among stipend holders)

Control	Division	Non-Duty Only B	Non-Duty Only A	TA Only B	TA Only A	RA Only B	RA Only A	TA Plus Non-Duty B	TA Plus Non-Duty A	RA Plus Non-Duty B	RA Plus Non-Duty A
Private	Natural Science	45 (86)	71 (97)	80 (35)	80 (35)	– (7)	80 (20)	85 (26)	84 (31)	93 (15)	81 (32)
	Soc-Hum	26 (140)	38 (101)	53 (15)	62 (26)	– (4)	– (6)	61 (18)	68 (38)	– (8)	– (8)
Public	Natural Science	38 (78)	67 (73)	14 (69)	38 (53)	41 (39)	58 (38)	34 (62)	54 (56)	46 (28)	66 (64)
	Soc-Hum	18 (85)	25 (51)	18 (55)	26 (66)	25 (16)	45 (11)	17 (46)	34 (56)	18 (11)	50 (10)

```
N . . . . . . . . . . . . . . . 1,715
Interdivisional or NA on Stage     23
No Stipend or NA or Ambiguous
   or Trainee or TA and RA . . .  965
NA on Amount or Tuition and
   Fees or Duty Stipend Hours. .  139
                                2,842
```

*B = Beginning, A = Advanced.

TABLE 6.11

NET VALUE OF STIPEND BY CONTROL, DIVISION, STAGE, AND TYPE OF STIPEND

(Mean value of stipend over and above tuition and fees among stipend holders)

Control	Division	Non-Duty Only B	Non-Duty Only A	TA Only B	TA Only A	RA Only B	RA Only A	TA Plus Non-Duty B	TA Plus Non-Duty A	RA Plus Non-Duty B	RA Plus Non-Duty A
Private	Natural Science	$931 (86)	$1,606 (97)	$1,459 (35)	$1,684 (35)	- (7)	$1,826 (20)	$1,636 (26)	$1,617 (31)	$2,026 (15)	$2,186 (32)
	Soc-Hum	$459 (140)	$696 (101)	$1,034 (15)	$1,480 (26)	- (4)	- (6)	$1,075 (18)	$1,431 (38)	- (8)	- (8)
Public	Natural Science	$1,095 (78)	$2,102 (73)	$1,388 (69)	$1,631 (53)	$1,701 (39)	$1,941 (38)	$1,540 (62)	$1,839 (56)	$1,885 (28)	$2,012 (64)
	Soc-Hum	$630 (85)	$912 (51)	$1,314 (55)	$1,575 (66)	$1,208 (16)	$1,892 (11)	$1,401 (46)	$1,594 (56)	$1,439 (11)	$1,722 (10)

```
N . . . . . . . . . . . . . . . . . 1,715
Interdivisional or NA on Stage . . .    23
No Stipend or NA or Ambiguous
  or Trainee or TA and RA . . . . .   965
NA on Amount or Tuition and Fees
  or Duty Stipend Hours . . . . . .   139
                                    2,842
```

*B = Beginning, A = Advanced

TABLE 6.12

AVERAGE HOURS PER WEEK FOR DUTY STIPEND HOLDERS BY CONTROL, DIVISION, STAGE, AND TYPE OF DUTY STIPEND

(Mean value of average hours per week reported by duty stipend holders)

Control	Division	TA Only B	TA Only A	RA Only B	RA Only A	TA Plus Non-Duty B	TA Plus Non-Duty A	RA Plus Non-Duty B	RA Plus Non-Duty A
Private	Natural Science	14.2 (35)	15.6 (35)	- (7)	27.6 (20)	14.6 (26)	15.7 (31)	13.2 (15)	10.4 (32)
Private	Soc-Hum	16.3 (15)	17.2 (26)	- (4)	- (6)	13.9 (18)	13.3 (38)	- (8)	- (8)
Public	Natural Science	15.5 (69)	14.7 (53)	20.2 (39)	25.4 (38)	15.4 (62)	15.1 (56)	17.4 (28)	10.0 (64)
Public	Soc-Hum	14.7 (55)	16.5 (66)	17.9 (16)	22.9 (11)	15.3 (46)	15.6 (56)	15.6 (11)	19.8 (10)

```
N . . . . . . . . . . . . . . . . . 1,004
Interdivisional or NA on Stage . .     9
No Stipend or NA or Ambiguous
  or Trainee or TA and RA or
  No Duty Stipend . . . . . . . . 1,690
NA on Amount or Tuition and Fees
  or Hours . . . . . . . . . . .   139
                                  ──────
                                  2,842
```

* B = Beginning, A = Advanced.

TABLE 6.13

ESTIMATED HOURLY WAGE FOR DUTY STIPEND HOLDERS BY CONTROL, DIVISION, STAGE, AND TYPE OF DUTY STIPEND

(Mean hourly wage over and above tuition and fees estimated on the basis of a 39 week year from average number of hours per week)

Control	Division	TA Only B	TA Only A	RA Only B	RA Only A	TA Plus Non-Duty B	TA Plus Non-Duty A	RA Plus Non-Duty B	RA Plus Non-Duty A
Private	Natural Science	$2.64 (35)	$2.77 (35)	$ - (7)	$1.69 (20)	$2.86 (26)	$2.63 (31)	$3.94 (15)	$5.38 (32)
	Soc-Hum	$1.62 (15)	$2.21 (26)	$ - (4)	$ - (6)	$1.98 (18)	$2.76 (38)	$ - (8)	$ - (8)
Public	Natural Science	$2.29 (69)	$2.84 (53)	$2.16 (39)	$1.96 (38)	$2.57 (62)	$3.13 (56)	$2.77 (28)	$5.15 (64)
	Soc-Hum	$2.29 (55)	$2.45 (66)	$1.73 (16)	$2.12 (11)	$2.35 (46)	$2.61 (56)	$2.36 (11)	$2.23 (10)

```
N . . . . . . . . . . . . . . . . . 1,004
Interdivisional or NA on Stage .      9
No Stipend or ambiguous or
   Trainee or TA and RA or No
   Duty Stipend . . . . . . . . . 1,690
NA on Amount or Tuition and Fees
   or Duty Stipend Hours . . . . .  139
                                   2,842
```

*B = Beginning, A = Advanced.

TABLE 6.14
SOURCES OF STIPENDS

Number of Sources	Source	Per Cent	
0		30	
1		59	
	University		32
	U.S. Federal Government		9
	G.I. or other Veterans Benefit		8
	Non-Governmental National Scholarship or Fellowship Programs		4
	Student's employer or future employer		2
	All other sources		4
2 or more		9	
	University Plus G.F.		5
	University Plus Non-University		2
	Combination of Non-University sources		2

Total* 98

N 2,825
NA   17
                             2,842

*Does not add to 100% because of rounding.

TABLE 6.15
DIVISION, STAGE, CONTROL AND RECEIPT OF STIPEND
FROM SPECIFIC SOURCES
(Per cent of all students receiving a stipend from . . .)

Source	Division			Stage		Control	
	Natural Science	Social Science	Humanities	Beginning	Advanced	Private	Public
One Source Only University . . .	34	27	32	30	35	23	41
Federal Government	16	7	*	6	13	8	10
Veterans Benefits	6	10	10	11	5	11	6
Private national program	5	4	3	4	5	4	4
Employer	2	2	2	2	2	3	1
Other and Multiple	16	13	10	12	17	11	17
Total	79	63	57	65	77	60	79
N	1,326	652	839	1,489	1,290	1,424	1,401

N 2,817   N 2,779   N . . . 2,825
NA, Inter-   NA on Source   NA on
divisional .   25   or Stage .   63   Source   17
             2,842   2,842   2,842

* - Less than one-half per cent.

TABLE 6.16

STIPENDS FROM UNIVERSITY FUNDS BY DIVISION, STAGE, AND CONTROL

(Per cent receiving a stipend from university funds, excluding students with multiple and "other" sources)

	Division			
Control	Natural Science		Social Science and Humanities	
	Beginning	Advanced	Beginning	Advanced

(a)

Private	33 (237)	33 (255)	17 (423)	30 (313)
Public	47 (328)	49 (272)	43 (323)	61 (223)

```
N . . . . . . . . . . . . 2,423
NA, Other and Multiple
  Sources . . . . . . . .   419
                          2,842
```

(b) Same Data, Excluding Students with a Teaching Assistantship

Private	11 (175)	14 (198)	11 (395)	13 (252)
Public	20 (214)	26 (186)	21 (232)	30 (123)

```
N . . . . . . . . . . . . 1,819
TA's . . . . . . . . . .    720
NA, Other and Multiple
  Sources . . . . . . . .   303
                          2,842
```

TABLE 6.17

STIPENDS FROM FEDERAL FUNDS BY DIVISION, STAGE, AND CONTROL

(Per cent receiving a stipend, other than veterans benefits, from the Federal Government, excluding students with multiple and "other" sources)

	Control			
Division	Private		Public	
	Beginning	Advanced	Beginning	Advanced
Natural Science	10 (237)	27 (255)	13 (328)	27 (272)
Social Sciences	5 (168)	9 (132)	9 (136)	12 (110)
Humanities	1 (255)	0 (181)	1 (187)	0 (113)

```
N . . . . . . . . . . . . 2,423
NA or Other or Multiple
  Sources . . . . . . . .   419
                          2,842
```

TABLE 6.18

STIPENDS FROM VETERANS BENEFITS, PRIVATE NATIONAL PROGRAMS, AND EMPLOYER BY DIVISION, STAGE, AND CONTROL

(Per cent receiving a stipend from veterans benefits, private national program, or employer, excluding students with multiple or "other" sources)

Control	Natural Science		Social Science and Humanities	
	Beginning	Advanced	Beginning	Advanced
Private	25 (237)	13 (255)	23 (423)	19 (313)
Public	13 (328)	11 (272)	13 (323)	10 (223)

```
                N . . . . . . . . . . . . 2,423
                NA or Other or Multiple
                    Sources . . . . . . . .  419
                                            -----
                                            2,842
```

TABLE 6.19

DISTRIBUTIONS OF ANSWERS TO QUESTIONS ON
ATTITUDES TOWARD ASSISTANTSHIPS

(a)

Answers to: "If financial considerations were unimportant to you, would you prefer . . ."

Pre-coded Answer	Per Cent
No part-time work at all	42
Part-time teaching assistantship during the year	31
Part-time research assistantship during the year	25
Other part-time work	2
Total	100

N 2,770
NA 72
2,842

(b)

Answers to: "Aside from the purely financial aspects of the stipend, how would you rate these duties as a training experience?" (Asked only of those reporting themselves as having a duty stipend.)

Pre-coded Answer	Per Cent
An unusual opportunity for training in my field	23
A good opportunity for training in my field	49
A fair opportunity for training in my field	23
Irrelevant for training in my field	5
Total	100

N 1,097
NA 27
Inapplicable . . . 1,718
2,842

(c)

Answers to: "Do you have any complaints about your stipend? . . If yes, what complaints do you have?" (Asked only of those reporting themselves as having a duty stipend.)

Answer	Per Cent
No	67
Yes	
Amount of money	29
Too time consuming	3
Duties disliked or irrelevant to training	1
Interpersonal relations	*
Total	100

N 1,080
NA 44
Inapplicable . . 1,718
2,842

* = Less than one-half per cent.

TABLE 6.20
PREFERENCE FOR ASSISTANTSHIP BY CURRENT EMPLOYMENT

Current Employment	Preference for Part-time Work					Total	N
	No	Yes	Type Preferred				
			TA	RA	Other		
None							
Fellows	63	37	15	21	1	100%	(344)
Other	48	52	26	22	4	100%	(433)
Employed, No Duty Stipend							
Full-time job . .	38	62	35	23	4	100%	(486)
Part-time job . .	36	64	35	24	5	100%	(462)
Assistants							
Teaching	38	62	42	18	2	100%	(716)
Research	28	72	17	54	1	100%	(329)

```
                          N . . . . . . . . . . . . . 2,770
                          NA on employment or preference
                                  for part-time work . . .    72
                                                            2,842
```

TABLE 6.21
RATING OF DUTY STIPEND AS A TRAINING OPPORTUNITY
(Per cent rating their assistantship as excellent or good)

	Type of Assistantship	
	Teaching	Research
Control		
Public	69 (470)	78 (166)
Private	74 (228)	67 (84)
Stratum		
I.	74 (200)	82 (76)
II.	70 (314)	68 (132)
III.	69 (184)	81 (42)
Division		
Natural Science	65 (376)	73 (176)
Social Science	73 (105)	78 (65)
Humanities	80 (217)	— (8)
Stage		
I.	71 (176)	74 (53)
II.	69 (154)	67 (61)
III.	72 (240)	77 (78)
IV.	69 (124)	80 (55)

```
Stratum and Control, N . . . .    948
NA . . . . . . . . . . . . . .     13
Students classified as RA's
  who did not define them-
  selves as such . . . . . . .     92
                                 1,053
```

In addition, for the data on division, N = 947; interdivisional = 1; for Stage, N = 941; NA on stage = 7.

TABLE 6.22

COMPLAINTS ABOUT INCOME FROM DUTY STIPEND

(Per cent complaining about amount of money
among duty stipend holders)

	Type of Assistantship	
	Teaching	Research
Control		
Public	33 (465)	18 (164)
Private	34 (223)	34 (82)
Stratum		
I.	35 (199)	23 (73)
II.	30 (308)	26 (131)
III.	35 (181)	17 (42)
Division		
Natural Science	29 (371)	23 (172)
Social Science	33 (103)	23 (65)
Humanities	39 (214)	— (8)
Stage		
I.	26 (173)	11 (53)
II.	33 (150)	26 (57)
III.	37 (240)	26 (78)
IV.	36 (121)	31 (55)

```
For Control and Stratum, N . . . . . .     934
NA or students classified as RA's who
    did not define themselves as such. .   119
                                         1,053
```

In addition, for division, N = 933; Interdivisional = 1;
For Stage, N = 927, NA on Stage = 7.

Table 7.1

NON-DUTY STIPEND AND EMPLOYMENT

(Per cent expecting full-time job, part-time job or duty stipend)

Non-Duty Stipend	Per Cent Expecting Employment	N
None	84	1,360
Scholarship* . . .	83	669
Fellowship** . . .	44	630
All students . .	74	2,659
NA		183
		2,842

*Scholarship = Non-duty stipend worth less than tuition plus $1,000.

**Fellowship = Non-duty stipend worth tuition plus $1,000 or more.

TABLE 7.2
CORRELATES OF EMPLOYMENT, CONTROLLING FOR FELLOWSHIP
(Per cent with a full-time job, part-time job, or assistantship)

(a) Stratum and Control

Fellowship	Stratum	Private	Public
No	I.	74 (328)	82 (250)
	II.	86 (393)	86 (499)
	III.	89 (302)	82 (256)
Yes	I.	34 (141)	52 (73)
	II.	40 (129)	52 (157)
	III.	35 (55)	55 (76)

N 2,659
NA on Stipend or Employment . . . 183
2,842

(b) Division

Fellowship	Natural Science	Social Science	Humanities
No	89 (892)	84 (463)	77 (668)
Yes	46 (368)	39 (123)	44 (138)
Total	76 (1,260)	75 (586)	71 (806)

N 2,652
NA and Inter-divisional . . 190
2,842

TABLE 7.2—Continued

(c) Father's Occupation

Fellowship	Low	High
No	87 (947)	79 (826)
Yes	48 (281)	43 (245)

```
N . . . . . . . . . . . 2,299
NA or uncodeable father's
  occupation . . . . .   360
NA on Stipend or Em-
  ployment . . . . . .   183
                        2,842
```

(d) Stage

Fellowship	Beginning	Advanced
No	72 (1,142)	77 (861)
Yes	38 (263)	49 (351)

```
N . . . . . . . . . . . 2,617
NA on stage . . . . .     42
NA on Stipend or Em-
  ployment . . . . . .   183
                        2,842
```

(e) Family Role

Fellowship	Sex	Single	Married, No Children	Married, Children
No	Female	76 (250)	78 (50)	55 (66)
	Male	83 (798)	86 (380)	94 (463)
Yes	Female	28 (78)	27 (11)	27 (11)
	Male	44 (218)	49 (116)	52 (190)

```
N . . . . . . . . . . . 2,631
NA on Family Role . .     28
NA on Stipend or
  Employment . . . .     183
                        2,842
```

TABLE 7.3
AGE, STAGE, FAMILY ROLE AND FULL-TIME NON-STIPEND WORK
(Per cent with a full-time non-stipend job)

Sex	Age	Stage	Family Role		
			Single	Married, No Children	Married, Children
Males	Under 27	Advanced	3 (208)	2 (129)	23 (57)
		Beginning	7 (456)	12 (149)	25 (85)
	27 or Older	Advanced	14 (227)	12 (154)	38 (335)
		Beginning	22 (169)	33 (89)	45 (196)
Females	Under 27	Advanced	11 (35)	12 (16)	— (4)
		Beginning	12 (187)	21 (29)	0 (11)
	27 or Older	Advanced	15 (72)	0 (11)	15 (27)
		Beginning	34 (47)	40 (10)	15 (34)

```
N . . . . . . . . . . . . . . 2,737
NA on Age, Stage, Family Role    73
NA on Employment . . . . . .     32
                              ------
                               2,842
```

TABLE 7.4
STRATUM, CONTROL, FATHER'S OCCUPATION AND FULL-TIME NON-STIPEND WORK
(Per cent with a full-time job)

Stratum	Father's Occupation					
	Low		High		N.A. and Uncodable	
	Private	Public	Private	Public	Private	Public
I.	14 (167)	9 (153)	5 (255)	6 (144)	4 (53)	15 (40)
II.	39 (296)	11 (341)	26 (183)	6 (269)	31 (77)	5 (101)
III.	46 (194)	14 (168)	45 (136)	9 (125)	49 (43)	6 (65)

```
                    N . . . . . . . . . . . . . 2,810
                    NA on Employment . . . . . .   32
                                                -------
                                                 2,842
```

TABLE 7.5
AGE, FAMILY ROLE, SCHOOL, AND FULL-TIME NON-STIPEND WORK
(Per cent with a full-time non-stipend job)

School Type	Family Role	Age	
		Under 27	27 or Older
Private II-III	Fathers	58 (40)	69 (226)
	Other	20 (340)	35 (315)
Other	Fathers	12 (104)	21 (321)
	Other	3 (889)	9 (544)

```
            N . . . . . . . . . . . . . . 2,779
            NA on Family Role or Age.      31
            NA on Employment . . . .       32
                                         -------
                                          2,842
```

TABLE 7.6

CLASSIFICATION OF FULL-TIME NON-STIPEND JOBS
BY SCHOOL TYPE AND DIVISION

Type of Job	Private II-III Natural Science	Private II-III Social Science	Private II-III Humanities	Other Natural Science	Other Social Science	Other Humanities
College Teaching	13	12	14	31	14	27
Research and Professional Practice in field	73	35	10	54	51	5
Other Professional or Executive work	9	31	19	4	23	19
Primary and Secondary Teaching	4	3	44	6	5	32
Clerical or Blue Collar	1	15	8	4	7	15
Other and uncodeable	1	5	6	4	2	3
*Total	101%	101%	101%	103%	102%	101%
N	139	101	113	54	43	59

```
N . . . . . . . . . . . . . . . .   509
NA on type or job or Interdi-
    visional . . . . . . . . . .     8
Not a full-time worker . . . . 2,325
                                   2,842
```

*Totals are greater than 100 per cent because of rounding and six full-time workers who hold multiple jobs.

TABLE 7.7

INCOME AMONG FULL-TIME WORKERS BY DIVISION AND TYPE OF SCHOOL

(Per cent of full-time workers making $500 per month or more)

Type of School	Division		
	Natural Science	Social Science	Humanities
Private II-III . . .	72 (141)	57 (99)	39 (112)
Other	64 (50)	44 (45)	22 (59)

```
                        N . . . . . . . . . . .  506
                        NA on Employment or
                          Income and Interdi-
                          visional  . . . . . .   11
                        Not a full-time
                          worker . . . . . . . .2,325
                                                2,842
```

TABLE 7.8

ANTICIPATED EMPLOYMENT BY NON-STIPEND EMPLOYMENT, DIVISION, AND SCHOOL TYPE

(Per cent expecting an academic job after completion of graduate study)

Type of School	Division					
	Natural Science		Social Science		Humanities	
	Full-Time Job					
	Yes	No	Yes	No	Yes	No
Private II-III	22 (139)	53 (230)	26 (98)	51 (150)	46 (114)	71 (175)
Other	57 (51)	51 (882)	44 (45)	60 (350)	66 (59)	83 (459)

```
                        N . . . . . . . . . . . . . . . 2,752
                        NA on Employment or Interdivi-
                          sional . . . . . . . . . . .    32
                        NA on Anticipated Employment. .   58
                                                        2,842
```

TABLE 7.9
FACULTY ABILITY RATING BY NON-STIPEND EMPLOYMENT, DIVISION, AND SCHOOL TYPE
(Per cent rated high in pooled rating of "native ability")

Type of School	Division						
	Natural Science		Social Science		Humanities	
	Full-Time Job					
	Yes	No	Yes	No	Yes	No
Private II-III	21 (119)	42 (221)	24 (84)	30 (144)	30 (101)	35 (168)
Other	40 (43)	38 (727)	31 (36)	39 (296)	29 (52)	39 (383)

```
N . . . . . . . . . . . . . . . . . 2,374
NA on Employment or Interdivisional.  32
NA on Native Ability . . . . . . . . 436
                                    2,842
```

TABLE 7.10
PART-TIME EMPLOYMENT, AND INCOME FROM STIPEND, CONTROLLING FOR INCOME FROM FULL-TIME EMPLOYMENT, SPOUSE, AND PARENTS
(Per cent reporting a part-time, non-stipend job)

Income From....		Stipend	
Full-Time Job	Spouse's Job or Parents	Yes	No
Yes	Yes or No	6 (79)	13 (438)
No	Yes	25 (758)	45 (366)
No	No	25 (946)	67 (223)

```
N . . . . . . . . . . . . . . 2,810
NA on Sources of Income .      32
                             2,842
```

TABLE 7.11
PART-TIME EMPLOYMENT BY SCHOOL TYPE, DIVISION, STAGE, AND STIPEND HOLDING
(Per cent with a part-time, non-stipend job, among students with no full-time job)

(a) Over-all

Type of School	Social Science and Humanities — Beginning	Social Science and Humanities — Advanced	Natural Science — Beginning	Natural Science — Advanced
Public	37 (313)	33 (217)	31 (350)	20 (314)
Private I	42 (112)	35 (129)	23 (78)	21 (112)
Private II-III	46 (176)	45 (117)	32 (100)	23 (121)

(b) Among Students With an Assistantship or Fellowship

Type of School	SS&H Beginning	SS&H Advanced	NS Beginning	NS Advanced
Public	27 (175)	30 (178)	24 (255)	18 (281)
Private I	21 (33)	26 (69)	18 (65)	14 (99)
Private II-III	29 (70)	38 (76)	21 (70)	16 (102)

(c) Among Students With Neither an Assistantship Nor Fellowship

Type of School	SS&H Beginning	SS&H Advanced	NS Beginning	NS Advanced
Public	49 (138)	44 (39)	49 (95)	42 (33)
Private I	51 (79)	45 (60)	46 (13)	69 (13)
Private II-III	57 (106)	59 (41)	57 (30)	63 (19)

```
N . . . . . . . . . . . . . . . . . . . . 2,139
   (N's for Tables b and c sum to 2,139)
NA on Stage, Interdivisional, and
   Stipend Holders not included in Stipend
   Typology . . . . . . . . . . . . . . .  154
Full-time Workers or NA on Employment . .  549
                                         2,842
```

TABLE 7.12
SPOUSE'S OCCUPATION BY SEX AND PRESENCE OF CHILDREN

Married Male Students

Spouse's Study	No Children Full-Time	No Children Part-Time	No Children None	No Children Total	Children Full-Time	Children Part-Time	Children None	Children Total
Yes ...	4	7	11	22	1	2	5	8
No ...	59	7	12	78	14	11	67	92
Total	63	14	23	100%	15	13	72	100%
			N = 521				N = 690	

Married Female Students

Spouse's Study	Full-Time	Part-Time	None	Total	Full-Time	Part-Time	None	Total
Yes ..	15	9	28	52	15	8	8	31
No ..	48	0	0	48	68	1	0	69
Total	63	9	28	100%	83	9	8	100%
			N = 67				N = 79	

```
N . . . . . . . . . . . . . . . . 1,357
NA on Spouse's Occupation . . .     10
NA or Single on Family Role
    Index . . . . . . . . . . . 1,475
                                  2,842
```

TABLE 7.13
SPOUSE'S TYPE OF EMPLOYMENT BY STUDENT'S SEX AND PRESENCE OF CHILDREN

	\multicolumn{6}{c}{Student's Sex and Family Role}
	\multicolumn{4}{c}{Male}	\multicolumn{2}{c}{Female}
Type	\multicolumn{2}{c}{No Children}	\multicolumn{2}{c}{Children}	No Children	Children
	Full-Time	Part-Time	Full-Time	Part-Time	Full or Part-Time	Full or Part-Time
High Status	3	1	6	6	57	59
Academic	2	1	3	6	32	21
Professional	1	0	2	0	21	27
Business	*	0	1	0	4	11
Middle Status	58	61	64	51	34	40
Professional	48	53	57	43	28	18
Supervisory	3	0	0	2	4	11
Other	7	8	7	6	2	11
Low Status	39	38	30	43	9	1
Clerical, Sales	39	31	28	29	9	1
Blue Collar, Service	*	7	2	14	0	0
Total	100%	100%	100%	100%	100%	100%
N	327	67	104	87	47	71

```
N . . . . . . . . . . . . . . . . . .  703
Spouse not employed or NA on type
    of employment . . . . . . . . . .  664
NA or single on Family Role . . . .  1,475
                                     ─────
                                     2,842
```

* = Less than one-half per cent.

TABLE 7.14

SOCIO-ECONOMIC STATUS AND WIVES' EMPLOYMENT,
CONTROLLING FOR PRESENCE OR ABSENCE
OF CHILDREN

(Per cent of married men whose spouse is employed)

Occupation of Husband's Father*	Children	No Children
Elite	23 (155)	79 (111)
Middle	26 (359)	78 (272)
Lower	31 (80)	72 (74)

```
N . . . . . . . . . . . . 1,051
NA on Father's Occupa-
    tion . . . . . . . .   164
NA on Spouse's Employ-
    ment . . . . . . . .     6
NA or not a married male
    on Family Role Index 1,621
                         ─────
                         2,842
```

*Categories of the classification are defined in Chapter III.

TABLE 7.15

STIPEND INCOME, INCOME FROM FULL-TIME JOB, AND WIVES' EMPLOYMENT, CONTROLLING FOR CHILDEN

(Per cent among married men whose spouse is employed)

Total Income From Full-Time Job	Children		
	Total Income From Stipends		
	None	Less than $2,000	$2,000 or More
None	42 (85)	39 (130)	26 (207)
Less than $4,500	19 (119)	9 (23)	— (2)
$4,500 or more	6 (94)	0 (11)	— (0)
	No Children		
None	84 (93)	82 (170)	79 (189)
Less than $4,500	50 (42)	— (6)	— (1)
$4,500 or more	40 (10)	— (5)	— (0)

N 1,187
NA on Spouse's Employment,
 Full-time Work, Stipend.   34
NA or Not Married Male on
 Family Role Index 1,621
                          2,842

TABLE 7.16
INCOME SOURCES, PRESENCE OR ABSENCE OF CHILDREN, AND WIFE'S EMPLOYMENT
(Per cent among married men whose spouse is employed)

Income From Full-Time Job	Income From Stipend	Children Yes	Children No
No	No	42 (85)	84 (93)
No	Less than $2,000	39 (130)	82 (170)
No	$2,000 or more	26 (207)	79 (189)
Less than $4,500	Any	18 (144)	51 (49)
$4,500 or more	Any	6 (105)	40 (15)

```
N . . . . . . . . . . . . . . . . . 1,187
NA on Spouse's Employment,
  Full-time Work, Stipend, or
  Income . . . . . . . . . . .        34
NA or Not a Married Male on
  Family Role Index . . . . .     1,621
                                   2,842
```

TABLE 7.17
SEX, EMPLOYMENT, CHILDREN AND SPOUSE'S RESISTANCE TO CONTINUED STUDY
(Per cent reporting spouse would probably or definitely disapprove of two or more further years of study)

Spouse's Employment	Male No Children	Male Children	Female No Children	Female Children
Yes	20 (366)	27 (185)	25 (45)	18 (69)
No	18 (117)	24 (472)	28 (18)	– (6)

```
N . . . . . . . . . . . . . . . . . 1,298
NA on Spouse's Employment . . . . .     9
NA or "Don't Know" on Disapproval .    60
NA or Not Married on Family Role .  1,475
                                    2,842
```

TABLE 7.18

FERTILITY EXPECTATIONS BY SPOUSE'S EMPLOYMENT, SPOUSE'S STUDENT STATUS AND PRESENCE OF CHILDREN AMONG MARRIED MALES

(a) Per Cent Expecting a Child in the Next Two Years

Number of Children Now	Wife's Employment	Wife's Study No	Wife's Study Yes
None	Full-Time	58 (288)	38 (21)
	Part-Time	67 (33)	37 (35)
	None	67 (57)	38 (56)
One	Full-Time	63 (59)	– (3)
	Part-Time	62 (32)	– (8)
	None	65 (172)	53 (17)
Two or More	Full-Time	21 (33)	– (6)
	Part-Time	24 (42)	– (4)
	None	33 (279)	20 (15)

```
N . . . . . . . . . . . . . . . . . . . . . 1,160
NA on Wife's Employment or Children Now or
   Fertility Expectations . . . . . . . . . . .   61
NA or Not a Married Male . . . . . . . . . . . 1,621
                                                2,842
```

(b) Correlation Coefficients (Q)
Between Spouse's Employment, Student Status and Fertility Expectations, Controlled for Number of Children Now

Children	Full-Time Work and Expectations	Study and Expectations
None	-.08	-.43
One	-.06	-.15
Two or More	-.27	-.28

TABLE 7.19

ANSWERS TO THE QUESTION: "WILL YOU RECEIVE ANY FINANCIAL SUPPORT FROM YOUR PARENTS THIS YEAR?"

Category	Per Cent Of Sample			Per Cent Of Students Receiving No Support, but One or Both Parents Living
<u>Yes</u>	23			
<u>No</u>	77			
Neither Parent Living		4		
One or Both Living		73		
Reason for Non-Support				
"I don't need any support from them"			44	61
"They are financially <u>unable</u> to spare any money"			20	28
"I am unwilling to receive support from them"			16	22
"They are unwilling to support my graduate education"			2	3
Other Reasons			2	3
No reason given			1	1
Total	100%	77%	85%*	118%**

N 2,816
NA 26
              2,842

*Sums to more than 77 per cent because of multiple answers.
**Sums to more than 100 per cent because of multiple answers.

TABLE 7.20
AGE, FAMILY ROLE, AND PARENTAL SUPPORT, AMONG STUDENTS WITH ONE OR BOTH PARENTS LIVING

	Males		Females	
Family Role	Age			
	Under 27	27 or Older	Under 27	27 or Older
(a) Per Cent Checking "I don't need any"				
Single	33 (662)	49 (365)	28 (218)	54 (108)
Married, No Children	52 (276)	55 (226)	67 (45)	80 (20)
Married, Children	44 (140)	54 (512)	56 (16)	68 (53)

```
                 N . . . . . . . . . . . . . . . . . 2,641
                 NA on Age or Family Role  . . . . . .    28
                 No Reason, NA or Neither Parent
                    Living, on Parental Aid . . . . . .  173
                                                       2,842
```

(b) Per Cent Receiving Aid From Parents or Spouse's Parents Among Those <u>Not</u> Checking "I don't need any."

Single	60 (444)	35 (186)	54 (157)	36 (50)
Married, No Children	44 (132)	33 (102)	45 (15)	— (4)
Married, Children	62 (78)	41 (235)	— (7)	35 (17)

```
                 N . . . . . . . . . . . . . . . . 1,427
                 "I don't need any"  . . . . . . . . 1,214
                 NA on Age or Family Role  . . . .      28
                 NA, No Reason, or Both Parents
                    Dead, on Parental Aid  . . . .    173
                                                    2,842
```

TABLE 7.21

AGE, FAMILY ROLE, AND AID FROM PARENTS AND SPOUSE'S PARENTS

(Per cent receiving aid among married students not checking "I don't need any" and with one or both parents living)

Age	Children	Aid from Both	Aid from Spouse's Parents Only	Parents Only	Total Spouse's Parents	Total Parents	N
			Males				
Under 27	Yes	18	5	39	23	57	78
Under 27	No	10	8	25	18	35	132
27 or Older	Yes	9	11	22	20	31	102
27 or Older	No	9	4	20	13	29	235
			Females				
Under 27		27	10	18	37	45	22
27 or Older		0	10	14	10	14	21

```
N . . . . . . . . . . . . . . . . . . . . .    590
Single . . . . . . . . . . . . . . . . . .    837
"I don't need any" . . . . . . . . . . . .  1,214
NA on Age or Family Role . . . . . . . . .     28
NA, No Reason, or Both Parents Dead, on
  Parental Aid . . . . . . . . . . . . . .    173
                                             2,842
```

TABLE 7.22

FULL-TIME EMPLOYMENT, SPOUSE'S EMPLOYMENT, STIPEND, SEX AND PARENTAL AID

Full-Time Employment	Spouse's Employment	Fellowship, or Assistantship	Per Cent "No Need" Male	"No Need" Female	Receiving Aid Male	Receiving Aid Female	Other Male	Other Female
Yes	Yes or No	Yes or No	69	67	7 (397)	6 (69)	24	27
No	Yes	Yes	50	72	20 (353)	12 (49)	30	16
No	Yes	No	45	62	28 (147)	16 (55)	27	22
No	No	Yes	43	43	27 (869)	25 (164)	30	32
No	No	No	26	21	48 (416)	49 (124)	26	30

```
N . . . . . . . . . . . . . . . . . .  2,643
Neither Parent Living, NA or No
  Reason on Parental Aid, NA on
  Income Sources . . . . . . . .          199
                                         2,842
```

*Base N's same as "Receiving Aid" columns.
**From parents or spouse's parents.

TABLE 7.23
FATHER'S OCCUPATION, ORIENTATION TO COLLEGE, AND PARENTAL AID

(a) Per Cent Receiving Aid From Parents Among Students <u>Not</u> Checking "I don't need any," for Students With One or Both Parents Living

Orientation	Father's Occupation*			
	Low Status, Respectable Working Class	Working Class Elite, Bottom Middle	Middle-Middle	Elite
"Naturally assumed the children would go to college"	35 (76)	50 (214)	55 (282)	64 (252)
"Wasn't assumed that all would go"	26 (138)	27 (154)	38 (74)	54 (28)
"Wasn't assumed that any would go"	18 (74)	18 (55)	— (5)	— (1)

(b) Per Cent "Naturally Assumed..."

Father's Occupation	Per Cent	N
Low Status, Respectable Working Class	26	288
Working Class Elite, Bottom Middle	51	423
Middle-Middle	78	361
Elite	90	281

N	1,353
"I don't need any"	1,121
NA on Father's Occupation	207
NA on Orientation or Aid	43
Neither Parent Living	118
	2,842

*Categories of Status Code are defined in Chapter III.

TABLE 7.24
FULL-TIME WORK, SPOUSE'S JOB, STIPEND, FATHER'S OCCUPATION, FAMILY ORIENTATION, SIBLINGS, AND AID FROM PARENTS
(Per cent receiving financial support from parents among those with one or both parents living)

Full-time Job	Spouse's Job	Fellowship or Assistantship	Parental Socio-Economic Index*					
			Low		Middle		High	
			Siblings					
			2+	0-1	2+	0-1	2+	0-1
No	No	No	29 (89)	30 (47)	33 (52)	54 (80)	49 (79)	66 (124)
No	No	Yes	13 (166)	17 (98)	22 (122)	32 (148)	30 (164)	35 (201)
No	Yes	No	5 (21)	18 (17)	12 (32)	25 (32)	21 (34)	45 (42)
No	Yes	Yes	9 (74)	12 (42)	9 (47)	15 (80)	16 (55)	31 (70)
Yes	-	-	2 (106)	1 (78)	3 (36)	5 (56)	10 (40)	7 (59)

```
N . . . . . . . . . . . . . . . . . . .   2,291
NA on Father's Occupation . . . . . .       216
NA on Orientation, Siblings, Parental
  Aid, Income Sources . . . . . . . .       217
Neither Parent Living . . . . . . . .       118
                                          ─────
                                          2,842
```

*High = middle-middle or elite, "naturally assumed."

Middle = middle-middle or elite, "wasn't assumed"
  or
  working class, bottom middle, low status, "naturally assumed."

Low = working class, bottom middle, low status, "wasn't assumed."

TABLE 7.25
DISTRIBUTIONS OF SAVINGS AND BORROWING

(a) Expected Borrowing and Non-Durable Debt

Amount of Non-Durable Debt
(Per Cent Expecting to Borrow)

$100 or More	Less than $100	All Students
27 (546)	5 (2,241)	9 (2,787)

N 2,787
NA on Borrowing or Debt . 55
                          2,842

(b) Simultaneous Distribution by Debt and Borrowing

		Non-Durable Debt of $100 or More		
		Yes	No	Total
Expect to Borrow	Yes	5	4	9
	No	14	77	91
		19	81	100%

N 2,787
NA on Borrowing or Debt. 55
                          2,842

(c) Savings Available at Beginning of Term

Amount	Per Cent
$1,500 or more	22
$500 - $1,499	25
$1 - $499	29
None	24
Total	100

N 2,705
NA   137
                          2,842

TABLE 7.26
STRATUM, CONTROL, DIVISION, AND DEBT AND SAVINGS

Stratum	Private Natural Science	Private Social Science	Private Humanities	Public Natural Science	Public Social Science	Public Humanities
\multicolumn{7}{c}{(a) Per Cent "Debtors"}
I.	20 (199)	26 (89)	26 (190)	21 (155)	25 (81)	27 (101)
II.	19 (222)	31 (148)	16 (190)	22 (396)	32 (158)	27 (158)
III.	15 (157)	24 (109)	16 (115)	20 (198)	39 (75)	28 (86)

```
N . . . . . . . . . . . . . . . . 2,827
Interdivisional, NA on Debt . . .   15
                                  ─────
                                  2,842
```

Stratum	Private Natural Science	Private Social Science	Private Humanities	Public Natural Science	Public Social Science	Public Humanities
\multicolumn{7}{c}{(b) Per Cent With $500 or More in Savings}
I.	56 (196)	59 (85)	54 (181)	55 (154)	57 (77)	43 (99)
II.	48 (209)	46 (139)	45 (168)	42 (388)	43 (156)	39 (154)
III.	53 (144)	54 (102)	49 (95)	46 (192)	36 (74)	37 (84)

```
N . . . . . . . . . . . . . . . . 2,697
Interdivisional . . . . . . . . .     8
NA on Savings . . . . . . . . . .   137
                                  ─────
                                  2,842
```

TABLE 7.27
AGE, FAMILY ROLE, AND DEBT AND SAVINGS

Family Role	Males		Females	
	Under 27	27 or Older	Under 27	27 or Older
(a) Per Cent "Debtors"				
Single	21 (668)	23 (410)	25 (224)	11 (137)
Married, No Children . . .	20 (279)	24 (246)	24 (45)	29 (21)
Married, Children.	30 (144)	28 (550)	19 (16)	19 (63)

```
                           N . . . . . . . . . . . . . . . .  2,803
                           NA on Age or Family Role . . . . .     32
                           NA on Debt                              7
                                                              -------
                                                               2,842
```

	(b) Per Cent With $500 or More in Savings			
Single	43 (652)	46 (380)	37 (216)	42 (105)
Married, No Children . . .	56 (277)	56 (235)	47 (45)	40 (20)
Married, Children.	50 (143)	52 (536)	53 (15)	38 (50)

```
                           N . . . . . . . . . . . . . . . .  2,674
                           NA on Age or Family Role . . . . .     31
                           NA on Savings . . . . . . . . . .    137
                                                              -------
                                                               2,842
```

TABLE 7.28
AGE, STAGE, AND DEBT AND SAVINGS

Age	Stage			
	I.	II.	III.	IV.
(a) Per Cent "Debtors"				
20-23	21 (400)	22 (132)	14 (59)	14 (21)
24-26	28 (183)	27 (205)	21 (226)	21 (145)
27-29	21 (124)	24 (161)	32 (220)	31 (143)
30 or older	16 (113)	20 (169)	21 (286)	27 (196)

N 2,783
NA on Age or Stage 52
NA on Debt 7
                                2,842

(b) Per Cent With $500 or More in Savings				
20-23	50 (387)	32 (129)	34 (59)	45 (20)
24-26	51 (179)	41 (203)	48 (221)	48 (145)
27-29	47 (120)	45 (150)	45 (212)	49 (140)
30 or older	60 (102)	47 (146)	55 (265)	49 (182)

N 2,660
NA on Age or Stage 45
NA on Savings 137
                                2,842

TABLE 7.29
FATHER'S OCCUPATION, DEBT, AND SAVINGS

Father's Occupation*	Per Cent "Debtors"	N	Per Cent With $500 or More in Savings	N
Elite	20	(453)	52	(432)
Middle-Middle	23	(664)	50	(639)
Working Class Elite Bottom Middle	23	(774)	47	(739)
Respectable Working Class	25	(395)	48	(384)
Low Status	30	(165)	41	(154)

N	2,451		N	2,348
NA on Father's Occupation	384		NA on Father's Occupation	357
NA on Debt	7		NA on Savings	137
	2,842			2,842

*Categories of Status Code are defined in Chapter III.

TABLE 8.1

DISTRIBUTION OF ANSWERS TO THE QUESTION,
"HOW MUCH DO YOU WORRY ABOUT YOUR
IMMEDIATE FINANCIAL SITUATION?"

Answer	Per Cent
It's my most serious problem right now	8
I worry about it a lot, but it isn't my most serious problem	23
I'm not very worried about it	53
I'm pleased with it	16
Total	100

N 2,806
NA   36
          2,842

TABLE 8.2

FINANCIAL WORRY, ACADEMIC WORRY, MARITAL STATUS, PEER GROUP MEMBERSHIP, AND MORALE

(Per cent low on morale index)

Concern About Grades[a]	Married	Peer Group Member[b]	Financial Worry[c] Low	Financial Worry[c] High
High	No	No	53 (95)	71 (45)
High	No	Yes	47 (88)	60 (54)
High	Yes	No	41 (69)	60 (56)
High	Yes	Yes	35 (60)	50 (48)
Low	No	No	38 (193)	54 (66)
Low	No	Yes	36 (212)	51 (82)
Low	Yes	No	29 (204)	45 (103)
Low	Yes	Yes	23 (212)	45 (88)

```
N . . . . . . . . . . . . . . . . . 1,675
NA on Concerns About Grades[d] . . .  570
NA on Family Role, Peer Group
   Membership, or Financial Worry .  558
NA on Esprit . . . . . . . . . . .    39
                                    2,842
```

[a] High = Very or Fairly Dissatisfied; Low = Very or Fairly Satisfied.

[b] Students were asked about the existence of informal groups in their department. "Yes" means students who say such groups exist and they are members, "No" means either students who say no groups exist or that they are not members.

[c] High = "Most serious problem" or "Worry about it a lot"; Low = "Not very worried" or "Pleased."

[d] The high NA on Concerns About Grades stems from 519 students who checked "This is my first term here so I have no idea."

TABLE 8.3
FAMILY ROLE AND FINANCIAL WORRY
(Per cent worried)

Sex	Single	Married, No children	Married, Children
Women	25 (346)	30 (66)	29 (77)
Men	30 (1,073)	29 (524)	39 (692)

```
           N . . . . . . . . . .  2,778
           NA on Family Role .       28
           NA on Worry . . . .       36
                                  2,842
```

TABLE 8.4
AGE, ACADEMIC STAGE AND FINANCIAL WORRY
(Per cent worried)

Age	Beginning	Advanced
Under 27	32 (915)	27 (450)
27 or Older . .	33 (554)	33 (839)

Stage shown above columns Beginning and Advanced.

```
           N   . . . . . . . . . .  2,758
           NA on Age or Stage . .      48
           NA on Worry . . . . . .     36
                                    2,842
```

TABLE 8.5
DIVISION AND FINANCIAL WORRY
(Per cent worried)

Division	Per Cent	N
Natural Science	28	1,324
Social Science	33	654
Humanities	36	820

N 2,798
Interdivisional . 8
NA on Worry . . . 36
2,842

TABLE 8.6
STRATUM, CONTROL, AND FINANCIAL WORRY
(Per cent worried)

Stratum	Natural Science Private	Natural Science Public	Social Science and Humanities Private	Social Science and Humanities Public
I.	26 (199)	22 (155)	36 (277)	32 (180)
II.	25 (219)	31 (396)	31 (333)	38 (314)
III.	23 (157)	34 (198)	31 (210)	45 (160)

N 2,798
Interdivisional . 8
NA on Worry . . . 36
2,842

TABLE 8.7
STIPEND HOLDING AND FINANCIAL WORRY
(Per cent worried)

Duty Stipend*	Non-Duty Stipend*		
	None	Low	High
None	35 (842)	33 (336)	22 (425)
Research Assistant	31 (150)	24 (86)	26 (97)
Teaching Assistant	36 (374)	35 (247)	36 (99)

```
N . . . . . . . . . . . . . . . . . . . 2,656
NA, RA-TA, Trainees, or Ambiguous
  on Stipend Typology . . . . . . .    153
NA on Worry . . . . . . . . . . . .     33
                                      2,842
```

*This classification is defined in Chapter VI.

TABLE 8.8
FATHER'S OCCUPATION AND FINANCIAL WORRY
(Per cent worried)

Father's Occupation*	Per cent	N
Elite	26	450
Middle-Middle	29	663
Working Class Elite Lower Middle	34	763
Respectable Working Class	32	392
Low Status	36	159

```
N . . . . . . . . . . . . . . . 2,427
NA on Father's Occupation .     379
NA on Worry . . . . . . . .      36
                               2,842
```

*This measure is defined in Chapter III.

TABLE 8.9

PERCEIVED ADEQUACY OF INCOME, SAVINGS, NON-DURABLE DEBT, DURABLE DEBT, AND FINANCIAL WORRY

(Per cent worried)

Perceived Adequacy of Income[a]	Savings	Durable Debt[b] Less than $500 Non-Durable Debt[c] Less than $100	$100 or More	Durable Debt[b] $500 or More Non-Durable Debt[c] Less than $100	$100 or More
Low	Less than $500	75 (126)	83 (18)	84 (135)	86 (22)
	$500 or More	67 (90)	- (7)	75 (32)	- (5)
High	Less than $500	24 (707)	37 (115)	45 (229)	52 (42)
	$500 or More	15 (936)	19 (132)	28 (67)	8 (12)

```
                    N . . . . . . . . . . . . . . . . . 2,675
                    NA on Adequacy, Savings or Debt . . .  131
                    NA on Worry . . . . . . . . . . . .     36
                                                         2,842
```

[a] Based on answers to the question, "Which of the following best describes your financial situation this academic year?" Low = "It's doubtful that I'll have enough money to cover my necessary expenses," and "I'm not sure whether I'll have enough money to cover my necessary expenses"; High = "I'll have enough money for my necessary expenses, but nothing left over for emergencies," and "I'll have enough money for my necessary expenses and enough left over for emergencies."

[b] Durable debt is defined as money owed for purchases with some re-sale value, e.g., automobile, house mortgage, life insurance, etc.

[c] Non-Durable Debt is defined as money owed and spent for purposes with no re-sale value, e.g., medical bills, living expenses.

TABLE 8.10

RELATIVE DEPRIVATION, PERCEIVED ADEQUACY,
AND FINANCIAL WORRY

(Per cent worried)

Financial Situation Compared With Other Graduate Students	Perceived Adequacy		
	Enough Left Over For Emergencies	Enough, but Nothing Left Over	Doubtful or Not Sure There Will Be Enough
Much better	6 (565)	26 (65)	57 (14)
Slightly better	12 (461)	33 (179)	75 (40)
Same	18 (355)	42 (438)	68 (158)
Slightly or Much Worse	47 (45)	56 (126)	88 (196)

```
N . . . . . . . . . . . . . . . . . . 2,642
NA on Worry or Perceived Adequacy . .   19
NA on Relative Standing . . . . . . .  181
                                      2,842
```

TABLE 8.11

SOURCES OF INCOME AND FINANCIAL WORRY

(Per cent worried)

Employment	Full-Time Job	Part-Time Job	Duty Stipend	Fellowship	Per cent	N
Full-time	Yes	-	-	-	28	(512)
Less than Full-time	No	Yes	Yes	-	38	(264)
	No	Yes	No	-	49	(425)
	No	No	Yes	-	32	(726)
None	No	No	No	No	26	(384)
	No	No	No	Yes	18	(331)

```
              N . . . . . . . . . . 2,642
              NA on Work Index . . .  164
              NA on Worry Now  . . .   36
                                     2,842
```

TABLE 8.12

EMPLOYMENT, ADEQUACY AND RELATIVE DEPRIVATION

Employment	Per Cent	N
(a) Per Cent Expecting "Enough Left Over for Emergencies"		
Full-time	71	(512)
None	59	(716)
Part-time or Duty Stipend	44	(1,410)

$$N \ldots 2{,}638$$
$$\text{NA on Work or Adequacy} \ldots \underline{204}$$
$$2{,}842$$

Employment	Per Cent	N
(b) Per Cent Checking "Much Better" or "Slightly Better"		
Full-time	69	(478)
None	58	(670)
Part-time or Duty Stipend	39	(1,352)

$$N \ldots 2{,}500$$
$$\text{NA on Work or Relative Deprivation} \ldots \underline{342}$$
$$2{,}842$$

TABLE 8.13
EMPLOYMENT, PERCEIVED ADEQUACY, RELATIVE DEPRIVATION AND FINANCIAL WORRY

Relative Standing	Perceived Adequacy — More Than Enough	Perceived Adequacy — Enough or Less Than Enough	Total
(a) Q Association Between Full-Time Employment (Versus Part-Time or Assistantship) and Worry[a]			
Better	+.058 (282-374)	+.320 (48-156)	-.028 (330- 530)
Same or Worse	-.093 (60-229)	+.199 (86-589)	-.016 (146- 872)
Total	-.099 (342-603)	+.172 (134-745)	-.236 (476-1,348)
(b) Q Association Between Part-Time or Assistantship Employment (Versus No Employment) and Worry[a]			
Better	+.273 (374-306)	+.188 (156- 75)	+.307 (530-381)
Same or Worse	+.190 (229- 94)	+.258 (589-187)	+.255 (818-281)
Total	+.308 (603-400)	+.265 (745-262)	+.363 (1,348-662)

[a]Tables are to be read as follows: In the lower right hand corner is the association for the entire sample (i.e., the association between part-time employment and worry for the total sample is -.236), the other coefficients are the partial relationships for other sub-groups (e.g., in Table (a), among those answering "Better" regardless of their perceived adequacy, Q = -.028; among those answering "Better" and also 'More than enough," Q = +.058).

In Table (a) the first N in parentheses is the number of full-time workers, the second, the number of part-time workers or assistants. In Table (b) the first number is the number of part-time workers or assistants, the second is the number of non-workers.

TABLE 8.14
EMPLOYMENT, PERCEIVED ADEQUACY, RELATIVE DEPRIVATION AND FINANCIAL WORRY
(Per cent worried)

Perceived Adequacy	Financial Situation Compared with Other Graduate Students					
	Better		Same		Worse	
	Employed					
	No	Yes	No	Yes	No	Yes
Doubtful or Not sure . .	67 (12)	74 (38)	47 (32)	76 (118)	81 (37)	88 (149)
Enough, but nothing left over	22 (63)	34 (166)	35 (99)	44 (306)	47 (19)	61 (102)
Enough left over for emergencies	6 (306)	10 (656)	14 (86)	20 (255)	- (8)	44 (34)

```
N . . . . . . . . . . . . . . . . . . . . . . . 2,486
NA on Adequacy or Relative Deprivation or Work .  320
NA on Worry Now . . . . . . . . . . . . . . .     36
                                                2,842
```

TABLE 8.15
RATINGS OF OCCUPATIONAL VALUES
(Per cent indorsing)

Item (Where wording of original Rosenberg items differs from that used in the survey, the original is given in parentheses.)	Graduate Students[*]	Undergraduates[**]
Opportunity to use my special aptitudes and abilities	94	78
Opportunity to be creative and original	80	48
Freedom from pressures to conform in my personal life	70	not asked
An opportunity to be helpful to others	67	43
A chance to earn enough money to live comfortably (A chance to earn a good deal of money)	64	39
An opportunity to be useful to society in general	64	not asked
A stable secure future	58	61
Opportunities to work with people (An opportunity to work with people rather than things)	54	44
A chance to receive recognition from others in my profession	46	not asked
Freedom from supervision (Leave me relatively free of supervision by others)	46	38
A chance to exercise leadership	39	32
Social standing and prestige in my community (Give me social status and prestige)	26	26

[*] = Per cent checking the item as "Extremely" or "Very Important" as opposed to "Somewhat Important" or "Not Important"; N's range from 2,817 to 2,830 depending on number of NA's.

[**] = Per cent checking "Highly Important" as opposed to "Medium Importance," "Little or No Importance," "Irrelevant" or "Distasteful." N = 4,585.

Data taken from Morris Rosenberg, *Occupations and Values* (Glencoe, Ill., Free Press, 1957), Table 1, p. 12.

TABLE 8.16
ANTICIPATED STARTING SALARY (ANNUAL INCOME FROM ALL SOURCES)

Amount	Per Cent	Cumulative
Less than $4,000	8	8
$4,000 - $4,999	26	34
$5,000 - $5,999	28	62
$6,000 - $6,999	18	80
$7,000 - $8,999	15	95
$9,000 or more	5	-
Total	100%	

N 2,618
NA . . . 224
2,842

TABLE 8.17
EXPECTED STARTING SALARY BY SEX, CAREER PLANS, DIVISION, DEGREE SOUGHT, AND PH.D. PLANS
(Per cent expecting $5,000 a year or more)

Sex	Degree Sought*	Ph.D. Plans**	Academic Humanities	Academic Social Science	Academic Natural Science	Non-Academic Humanities	Non-Academic Social Science	Non-Academic Natural Science
Male	Ph.D.	-	52 (236)	72 (163)	84 (346)	43 (23)	79 (92)	96 (288)
Male	Master's	Yes	37 (111)	58 (72)	74 (101)	50 (12)	94 (31)	90 (71)
Male	Master's	No	37 (75)	48 (25)	70 (50)	39 (70)	61 (98)	81 (220)
Female	Ph.D.	-	31 (52)	56 (25)	64 (45)	- (7)	79 (29)	79 (14)
Female	Master's	Yes	23 (22)	69 (13)	- (8)	- (2)	- (5)	- (5)
Female	Master's	No	17 (48)	- (8)	47 (19)	12 (50)	50 (26)	53 (38)

N 2,500
NA on Sex, Degree Sought, Ph.D. Plans, Career Plans,
Division, or Interdivisional 118
NA on Starting Salary 224
2,842

*Degree for which student is now working.

**Answers to "What are your eventual plans concerning the doctoral degree?" Yes = "I definitely plan to get a doctorate"; No = all other answers.

TABLE 8.18
SEX, CAREER PLANS, DIVISION AND SALARY EXPECTATIONS

(a) Mean Annual Income Predicted

Sex	Career Plans	Division	Starting Salary	After 5 Years	Age 45
Male	Non-Academic	Natural Science	$6,903 (581)	$9,258 (570)	$13,176 (556)
		Social Science	$5,769 (222)	$8,254 (222)	$12,622 (217)
		Humanities	$4,669 (105)	$6,229 (104)	$9,508 (100)
	Academic	Natural Science	$5,755 (498)	$7,556 (482)	$9,912 (472)
		Social Science	$5,246 (260)	$7,141 (257)	$10,027 (252)
		Humanities	$4,659 (423)	$6,110 (415)	$8,598 (405)
Female	Non-Academic	Natural Science	$5,211 (57)	$6,763 (52)	$8,342 (40)
		Social Science	$5,356 (61)	$7,117 (60)	$7,946 (54)
		Humanities	$3,944 (59)	$5,076 (55)	$6,552 (40)
	Academic	Natural Science	$4,733 (72)	$6,256 (71)	$7,100 (62)
		Social Science	$4,796 (46)	$6,458 (45)	$7,834 (41)
		Humanities	$4,267 (122)	$5,397 (116)	$6,957 (102)

N 2,506	2,449	2,341
NA on Sex, Career Plans, Division or Interdivisional . 156	156	156
NA on Salary 180	237	345
Total 2,842	2,842	2,842

TABLE 8.18—Continued

(b) Expectation as a Per Cent of Starting Salary in Table 8.18a

Sex	Career Plans	Division	After 5 Years	Age 45
Male	Non-Academic	Natural Science	134	191
		Social Science	143	219
		Humanities	133	204
	Academic	Natural Science	131	172
		Social Science	136	191
		Humanities	131	185
Female	Non-Academic	Natural Science	130	160
		Social Science	133	148
		Humanities	129	167
	Academic	Natural Science	132	150
		Social Science	135	163
		Humanities	126	163

TABLE 8.19

CURRENT INCOME, EXPECTED STARTING SALARY AND
ESTIMATED LENGTH OF TIME FOR COMPLETING PH.D.

(Per cent expecting to complete the Ph.D. in 5 years
or less from date of beginning graduate study,
among Ph.D. candidates)

Total Income for Academic Year	Expected Starting Salary		
	Less than $5,000	$5,000 to $6,999	$7,000 or More
$4,500 or more	31 (113)	41 (223)	48 (163)
$2,700 - $4,499	36 (108)	55 (213)	63 (112)
Less than $2,700	57 (92)	65 (172)	74 (80)

```
N . . . . . . . . . . . . . . . . . . . . . . . . . 1,276
NA on Income, Starting Salary or Degree Time .  159
NA or Not a Ph.D. Candidate on Degree Status . 1,407
                                                2,842
```

TABLE 8.20

ABILITY RATING, ECONOMIC OPPORTUNITY STRUCTURE AND
TIME FOR COMPLETION OF THE PH.D.

(Per cent expecting to complete the Ph.D. in 5 years
or less from date of beginning graduate study,
among Ph.D. candidates)

Economic Opportunity Structure			Faculty Rating of Native Ability*		
Current Income	Starting Salary		High	Middle	Low
Less than $3,600	$5,000 or more	Plus	69 (154)	63 (126)	57 (70)
Less than $3,600 (or) $3,600 or more	Less than $5,000 $5,000 or more	Zero	53 (288)	37 (212)	43 (92)
$3,600 or more	Less than $5,000	Minus	30 (64)	22 (49)	29 (28)

```
N . . . . . . . . . . . . . . . . . . . . . . . . . . . . . 1,083
NA on Ability, Income, Starting Salary, or Time . . . . . . .  352
NA or Not a Ph.D. Candidate on Degree Status  . . . . . . . 1,407
                                                            2,842
```

*This index has been explained in Chapter VI.

TABLE 8.21

DIVISION, ECONOMIC OPPORTUNITY STRUCTURE AND TIME
FOR COMPLETION OF THE PH.D.

(Per cent expecting to finish in five years or less)

Opportunity Structure	Division		
	Natural Science	Social Science	Humanities
Plus	74 (269)	53 (83)	48 (63)
Zero	50 (359)	47 (175)	42 (157)
Minus	38 (40)	33 (45)	27 (82)

```
N . . . . . . . . . . . . . . . . . . . . . . . 1,273
NA on Opportunity Structure or Time or Inter-
    divisional . . . . . . . . . . . . . . . . .   162
NA or Not a Ph.D. Candidate on Degree Status . 1,407
                                                 2,842
```

TABLE 8.22

CAREER PLANS, ECONOMIC OPPORTUNITY STRUCTURE
AND TIME FOR COMPLETION OF THE PH.D.

(Per cent expecting to finish in five years or less)

Opportunity Structure	Expected Job	
	Academic	Non-Academic
Plus	62 (247)	73 (157)
Zero	48 (442)	47 (233)
Minus	33 (133)	19 (31)

```
N . . . . . . . . . . . . . . . . 1,243
NA on Opportunity Structure or
    Time or Expected Job . . . .   192
NA or Not a Ph.D. Candidate on
    Degree Status . . . . . . . . 1,407
                                   2,842
```

TABLE 8.23

STRATUM OF SCHOOL, ECONOMIC OPPORTUNITY STRUCTURE AND TIME FOR COMPLETION OF THE PH.D.

(Per cent expecting to finish in five years or less)

Opportunity Structure	Stratum I	Stratum II	Stratum III
Plus	68 (160)	62 (179)	69 (77)
Zero	54 (223)	47 (328)	38 (142)
Minus	40 (60)	31 (81)	12 (26)

```
N . . . . . . . . . . . . . . . . . . . . . . 1,276
NA on Opportunity Structure or Time .     159
NA or Not a Ph.D. Candidate on
   Degree Status . . . . . . . . . . . . 1,407
                                          2,842
```

TABLE 8.24

FAMILY ROLE, ECONOMIC OPPORTUNITY STRUCTURE AND TIME FOR COMPLETION OF THE PH.D.

(Per cent expecting to finish in five years or less)

Opportunity Structure	Men — Single	Men — Married, No Children	Men — Married, Children	Women — Single	Women — Married
Plus	71 (262)	69 (42)	59 (64)	50 (38)	– (6)
Zero	54 (158)	60 (199)	35 (254)	48 (48)	43 (28)
Minus	36 (22)	40 (53)	20 (59)	– (7)	35 (23)

```
N . . . . . . . . . . . . . . . . . . . . . . . . . . . 1,263
NA on Opportunity Structure, Years, or Family
   Role . . . . . . . . . . . . . . . . . . .           172
NA or Not a Ph.D. Candidate on Degree Status . 1,407
                                                      2,842
```

TABLE 8.25

EMPLOYMENT, ECONOMIC OPPORTUNITY STRUCTURE AND
TIME FOR COMPLETION OF THE PH.D.

(Per cent expecting to finish in five years or less)

Opportunity Structure	Employment Status		
	Full-Time Workers	Part-Time or Duty Stipend	Not Employed
Plus	– (6)	67 (287)	65 (123)
Zero	23 (137)	55 (413)	50 (143)
Minus	10 (61)	46 (76)	37 (30)

```
N . . . . . . . . . . . . . . . . . . . . . 1,276
NA on Opportunity Structure, Employment,
   or Time . . . . . . . . . . . . . . . . .   159
NA or Not a Ph.D. Candidate on Degree Status. 1,407
                                              2,842
```

TABLE 8.26

TRANSFER STATUS, ECONOMIC OPPORTUNITY STRUCTURE
AND TIME FOR COMPLETION OF THE PH.D.

(Per cent expecting to finish in five years or less)

Opportunity Structure	Number of Graduate Schools Attended	
	One	Two or More
Plus	82 (256)	39 (160)
Zero	63 (395)	28 (296)
Minus	43 (82)	20 (85)

```
N . . . . . . . . . . . . . . . . . . 1,274
NA on Opportunity Structure, Time,
   or Transfer Status . . . . . . . .   161
NA or Not a Ph.D. Candidate on
   Degree Status . . . . . . . . . . . 1,407
                                       2,842
```

TABLE 8.27*

TYPE OF EMPLOYMENT, STIPEND, TRANSFER STATUS AND TIME FOR COMPLETION OF THE PH.D.

(Per cent expecting to finish in five years or less)

| | One Graduate School Only || Two or More Graduate Schools ||
| Employment | Assistantship or Fellowship || Assistantship or Fellowship ||
	No	Yes	No	Yes
Full-Time	32 (97)	-	9 (124)	-
Part-Time	59 (100)	73 (342)	31 (62)	41 (237)
None	68 (80)	80 (106)	21 (70)	28 (81)

```
N . . . . . . . . . . . . . . . . . . . . . . . . . 1,299
NA on Stipend, Employment, Transfer Status or Time . .   136
NA or Not a Ph.D. Candidate on Degree Status  . . . . . 1,407
                                                        2,842
```

*NOTE: The above table was actually defined by residual sorting rather than cross-tabulations. The definitions of the various categories are as follows:

(a) Full-time No--Full-time workers, regardless of stipend status or additional part-time job.

(b) Part-Time No--Non-full-time workers, with a part-time job and no duty stipend or fellowship.

(c) None No--Non-workers with no duty stipend or fellowship.

(d) Part-time Yes--Non-full-time workers with a duty stipend, regardless of additional part-time work or non-duty stipend.

(e) None Yes--Non-workers with a fellowship.

TABLE 9.1

FOLLOW-UP STATUS OF THE SAMPLE ONE YEAR AFTER THE ORIGINAL SURVEY

(a) General

Outcome	Per Cent	N
In School*		
Same School and Field of Study	59	1,666
Change in School or Field	7	179
Disappeared**	6	176
Out of School	28	785
Total	100%	2,806

```
              N . . . . . . . . . . . . . 2,806
              NA . . . . . . . . . . . .    36
                                          2,842
```

(b) Status of Those in School

Field of Study	Institution Same	Institution Different	Total
Same	90	6	96
Different	3	1	4
Total	93	7	100%

N = 1,845

(c) Occupation of Those out of School

Occupation	Per Cent
Academic Job (research or teaching for a university or college)	39
Non-Academic Research	15
Primary or Secondary Teaching	12
Other employment	25
Not in Labor Force	9
Total	100

```
                  N . . . . . . . 694
                  NA on Occupation  91
                                   785
```

*Includes a small number of Post-doctoral Fellows.

**Students no longer registered, for whom faculty informants were found, but informants knew nothing about current activities.

TABLE 9.2
STAGE OF STUDY AND OUTCOME

Status Fall, 1959	\multicolumn{4}{c}{Stage of Study and Outcome}
	I.	II.	III.	IV.
In School				
Same Institution and Field of Study	60	50	73	53
Shift in Institution or Field	9	8	4	4
Out or Disappeared				
Received Ph.D.	0	0	2	17
Terminal M.A.*	1	4	0	0
Other	30	38	21	26
Total	100%	100%	100%	100%
N	814	654	787	504
NA	9	18	5	3

```
Total N . . . . . . . . . . . . . . 2,759
NA on Outcome . . . . . . . . . . .    35
NA on Stage . . . . . . . . . . . .    48
                                    ------
                                     2,842
```

* Terminal M.A. is defined as a student who in the 1958-1959 questionnaire did not check "I definitely plan to get the Ph.D." It is thus subjectively defined and does not necessarily correspond to the faculty evaluation of the master's degree awarded.

TABLE 9.3
STAGE, FACULTY RATING OF NATIVE ABILITY, AND DROP OUT
(Per cent dropping out*)

Faculty Ability Rating**	Beginning (I-II)	Advanced (III-IV)	Total
High	21 (316)	22 (460)	21 (776)
Middle	29 (370)	27 (365)	28 (735)
Low	41 (521)	37 (184)	40 (705)
Total	32 (1,207)	27 (1,009)	
Per Cent High and Middle	57 (1,207)	82 (1,009)	

```
N . . . . . . . . . . . . . . 2,216
NA on Ability or Stage. . . .   423
NA or Graduated on Outcome. .   203
                              ─────
                              2,842
```

*A Drop Out is defined as a student known to be out of school in 1959, except for: (a) those awarded the Ph.D. and (b) those awarded the master's degree who had not checked "I definitely plan to get the Ph.D." Students who "disappeared" are excluded from the tabulations.

**The faculty rating of native ability is described in detail in Chapter VI.

TABLE 9.4

GRADE POINT AVERAGE, FACULTY ABILITY RATING
AND DROP OUT

(Per cent dropping out)

Grade Point Average*	Faculty Ability Rating	
	High and Medium	Low
4.00	26 (259)	15 (26)
3.00–3.99	20 (989)	36 (396)
2.00–2.99	21 (107)	33 (197)
Less than 2.00	– (9)	71 (34)

```
N . . . . . . . . . . . . . . . 2,017
NA on Grades  . . . . . . .  229
NA on Ability . . . . . . .  393
NA or Graduated on Outcome.  203
                             2,842
```

*A = 4.0, B = 3.0, C = 2.0

TABLE 9.5

FACULTY RATING OF RESEARCH PRODUCTION, FACULTY
ABILITY RATING, AND DROP OUT

(Per cent dropping out)

Predicted Publications*	Faculty Ability Rating	
	High and Medium	Low
None	39 (70)	49 (281)
Only 2 or 3 publications	30 (426)	36 (292)
Regularly, although not frequently	20 (774)	22 (68)
Will publish a large amount	21 (112)	– (7)

```
N . . . . . . . . . . . . . . . 2,030
NA on Research Rating . . . . . 216
NA on Ability . . . . . . . . . 393
NA or Graduated on Outcome . . 203
                               2,842
```

*Answer to "Ignoring for the moment the quality of the work, what would be your guess as to this student's eventual production of scholarly or scientific work?" Tabulation based on one rater per student.

TABLE 9.6

FACULTY RATING OF COLLEGE TEACHING ABILITY, FACULTY ABILITY RATING, AND DROP OUT

(Per cent dropping out)

Teaching Ability*	Faculty Ability Rating	
	High and Medium	Low
Outstanding	25 (394)	- (9)
Capable	25 (1,011)	36 (355)
Not Suited for College Teaching	34 (59)	47 (298)

```
N . . . . . . . . . . . . . . . . . . .  2,126
NA on Teaching Ability . . . . . . .      120
NA on Ability. . . . . . . . . . . .      393
NA or Graduated on Outcome . . . . .      203
                                        -----
                                        2,842
```

*Answers to the question, "If this student were to do college teaching, how would you rate his ability?" Tabulation based on one rating per student.

TABLE 9.7

PERCEIVED ACADEMIC STANDING, FACULTY ABILITY RATING AND DROP OUT

(Per cent dropping out)

Faculty Ability Rating	Perceived Standing			
	Top Fifth	Second Fifth	Third Fifth or Lower	Don't Know
High and Middle	25 (575)	23 (411)	27 (156)	25 (319)
Low	31 (93)	40 (154)	43 (199)	41 (239)
Total	26 (668)	28 (565)	36 (355)	-
Per Cent High and Middle	86	73	44	-

```
N . . . . . . . . . . . . . . . . . . .  2,146
NA on Ability or Perceived Standing.      493
NA or Graduated on Outcome . . . . .      203
                                        -----
                                        2,842
```

TABLE 9.8
PERSONAL ADJUSTMENT, FACULTY ABILITY RATING AND DROP OUT
(Per cent dropping out)

(a) Morale Index*

Faculty Ability Rating	High	Low	Per Cent High Morale
High and Medium	24 (840)	25 (669)	56 (1,509)
Low	42 (329)	40 (378)	47 (707)
Total	29 (1,169)	30 (1,047)	

```
N . . . . . . . . . . . . . . 2,216
NA on Morale . . . . . . . .     30
NA on Ability . . . . . . . .   393
NA or Graduated on Outcome. .   203
                              2,842
```

*This Index is defined in Chapter VIII.

(b) Faculty Rating on Personality Problems

Faculty Rater's answer to: "Does this student have any personality characteristics which you feel may hinder him in his career?"

Faculty Ability Rating	Yes	No	Per Cent Yes on Personality Characteristics
High and Medium	26 (226)	25 (1,258)	15 (1,484)
Low	36 (208)	41 (485)	30 (693)
Total	31 (434)	29 (1,743)	

```
N . . . . . . . . . . . . . . 2,177
NA on Personality Charac-
   teristics . . . . . . . . .   69
NA on Ability . . . . . . . .   393
NA or Graduated on Outcome. .   203
                              2,842
```

TABLE 9.9

CRITICISMS OF GRADUATE SCHOOL, FACULTY ABILITY
RATING, AND DROP OUT

(Per cent dropping out)

Criticism	Faculty Ability Rating			
	High and Medium		Low	
	No*	Yes*	No*	Yes*
It encourages over-specialization	24 (863)	26 (653)	40 (375)	41 (328)
It stifles the creativity of its students	24 (927)	26 (581)	39 (439)	43 (259)
The training has little or nothing to do with the jobs the students will eventually get	24 (1,139)	27 (367)	37 (487)	47 (210)
It has too many purely formal "hurdles" which are really initiation rituals, not genuine training	25 (725)	25 (783)	39 (368)	42 (331)
It doesn't provide enough training for teaching	24 (773)	25 (735)	38 (356)	43 (345)
It doesn't provide enough training for research and scholarly activities	24 (1,095)	26 (412)	40 (501)	42 (202)
It accepts and encourages more students than it can ultimately place in desirable jobs	23 (1,145)	28 (337)	39 (543)	45 (146)
Admission standards are too low	25 (1,057)	25 (446)	40 (561)	42 (139)
It exploits its students by using them for cheap labor	24 (995)	26 (503)	42 (499)	38 (198)
It rewards conformity and punishes individualism	24 (1,064)	26 (432)	40 (500)	41 (198)
It discourages students who wish to apply their knowledge to practical problems	25 (1,211)	27 (280)	39 (542)	47 (151)
Faculty members tend to become more more involved in building research empires than in making creative contributions to the field	24 (990)	25 (496)	40 (475)	43 (216)

```
N (Difference between Total N in each row and 2,246
    is due to NA on the item in question) . . . . . . . 2,246
NA on Ability . . . . . . . . . . . . . . . . . . . .  393
NA or Graduated on Outcome . . . . . . . . . . . . .  203
                                                     2,842
```

*Yes = "Valid" or "Somewhat Valid" as a criticism; No = "Not Valid" or "Dead Wrong."

TABLE 9.10

FINANCIAL WORRY, FACULTY ABILITY RATING, AND DROP OUT

(Per cent dropping out)

Faculty Ability Rating	Worry About Immediate Financial Situation	
	Worried	Not Worried
High and Medium	26 (465)	24 (1,048)
Low	44 (243)	39 (462)

```
                N . . . . . . . . . . . . . 2,218
                NA on Worry . . . . . . .      28
                NA on Ability . . . . . .     393
                NA or Graduated on Outcome    203
                                            2,842
```

TABLE 9.11

PERCEIVED ADEQUACY OF INCOME, SAVINGS, INDEBTEDNESS, FACULTY ABILITY RATING AND DROP OUT

(Per cent dropping out)

Faculty Ability Rating	Debt*	Savings**	Perceived Adequacy of Income	
			High***	Low***
High or Middle	High	Low	28 (189)	30 (106)
	High (or) Low	High High	24 (495)	27 (74)
	Low	High	22 (553)	30 (46)
Low	High	Low	38 (72)	58 (50)
	High (or) Low	High High	37 (224)	39 (49)
	Low	High	42 (246)	38 (21)

```
                N . . . . . . . . . . . . . 2,125
                NA on Perceived Adequacy,
                  Savings, Debt, or Ability .  514
                NA or Graduated on Outcome. .  203
                                             2,842
```

*High debt = Students who indended to borrow during the year and or those with $100 or more outstanding in non-durable debts. Low = All other.

**High = $500 or more; Low = Less than $500.

***This measure is defined in Chapter V. High = "Enough for my necessary expenses"; Low = "Not sure" or "Doubtful" that there will be enough.

TABLE 9.12
PREFERRED ACTIVITY, SELF CONCEPTION AS AN INTELLECTUAL FACULTY ABILITY RATING, AND DROP OUT

(a) Per Cent Dropping Out

Faculty Ability Rating	Intellectual*	Preferred Activity		
		Research	College or University Teaching	Other
High and Medium	Yes	21 (302)	25 (291)	28 (144)
	No	19 (266)	27 (285)	33 (165)
Low	Yes	30 (106)	33 (99)	48 (67)
	No	34 (131)	46 (148)	53 (128)

N (also Table b) 2,132
NA on Preferred Activity, Intellectual or Ability 507
NA or Graduated on Outcome 203
                                                              2,842

(b) Motivational Index, Faculty Ability Rating, and Drop Out

Faculty Ability Rating	(Per Cent Dropping Out)	
	Index**	
	Low	High
High and Medium	29 (594)	22 (859)
Low	49 (336)	32 (343)

*Answer to: "Do you think of yourself as an 'intellectual'?" Yes = "Definitely" or "In many ways"; No = "In some ways" or "Definitely not."

**High = Researchers plus Teachers who are high on intellectualism; Low = Others, plus Teachers who are low on intellectualism.

TABLE 9.13

DIVISION, MOTIVATION INDEX, FACULTY
ABILITY RATING, AND DROP OUT

Division	Faculty Ability Rating			
	High and Medium		Low	
	Motivation			
	High	Low	High	Low
Humanities	28 (224)	35 (213)	45 (69)	53 (131)
Social Science	26 (161)	29 (193)	40 (61)	49 (97)
Natural Science	17 (484)	21 (193)	26 (205)	45 (116)

```
N . . . . . . . . . . . . . . .   2,147
NA on Motivation Index, or
    Ability or Interdivisional. .   492
NA or Graduated on Outcome. . .     203
                                  -------
                                    2,842
```

TABLE 9.14

EMPLOYMENT, STIPEND HOLDING, FACULTY ABILITY RATING AND DROP OUT

(Per cent dropping out)

(a) Detailed Classification

Full-time Job	Part-time Job or Duty Stipend			Faculty Ability Rating			
				High and Middle		Low	
Yes	–			41 (244)		48 (169)	
No	Yes			Duty Stipend		Duty Stipend	
				Yes	No	Yes	No
		Part-time Job	Yes	21 (179)	31 (195)	Yes 32 (44)	44 (140)
			No	17 (453)	–	No 31 (134)	–
No	No						
		Fellowship	No	21 (179)		No 35 (115)	
			Yes	26 (171)		Yes 49 (76)	

(b) Same Data Grouped

Full-time job	Duty Stipend	Faculty Ability Rating	
		High and Middle	Low
Yes	–	41 (244)	48 (169)
No	No	26 (545)	42 (331)
No	Yes	18 (632)	31 (178)

```
N, for both tables . . . . . . . . . . 2,099
NA on Ability or Employment or
    Stipend . . . . . . . . . . . . . .  540
NA on Graduated on Outcome . . . . . .  203
                                       ─────
                                       2,842
```

TABLE 9.15

MEMBERSHIP IN STUDENT GROUPS, EMPLOYMENT STATUS, FACULTY ABILITY RATING AND DROP OUT

(Per cent dropping out)

Faculty Ability Rating	Full Time Job	Duty Stipend	Membership in Informal Student Groups — No Membership	Membership in Informal Student Groups — Membership	Per Cent Yes on Membership
High and Middle	Yes	-	37 (174)	49 (55)	24 (229)
	No	No	27 (310)	24 (247)	44 (557)
	No	Yes	17 (233)	19 (463)	67 (696)
Low	Yes	-	44 (130)	63 (27)	17 (157)
	No	No	46 (185)	34 (143)	44 (328)
	No	Yes	38 (71)	28 (121)	63 (192)

```
N . . . . . . . . . . . . . . . . . 2,159
NA on Ability, Employment Status,
    or Group Membership . . . . . .   480
NA or Graduated on Outcome  . . .     203
                                    ─────
                                    2,842
```

TABLE 9.16

FACULTY ENCOURAGEMENT INDEX, EMPLOYMENT STATUS, FACULTY ABILITY RATING, AND DROP OUT

(Per cent dropping out)

Faculty Ability Rating	Full Time Work	Duty Sti-pend	Perceived Encouragement No	Perceived Encouragement Yes	Per Cent Yes on Encouragement
High and Middle	Yes	–	34 (65)	43 (176)	73 (241)
	No	No	29 (163)	24 (392)	71 (555)
	No	Yes	10 (120)	20 (575)	83 (695)
Low	Yes	–	48 (79)	54 (78)	50 (157)
	No	No	48 (163)	35 (175)	52 (388)
	No	Yes	33 (64)	33 (122)	66 (186)

```
N . . . . . . . . . . . . . . . 2,172
NA on Ability, Employment Status,
   or Faculty Encouragement. . . .   467
NA or Graduated on Outcome. . . .    203
                                   2,842
```

Tables 275

TABLE 9.17

AGE, FACULTY ABILITY RATING AND DROP OUT

(Per cent dropping out)

Faculty Ability Rating	Age Under 27	Age 27 or Older
High and Middle	18 (751)	32 (773)
Low	38 (347)	43 (369)
Total	24 (1,098)	36 (1,142)

```
N . . . . . . . . . . . . . . . 2,240
NA on Age or Ability. . . . .   399
NA or Graduated on Outcome. .   203
                              ─────
                              2,842
```

TABLE 9.18

AGE, EMPLOYMENT STATUS, AND DROP OUT

(Per cent dropping out)

Full Time Work	Duty Stipend	Age Under 27	Age 27 or Older	Per Cent 27 or Older
Yes	—	45 (128)	47 (359)	74 (487)
No	No	29 (573)	36 (518)	47 (1,091)
No	Yes	20 (616)	24 (411)	40 (1,027)

```
N . . . . . . . . . . . . . . . 2,605
NA on Employment Status or
    Age . . . . . . . . . . . .    34
NA or Graduated on Outcome. .    203
                               ─────
                               2,842
```

TABLE 9.19
FAMILY ROLE, AGE, EMPLOYMENT STATUS, FACULTY
ABILITY RATING, AND DROP OUT

(a) Per cent Dropping Out

Faculty Ability Rating	Full-Time Work	Duty Stipend	Age*	Family Role – Father	Family Role – Other
High and Middle	Yes	–	Older	47 (113)	40 (67)
			Younger	17 (18)	35 (43)
	No	No	Older	42 (91)	28 (200)
			Younger	19 (21)	19 (250)
	No	Yes	Older	25 (103)	19 (178)
			Younger	24 (41)	15 (374)
Low	Yes	–	Older	49 (67)	44 (54)
			Younger	42 (12)	53 (34)
	No	No	Older	53 (36)	41 (123)
			Younger	45 (11)	40 (164)
	No	Yes	Older	48 (23)	44 (54)
			Younger	– (5)	30 (120)
Total				39 (541)	27 (1,661)

```
N . . . . . . . . . . . . . . . . . . . . . . .  2,202
NA on Ability, Employment Status, Age, or
   Family Role . . . . . . . . . . . . . . . . .   437
NA or Graduated on Outcome . . . . . . . . . . .   203
                                                 2,842
```

*Older = 27 or older, Younger = Under 27.

(continued)

TABLE 9.19—Continued

(b) Per Cent Fathers

(Same Data Re-Percentaged To Show Relationship Between Family Role and Other Variables)

		Faculty Ability Rating			
Full-Time	Duty	High and Middle		Low	
Work	Stipend	Younger	Older	Younger	Older
Yes	-	30 (61)	63 (180)	26 (46)	55 (121)
No	No	8 (271)	31 (291)	6 (175)	23 (159)
No	Yes	10 (415)	37 (281)	4 (125)	30 (77)

```
N . . . . . . . . . . . . . . . . . . . . . . 2,202
NA on Ability, Employment Status, Age, or
  Family Role . . . . . . . . . . . . . . . .   437
NA or Graduated on Outcome . . . . . . . . . .   203
                                               2,842
```

(c) Per Cent Dropping Out

(Same Data Re-Percentaged on Family-Age Index)

Faculty Ability Rating	Full-Time Work	Duty Stipend	Family-Age		
			Fathers 27 or Older	Other	Non-Fathers Under 27
High and Middle	Yes	-	47 (113)	35 (85)	35 (43)
	No	No	42 (91)	27 (221)	19 (250)
	No	Yes	25 (103)	20 (219)	15 (374)
Low	Yes	-	49 (67)	44 (66)	53 (34)
	No	No	53 (36)	41 (134)	40 (164)
	No	Yes	48 (23)	44 (59)	30 (120)

```
N . . . . . . . . . . . . . . . . . . . . . . . . . . . 2,202
NA on Ability, Employment Status, Age, or Family Role . . . .   437
NA or Graduated on Outcome . . . . . . . . . . . . . . . . .   203
                                                              2,842
```

278 *Tables*

TABLE 9.20

FACULTY ABILITY RATING, DIVISION, "INVOLVEMENT INDEX" AND DROP OUT

(Per cent dropping out)

Faculty Ability Rating	Division	Score on Involvement Index*		
		4	3-2	1-0
High and Middle ...	Natural Science	10 (97)	14 (444)	37 (145)
	Social Science	14 (50)	24 (224)	46 (93)
	Humanities	22 (55)	28 (256)	42 (126)
Low	Natural Science	17 (30)	31 (198)	44 (102)
	Social Science	- (6)	43 (99)	46 (59)
	Humanities	- (6)	46 (120)	58 (78)

```
                N. . . . . . . . . . . . . .   2,188
                NA on Ability, Age, Employment
                   Status, Self-Conception, or
                   Interdivisional. . . . . . . .   451
                NA or Graduated on Outcome . . . .   203
                                                   -----
                                                   2,842
```

*Scores on the involvement index are the sum of arbitrary weights for the following characteristics:

Characteristic	Weight
Age:	
Under 27	1
27 or Older.	0
Employment Status:	
Duty Stipend	2
Neither.	1
Full-Time Job.	0
Intellectual Self-Conception:	
"Definitely" or "In Many Ways" . .	1
"In Some Ways" or "Definitely Not"	0

TABLE 9.21

CORRELATES OF TRANSFER STATUS

(Per cent shifting to a new institution among students known to be in school in 1959)

(a) Family Role

Sex	Single	Married, No Children	Married, Children
Female	10 (222)	2 (45)	4 (46)
Male	8 (762)	6 (378)	5 (380)

N 1,833
NA on Family Role 12
NA on Outcome or Not in School . . . 997
                                    2,842

(b) Stipend Typology

Duty Stipend	Non-Duty Stipend*		
	None	Low	High
None	6 (470)	6 (212)	9 (272)
Teaching	10 (266)	7 (195)	7 (74)
Research	3 (108)	3 (70)	4 (69)

N 1,736
NA or RA-TA or Trainee on Stipend . 109
NA on Outcome or Not in School . . . 997
                                    2,842

(c) Satisfaction With Choice of School

Answer	Per Cent	N
I definitely made the best decision by coming here	7	704
I'm pretty sure I made the best decision by coming here	6	660
This decision was no better and no worse than another I might have made	7	350
I'm pretty sure I should have gone elsewhere	12	82
I definitely made a bad decision	29	24

N 1,820
NA on Satisfaction 25
NA on Outcome or Not in School . . . 997
                                    2,842

* This classification is defined in Chapter VI.

TABLE 9.22
FACULTY ABILITY RATING, STRATUM AND TRANSFER

(a) Per Cent Transferring Schools Among Students in School 1959

Stratum	Faculty Ability Rating		Total*
	High and Middle	Low	
I.	7 (306)	12 (91)	7 (566)
II.	6 (571)	7 (203)	6 (845)
III.	9 (287)	10 (135)	9 (434)

*Includes NA on Ability.

N 1,593
NA on Ability 252
NA on Outcome or Not in
  School 997
                           2,842

N 1,845
NA on Outcome or Not in
  School 997
                           2,842

(b) Control of Old and New School For Transfers (N)

Year	School	1959	
		Private	Public
1958	Private	25	11
	Public	15	35

N 86

(c) Stratum of Old and New School for Transfers

Year	Stratum	1959		
		I	II	III
1958	I	8	5	5
	II	16	16	8
	III	7	12	9

N 86

Per Cent				
Moving Up	No Change	Moving Down	Total	N
41	38	21	100%	86

(continued)

TABLE 9.22—Continued

(d) Ability and Destination

Faculty Ability Rating	Change in Stratum				N
	Moved Up	No Change	Moved Down	Total	
High and Middle . . .	52	35	13	100%	52
Low	30	40	30	100%	27

N 79
NA on Ability 7
────
86

(e) Per Cent High and Middle Ability by Stratum of Destination

Destination of Transfers		
I.	II.	III.
83 (29)	61 (31)	47 (19)

N 79
NA on Ability 7
────
86

TABLE 9.23

PREFERENCE, EXPECTATIONS AND EMPLOYMENT

(Per cent with academic jobs)

Expectation Five Years After Completing Graduate Study	Prefer Academic Jobs	
	Yes	No
Academic	66 (311)	43 (23)
Non-Academic	22 (95)	14 (173)

```
                N . . . . . . . . . . . . . . . . . . . .  602
                NA on Preference or Expectation . . . . .   31
                NA on Occupation or Non-Labor Force . . .  152
                In School, Disappeared, or NA on Outcome. 2,057
                                                          -----
                                                          2,842
```

TABLE 9.24

STAGE, PREFERENCE AND EMPLOYMENT

(Per cent with academic jobs)

Prefer Academic Jobs	Stage	
	Beginning	Advanced
Yes	31 (156)	72 (233)
No	15 (117)	20 (70)

```
                N . . . . . . . . . . . . . . . . . . . .  576
                NA on Preference or Stage . . . . . . . .   57
                NA on Occupation or Non-Labor Force . . .  152
                In School, Disappeared, or NA on Outcome. 2,057
                                                          -----
                                                          2,842
```

TABLE 9.25
FACULTY ABILITY RATING, STAGE, PREFERENCE AND EMPLOYMENT
(Per cent with academic jobs)

Preference	Stage	Ability Rating High and Middle	Ability Rating Low
Academic	Advanced	76 (170)	60 (40)
	Beginning	39 (76)	22 (64)
Non-Academic	–	20 (108)	9 (65)

```
N . . . . . . . . . . . . . . . . . . . . . .           522
NA on Preference, Stage, or Ability . . . .             111
NA on Occupation or Non-Labor Force. . . . .            152
In School, Disappeared, or NA on Outcome. .           2,057
                                                      ─────
                                                      2,842
```

TABLE 9.26
STRATUM, CONTROL AND EMPLOYMENT, CONTROLLING FOR PREFERENCE, STAGE, AND FACULTY ABILITY RATING
(Per cent with an academic job)

	Group A* Private	Group A* Public	Group B* Private	Group B* Public
I.	77 (26)	80 (10)	22 (41)	– (9)
II.	83 (47)	83 (48)	27 (67)	42 (80)
III.	46 (13)	65 (26)	14 (58)	39 (49)

Group C* – 9% (65)

```
N . . . . . . . . . . . . . . . . . . . . .             539
NA on Preference, Stage or Ability . . . .               94
NA on Occupation or Non-Labor Force . . . .             152
In School, Disappeared or NA on Outcome . .           2,057
                                                      ─────
                                                      2,842
```

*Groups are defined by combinations of the categories in Table 9.25. A = Advanced students, rated high or middle who prefer academic jobs; Group C = Students low on ability who do not prefer academic jobs; Group B = All other combinations.

TABLE 9.27

DI DIVISION AND EMPLOYMENT, CONTROLLING FOR PREFERENCE, STAGE, AND FACULTY ABILITY RATING

(Per cent with an academic job)

Group	Division		
	Natural Science	Social Science	Humanities
A . . .	70 (71)	61 (36)	92 (63)
B . . .	33 (123)	28 (72)	31 (108)
C . . .	–	–	9 (65)

N 538
NA on Preference, Stage, Ability, or Interdivisional . 95
NA on Occupation or Non-Labor Force 152
In School, Disappeared or NA on Outcome 2,057
                                                              2,842

TABLE 9.28

FACULTY ENCOURAGEMENT AND EMPLOYMENT, CONTROLLING FOR PREFERENCE, STAGE, AND FACULTY ABILITY RATING

Group	Perceived Encouragement	
	No	Yes
A	65 (17)	77 (149)
B	19 (99)	37 (199)
C	–	– 9 (65)

N 529
NA on Preference, Stage, Ability or Encouragement . . 104
NA on Occupation or Non-Labor Force 152
In School, Disappeared or NA on Outcome 2,057
                                                               2,842

TABLE 9.29

IMPORTANCE OF COMFORTABLE HOME AND EMPLOYMENT, CONTROLLING FOR PREFERENCE, STAGE, AND FACULTY ABILITY RATING

(Per cent with an academic job)
Answer to: "How important is it eventually to have a comfortable home, nice furniture, etc?"

Group	Importance to Me			Importance to My Spouse		
	Extremely Important	Quite Important	Somewhat or Unimportant	Extremely Important	Quite Important	Somewhat or Unimportant
A	76 (21)	73 (44)	68 (38)	65 (37)	73 (48)	79 (19)
B	28 (43)	30 (82)	39 (54)	25 (60)	34 (91)	43 (28)

Group C - 9 (65)

N 347	N 348
NA on Preference, Stage, Ability, Not Married, or NA on Importance. 286	NA on Preference, Stage, Ability, Not Married, or NA on Importance . 285
NA on Occupation or Non-Labor Force 152	NA on Occupation or Non-Labor Force 152
In School, Disappeared, or NA on Outcome 2,057	In School, Disappeared, or NA on Outcome . . . 2,057
2,842	2,842

Index

Ability
  and academic expectations, 102
  and career expectations-realization, 117–18
  collection of ratings of, 63–64
  and course loads, 56
  and drop-out, 109, 111, 114
  and full-time employment, 77
    and division and stratum, 77
  and jobs, 56
  and stipends, 63, 64, 66
  and transfers, 115–16
Academic expectations
  and ability, 102
  and career expectations, 103
  and division, 103
  and employment, 103
  and family role, 103
  and full-time job, 55
  and starting salary, anticipated, 102, 103
  and stipend, 103
  and stratum, 103
  and total income, 102
  and transfers, 103
Academic worry
  and morale, 94
Administrative control of school (*see* Control)
Age, 24
  at bachelor's degree, 27, 28
    and father's occupation, 27
    and hiatus, 28, 29
    and sex, 27
  and undergraduate self-support, 27
  and control, 30
  and course load, 56–57
  and debt and savings, 89
  and division of study, 30
  and drop-out, 111, 113
  and family role, 33, 44, 45
  and father's occupation, 26
  and fertility, 32
  and financial worry, 95
  and full-time employment, 75, 77
  and marital status, 31, 44
  and parental support, 85
  and perceived adequacy of income, 46
  and stage of study, 30, 33
  and stratum, 30
  of students in sample, 25
  and total income, 43, 45
Assistantships; *see* Stipends
Association of Graduate Schools, 15

Bruner, J. S., 92 fn.

Caplow, Theodore, 17 fn., 21 fn.
Career expectations, 20
  and academic expectations, 103
  and control, 21
  and course load, 56
  and division of study, 20
  and father's occupation, 26
  and fertility, 32
  and full-time employment and division and stratum, 77
  and income, anticipated, 101

287

288 *Index*

and perceived adequacy of income, 46
realization of, 116–19
   and ability, 117–18
   and control, 118
   and division, 118
   and faculty encouragement, 118
   and marital status, 118
   and stage, 117
and stage of study, 20
and starting salary, 100–101
and stratum, 20
See also Income, anticipated
Catholics; *see* Religion
Census, U.S. (1958), 41
Class; *see* Father's occupation
Cloward, Richard A., 102 fn.
Children; *see also* Fertility; Family Role Index
   and dissatisfaction of working spouse, 83
   and father's occupation and spouse's employment, 82
   and parental support, 85
   and spouse's employment, 81
   and type of spouse's employment, 81–82
Coefficient of reproducibility, 15
Control, 16
   and age, 30
   and career expectations, 21
   and career realization, 118
   and course load, 56
   and debt and savings, 88–89
   and division, 18
   and duty stipend hours per week, 67
   and duty stipend as training opportunity, 72
   and employment, 75
   and estimated hourly wage, 68
   and federal government as stipend source, 70–71
   and financial worry, 95
   and full-time employment, 76
   and graduate schools as stipend source, 70
   and others as stipend source, 71
   and perceived adequacy of income, 46
   and proportional expenses, 53
   and stage of study, 19
   and stipend sources, 69
   and stipends, 60–61, 62, 64, 67–68
   and stratum, 18
   and transfer, 115
   and tuition, 52, 53
   distribution of students by stratum and, 16
Course load, 44, 53
   and ability, 56
   and age, 56, 57
   and career expectations, 56
   and control, division, stage, and stratum, 56
   and employment, 56
   and family role, 56
   and father's occupation, 56
   and full-time employment, 55, 56
   and proportional expenses, 53
   and teaching, research assistantships, 55
   and total income, 56, 57
   and tuition, 53
   work completed, 1958–59, 55

Davis, James A., 15 fn., 96 fn.
Debt and savings, 41, 88–89
   and age, 89
   and control, division, stage, stratum, 88–89
   and family role, 88–89
   and father's occupation, 89
   and financial worry, 96
   students with regard to, 88
   withdrawal from (savings), 36, 37, 40
Division of study, 17
   and ability and employment, 77
   and academic expectations, 103
   and age, 30
   and anticipated income, 10
   and career expectations, 20
   and career realization, 118
   and course load, 56
   and debt and savings, 88–89
   and drop-out, 111
   and duty stipend as training opportunity, 72
   and employment, 75
   and estimated hourly wage, 68
   and father's occupation, 26
   and federal government as stipend source, 70, 71
   and financial worry, 95

and full-time employment, 77
and graduate schools as stipend source, 70
and hiatus, 29, 30
and hours per week for duty stipends, 67–68
and income for full-time employment, 77
and others as stipend source, 71
and part-time employment, 79
and perceived adequacy of income, 46
and stage of study, 19
and starting salary, 100–101
and stipend sources, 69
and stipends, 59–60, 61, 62, 64, 65
and stratum and control, 18
departments grouped into, 17
Drop-out, 44, 108–15
  and ability, 109, 110, 111
    and financial worry, 110, 111
    and grades, 109
    and morale, 110
    and satisfaction with choice of school, 110
  and age, 111, 113
  and career expectations, 111
  and division, 111
  and employment, 111, 112, 114
  and faculty encouragement, 113
  and faculty rating of teaching ability, 109, 114
  and family role, 111, 113
  and father's occupation, 113
  and motivation, 111
  and peer group, 112–13
  and religion, 113
  and stage, 109
  and stipends, 112
  and student's self rating, 109
  relation of financial worry and, 110, 111
Duty stipend; *see* Stipends

Employment; *see also* Stipends
  and academic expectations, 103
  and control, 75
  and course load, 56
  and division, 75
  and drop-out, 111, 112, 114
  and father's occupation, 75
  and family role, 75
  and financial worry, 98
  and peer group, 112–13
  and stage, 75
  fellowships and, 74–75
  frequency in graduate school, 74
  full-time, 36, 38, 40, 42
    and ability, 77
    and academic expectations, 103
    and age, 75, 77
    and career expectations, 77
    and control, 76
    and course loads, 55
    and division, 77
    and family role, 42, 75, 77
    and father's occupation, 76
    and parental support, 86, 87
    and part-time employment, 79
    and stage, 75
    and stratum, 76, 77
    income from, 77
  part-time, 36, 37, 40, 78–80
    and academic expectations, 103
    and course load, 55
    and division, stage, and stratum, 79
    and full-time employment, 79
    and non-duty stipends, 79
    and parental aid, 79
    and spouse's employment, 79
    and stipends, 79
  spouse's, 36, 37, 40, 42, 80–84
    and children, 81, 83, 84
    and family role, 42
    and father's occupation, 82
    and fertility, 83–84
    and marital status, 44
    and parental aid, 86, 87
    and part-time work, 79
    and sex, 81
    and stage, 83–84
    and stipend income, 82–83
    and spousal dissatisfaction, 83
    type of, 81–82
Enrolment, 15
  distribution of graduate schools, by, 14
Erbe, William, 64 fn.
Evaluations of job opportunities, 21
  and stage, 102–3
Expenses; *see also* Tuition
  academic, 41, 50–54
    books, journals, thesis, 50
    fees, 50
    total, 51

proportional, 51
  and control, 53
  and course load, 53
  and family role, 53
  and perceived adequacy of income, 53-54

Faculty encouragement
  and drop-out, 113
  and career realization, 117
Faculty ratings of student ability (*See* Ability)
Family Role Index; *see also* Marital Status
  definition, 32-33
  and academic expectations, 103
  and age, 33, 45
  and course load, 56
  and debt and savings, 88-89
  and drop-out, 111, 113
  and financial worry, 95
  and full-time employment, 42, 75, 77
  and spouse's employment, 42, 44
  and parental support, 85
  and perceived adequacy of income, 45, 46
  and proportional expenses, 51
  and stage of study, 33
  and stipends, 65-66
  and total income, 43
Father's occupation, 25
  and age, 26
  and age at bachelor's, 27
  and career expectations, 26
  and course load, 56
  and debt and savings, 89
  and division of study and stratum, 26
  and drop-out, 113
  and employment, 75
  and financial worry, 95
  and full-time employment, 76
  and hiatus, 28-29
  and orientation to college, 86-87
  and parental support, 86-87
  and perceived adequacy of income, 46
  and spouse's employment, 82
    and children, 82
  and stage of study, 26
  and stipends, 65
  and undergraduate self-support, 27
  as a measure of prestige, 25-26
Feld, Shiela, 92 fn.

Fellowships (*See* Stipends)
Fertility, 31-33; *see also* Family Role Index
  and age, 32
  and career expectations, 32
  and duration of marriage, 31-32
  and religion, 32
  and spouse's employment, 83-84
  expectations, 32
Field of study; *see also* Division of Study
  Ph.D. and age, 29
Financial need; *see also* Income, perceived adequacy of
  and parental support, 85
  and stipend allocation, 65
Financial worry, 93-99
  and age, 95
  and control, division, stage, and stratum, 95
  and debt and savings, 96
  and drop-out, 110, 111, 112
  and employment, 98
  and family role, 95
  and father's occupation, 95
  over immediate situation, 93
  and morale, 94
  and perceived adequacy of income, 96, 97, 98
  and relative deprivation, 97, 98
  in sample, 93
  and sources of income, 97
  and stipend, 95
Follow-up study, 53, 106-19; *see also* Academic expectations; Career expectations; Drop-out; Transfers
  course load in, 53
  extent and method of, 106-7
  general status of sample in, 107-8
  proportional expenses in, 53
  tuition in, 53
Ford Foundation fellowships, 69
Fund for the Republic, 93

Gallop Poll, 93
Goodman, C. C., 92 fn.
Graduate schools; *see also* Control; Stratum
  distribution by enrolment, 4-15
  geographic location, 16
  Keniston ranking, 14

Gurin, Gerald, 92 fn.
Guttman scale, 15

Hiatus, 28–30
  and age at bachelor's degree, 28, 29
  and division of study, 29, 30
  and father's occupation, 28–29
  nature of, 28
  and stratum, 30

Income, anticipated, 99–104
  and career expectations, 101
  and division, 101
  and sex, 101
  graduate and undergraduate students', 99–100
  starting salary in,
    and academic expectations, 100–101, 102, 103
    and career expectations, 100–101
    and division, 100–101
    and sex, 100–101
    and stage, 100–101, 102–3
Income, perceived adequacy of, 45–46
  and age, 46
  and career expectations, 46
  and control, division, stage, and stratum, 46
  and family role, 45, 46
  and father's occupation, 46
  and financial worry, 96, 97, 98
  and marital status, 45, 46
  and proportional expenses, 53–54
  and relative deprivation, 97–98
  and total income, 45, 53–54
Income, sources of, 36–40; *see also* Debt and savings; Employment; Investments; Loans; Parental support; Stipends; Veteran's benefits
  and financial worry, 97
  and relative deprivation, 97–98
  and total income, 42
  other, 37, 38, 40
Income, total, 40–45; *see also* Expenses
  and academic expectations, 102
  and age, 43, 44, 45
  as compared to general population, 41–42
  and course load, 56, 57
  and family role, 43
  and marital status, 43, 44

  and perceived adequacy of income, 45, 53–54
  and sources of income, 42
  and stage of study, 43
Intellectualism
  and drop-out, 109, 111
Interim between undergraduate and graduate school (*see* Hiatus)
Investments, 36, 38, 40, 41

Jews; *see* Religion
Jobs; *see* Employment

Keniston, Hayward, 14 fn.
  ranking by, 14, 15
Kitt, Alice S., 96 fn.

Lauriate, Patience, 31 fn.
Lazarsfeld, Paul F., 96 fn.
Loans, 37, 38, 40; *see also* National Defense Act Loans

Marital status, 30–33; *see also* Family Role Index
  and age, 31, 43
  and career realization, 118
  and full-time employment, 44, 76
  and morale, 94
  and parental support, 85
  and perceived adequacy of income, 45–46
  and sex, 31
  and stage of study, 44
  and total income, 43, 44
  and transfers, 115
Master's degree; *see* Stage of study
Matza, David, 102 fn.
McGee, Reece, 17 fn., 21 fn.
Merton, Robert K., 96 fn.
Motivation index
  definition, 111
  and drop-out, 111
Morale, 22
  and ability, 110
  and academic worry, 94
  and drop-out, 110
  and financial worry, 94
  and marital status, 94
  and peer group, 94
  compared with soldiers, 94
  index, 94

Index

National Academy of Sciences–National Research Council, 29 fn.
National Defense Act loans, 38, 69, 90
National Opinion Research Center, 53, 131 fn.
National Science Foundation, 35
  fellowships, 63
Non-duty stipends; *see* Stipends

Ohlin, Lloyd E., 102 fn.

Parental support, 27, 36, 37, 40, 84–88
  and age, 85
  and children, 85
  and family climate, 86–87
  and family role, 85
  and father's occupation, 86–87
  and financial need, 85
  and full-time employment, 86, 87
  and marital status, 85
  and part-time employment, 79
  and siblings, 87
  and sex, 85
  and spouse's employment, 86, 87
    and sex, 86
  and stipends, 86, 87
  spouse's, 37, 40
  students receiving, 84–85
Peer groups; *see also* Relative deprivation
  and drop-out, 112–13
  and employment, 112–13
  and morale, 94
Ph.D.; *see* Stage of study
Prestige, of school; *see* Stratum; Father's occupation
Protestants; *see* Religion

Relative deprivation, 96–99; *see also* Peer groups
  definition, 96–97
  and financial worry, 97–98
  and perceived adequacy of income, 97–98
  and source of income, 97–98
Religion
  and drop-out, 113
  distribution in sample, 26
  and fertility expectations, 32
Rosenberg, Morris, 99 fn.

Sample, the, 131–44
  academic work completed in 1958–59 by, 55
  description of, 16
  financial worry in, 93
  full-time employment in, 75
  median income in, 43
  types of stipend in, 58–59
Sampling error, 139
Satisfaction with school choice, 21
  and drop-out, 110
  and transfer, 115
Savings; *see* Debt and savings
Scholarships; *see* Stipends, non-duty
Sex; *see also* Family Role Index; Women as graduate students
  and age at bachelor's degree, 27
  and anticipated income, 101
  and dissatisfaction of working spouse, 83
  and marital status, 31
  and parental support, 85
  and spouse's employment, 81
  and starting salary, 100–101
  and type of spouse's employment, 81
  and undergraduate self-support, 27
Siblings
  and parental support, 87
Social Science Research Council (SSRC) fellowships, 69
Spaeth, Joe L., 20, 99 fn.
Spouses; *see* Income, sources of; Marital status; Family Role Index; Employment
Stage of study
  definition, 18–19
  and age, 30, 33
  and career expectations, 20
  and career realization, 117
  and complaints about income from duty stipend, 72
  and control, 19
  and course load, 56
  and debt and savings, 89
  distribution of students by, 18–19
  and division of study, 19
  and drop-out, 109
  and duty stipend as training opportunity, 72
  and duty stipend hours per week, 67–68

and employment, 75
and estimated hourly wage, 68
and Family Role Index, 33
and father's occupation, 26
and federal government as stipend source, 70–71
and financial worry, 95
and full-time employment, 75
and graduate schools as stipend source, 70
and marital status, 44
and others as stipend source, 71
and part-time employment, 79
and perceived adequacy of income, 46
and starting salary, 100–101
and stipend sources, 69
and stipends, 59–60, 61, 62, 64, 65
and stratum, 19–20
and students in follow-up study, 108
and total income, 44
and transfers, 115
Stipends
  ascriptive characteristics of, 59
  definitions, 36, 58
  allocation of, 59 (*see below* sources of stipends)
  and ability, 63, 64, 66
  and academic expectations, 103
  classification of (typology), 58–59
  and control, 60–1, 62, 64, 67
  and division of study, 59, 60, 61, 62, 64, 65
  and drop-out, 112
  duty, 59
    and average hours per week, 67–68
    and estimated hourly wage, 68
    and part-time employment, 79
    as a training opportunity, 72
    complaints about income from, 72
    student opinion on, 71–73
  and father's occupation, 65
  and family role, 65–66
  and financial need, 65, 66
  and financial worry, 95
  income from, 82–83
    and income from employment, 82–83
    and children, 82–83
  minus tuition, 67
  non-duty, 59, 60
    fellowships, 59, 61, 64, 65
    scholarships, 59, 61, 64
    and parental support, 86, 87
    and part-time employment, 79
    research assistantships, 59, 60, 61, 64, 65, 72, 79
    and course load, 55
  in the sample, 58–59
  sources of, 69–71
    and control, division, and stage, 69
    federal government as, 69
    graduate school as, 69–70
    others as, 71
    private funds as, 69
    and stage of study, 59, 60, 61, 62, 64, 65
    and stratum, 59, 60–61, 62, 65
    supplemented by non-stipend income, 74–75
  teaching assistantships, 59, 60, 61, 62, 64, 65, 70, 71, 79
    and course loads, 55
  traineeship and internship, 58
  and transfer, 115
  and tuition, 50–51
  value of, 67
Stouffer, Samuel, 93, 93 fn.
Stratum
  definition, 14–16
  and ability and employment, 77
  and academic expectation, 103
  and age, 30
  and career expectations, 20
  and control, 52
  and course load, 56
  and debt and savings, 88–89
  and division and control, 18
  and duty stipends as training opportunity, 72
  and employment, 75
  and father's occupation, 26
  and financial worry, 95
  and full-time employment, 76, 77
  and hiatus, 30
  and income from full-time employment, 77
  and part-time employment, 79
  and perceived adequacy of income, 46
  and proportional expenses, 53
  and stage of study, 19–20
  and stipends, 59, 60–61, 62, 65

and transfer, 115–16
and tuition, 53

Tietze, Christopher, 31 fn.
Traineeship and internship; *see* Stipends
Transfers, 108, 115–16
    and ability, 115–16
    and academic expectation, 103
    and control, 115
    and marital status, 115
    and satisfaction with school choice, 115
    and stage, 115
    and stipend, 115
    and stratum, 115–116
Tuition, 50, 51, 52, 61
    and control, 52, 53
    in follow-up study, 53
    and stratum, 53
    stipends minus, 67
    and total costs, 51

Undergraduate self-support, 27
    and age at bachelor's degree, 27
    and sex, 27

Veroff, Joseph, 92 fn.
Veteran's benefits, 36, 38, 40
    and stipends combined in analysis, 37

Warner Occupational Prestige Scale, 25 fn.
Wolfe, Dael, 13 fn.
Women as graduate students
    finances, 43
Woodrow Wilson fellowships, 69